PRAISE FOR *BUILDING A CULTURE OF INNOVATION*

"Clear practical steps to embed a culture of innovation and an enjoyable read. This is a really practical guide for any organization aiming to put innovation at the centre of its business strategy. It does what it claims to do; defining a culture of innovation and giving some easy to use tools within a six-stage framework to make the journey successful. The concepts and tools in this book are clear, practical and easy to use – it will help to make innovation central to your strategy." **Irene Stark, Group HR Director, ATS Euromaster**

"To read this book is just like sitting down for a chat with the authors who share years of experience wrapped up in a single book, in a conversational style, punctuated with concepts, perspectives and leading case studies along the way. A useful touchpoint for leaders who know that innovation is critical for business success and are navigating this cultural journey." **Sarah Salter, Group HR Director, Northumbrian Water**

"I found the book to be one of the few that look at life as it is today – too many management books still look backwards. All the examples quoted are current and the topic is definitely the number one issue facing all business areas today. A great book that I will definitely recommend to any change professional or business leader responsible for keeping their business current."
Catherine Rutter, Group Operations Change Director, Lloyds Banking Group

"Building an innovation culture into a business is a huge opportunity for many organizations. This book builds frameworks which can help navigate us through the innovation journey, how you create the culture and build momentum through trust and empowerment of teams. It recognizes many of the big hurdles, such as getting the right people into the organization and the barriers that get built to slow down or prevent change. A valuable insight that can help many of us go on these change journeys to create the next generation organization for our businesses to succeed in the future." **Stephen Shurrock, CEO, Telefonica Global Consumer Group**

D1636729

"*Building a Culture of Innovation* provides a real world examination of the issues around innovation and culture that large companies are grappling with in the light of rapidly changing consumer behaviour and emerging competition. It provides a structured and pragmatic approach to embedding innovation capabilities in to organizations." **Duncan Mosely, Director of Corporate Development, Prudential**

"Does the culture of your organization enable innovative thinking, or prevent it from taking root in the first place? Too often, leaders fail to recognize that the innovation they seek simply isn't possible within the framework of the current culture and that becoming more innovative requires changes in unexpected places. This book addresses that issue, making it a valuable and relevant work on the topic." **Colin J Browne, author of *How to Build a Happy Sandpit***

"What makes this such a vital read is that it's not just another innovation book but an essential practical guide for anyone who is looking for the framework to move from talking about innovation in the workplace to actually making it a reality. The pioneering organization is transformed by leadership that can lead on innovation, managers who then manage innovation and a community that are more effectively engaged in the culture of innovation. The authors clearly have an abundance of hands on experience across this innovation value chain and draw on this to deliver a digestible and practical guide for practitioners at all levels." **Andrew Grahame, Co-founder, Mr & Mrs Smith Hotels**

"In a time when everyone is talking about innovation, it's clear that not enough business leaders understand the difference between invention and innovation or between innovative people and an innovative organization. Sustainable innovation can only be achieved by embarking on the journey towards a culture of innovation. This book serves as a useful guide for what will always be a long and difficult adventure. Providing frequent, practical tools, case studies and helpful commentary, *Building a Culture of Innovation* will ensure that more of us arrive at our destination in one piece." **Andy Hedge, Global Director of Learning and Development, Xchanging**

"There can be few business leaders who aren't wrestling with the challenge of how to create or re-energize the innovative DNA of their organization. Delivering the demands of today and at the same time ensuring that you can remain relevant to and meet the demands of your customers tomorrow has never been a more challenging leadership issue. There's no single route or magic formula to achieving an innovative culture any more than meeting any other business challenge, but there are key components requiring leadership attention and *Building a Culture of Innovation* surfaces and explores these dimensions using some refreshing and insightful real life examples to help bring the theory and concepts to life. It's proved to be a helpful reminder that leadership persistency and having the right people capabilities and mind-set are a constant. With plenty of nuggets to take away and think about how to apply to your own cultural environment I am sure it's a book I will keep coming back to for a refresh." **Mark Howes, CEO, AXA Direct Protection and Director, AXA PPP healthcare**

"*Building a Culture of Innovation* superbly underpins the value of innovation being driven from the engine room of business culture as a commercial differentiator. Everything about this book is practical which makes it essential reading for both HR professionals and business leaders continuously adapting to growing regulation, digital advancements and new generations of consumers. Using case studies, best practice insights, stakeholder strategies and frameworks – it's a useful refresh to those already making progress or to identify future growth opportunities." **Beth Robotham, Head of Business Development, Bupa UK**

"Right from the outset *Building a Culture of Innovation* helps demystify innovation and how to embed it into the culture of the big, complex corporate company. It helps set innovation, and even the very definition of it, in the context of the individual organization and most importantly helps outline how to measure innovation itself as well as, and more importantly, your progress along your innovation journey. It's a refreshing change from the usual innovation books that reinforce why we need to innovate, this time the authors have shown us how to communicate innovation, engage people in it and ultimately, make it happen." **Nikki Wray, Delivery Director and Head Of People Faculty, QinetiQ**

"Innovation, the Holy Grail to which the majority of forward-thinking organizations aspire, has at last been turned into an understandable and very readable step-by-step guide to creating a culture of innovation. Make no mistake, this is not a prescriptive 'one size fits all' model for creating a culture of innovation and the challenge to achieve it is certainly not for the faint-hearted, but what the authors set out to do (and achieve) is to provide clear direction and simple models through which there is a clear journey for any organization to follow in order to move towards creating an innovative culture."
Dr Sue Waldock, Group HR Director, The Rank Group Plc

"A highly useful practical guide to develop a culture of innovation in your business. Very clear and straight to the point. It will prove invaluable to practitioners who strive to change their organization for the better. The authors offer an exciting vision and, at the same time, provide a step-by-step approach to manage change. This book will have a high impact on its readers."
Prof Reinhard Bachmann BA MSc PhD, Chair in International Management, SOAS, University of London

Building a Culture of Innovation

A practical framework for placing innovation at the core of your business

Cris Beswick, Derek Bishop and Jo Geraghty

LONDON PHILADELPHIA NEW DELHI

Publisher's note

Every possible effort has been made to ensure that the information contained in this book is accurate at the time of going to press, and the publishers and authors cannot accept responsibility for any errors or omissions, however caused. No responsibility for loss or damage occasioned to any person acting, or refraining from action, as a result of the material in this publication can be accepted by the editor, the publisher or any of the authors.

First published in Great Britain and the United States in 2016 by Kogan Page Limited

2nd Floor, 45 Gee Street
London
EC1V 3RS
United Kingdom

1518 Walnut Street, Suite 1100
Philadelphia PA 19102
USA

4737/23 Ansari Road
Daryaganj
New Delhi 110002
India

ISBN   978 0 7494 7447 8
E-ISBN 978 0 7494 7448 5

British Library Cataloguing-in-Publication Data

A CIP record for this book is available from the British Library.

Library of Congress Cataloging-in-Publication Data

Names: Beswick, Cris, author. | Bishop, Derek, author. | Geraghty, Jo, author.
Title: Building a culture of innovation : a practical framework for placing
    innovation at the core of your business / Cris Beswick, Derek Bishop, Jo
    Geraghty.
Description: London ; Philadelphia : Kogan Page, 2015.
Identifiers: LCCN 2015036071| ISBN 9780749474478 | ISBN 9780749474485
Subjects: LCSH: Creative ability in business. | Corporate culture. |
    Diffusion of innovations. | New products. | Technological
    innovations—Management.
Classification: LCC HD53 .B4768 2015 | DDC 658.3/14—dc23 LC record available at
http://lccn.loc.gov/2015036071

Typeset by Amnet
Print production managed by Jellyfish
Printed and bound by CPI Group (UK) Ltd, Croydon CR0 4YY

CONTENTS

List of figures viii
Acknowledgements ix

01   Introduction: So you think your organization innovates? 1

Invention versus innovation 3
Why innovation? 6
The drivers of change 8
The culture of innovation 12
Next Generation Organizations 16
Pointing the way towards innovation 20
Overcoming barriers to innovation 24
In summary 30
References 32

02   Understanding where you are today 35

Why not simply buy innovation? 37
Know thyself – the cultural assessment 38
Innovation maturity 42
The strategic innovation decision 49
Owning the innovation agenda 55
In summary 65
References 67

03   Building an innovation leadership team 69

If it's not on the top team's agenda, it's not going to
   be in the culture 69
Aligning strategy with the organization's appetite
   for innovation 70
The key drivers of innovation 72

Making your innovation strategy and vision your own 78
Positioning innovation for everyone 79
Building leadership team agreement 81
Creating capability 87
Leading through change 89
In summary 91
References 92

04   Designing the future 95

Shaping the vision 96
Defining the values 99
Translating values into competencies 102
Shaping the journey 104
Dual operating system 108
Employee engagement 111
Creating alignment 113
Benefits of change 115
In summary 116
References 117

05   Communication and people engagement 119

Developing engagement 120
Employee-led engagement programmes 123
The engagement plan 124
Innovation agents (i-agents) 126
The communication and engagement plan 134
Creating the communication plan 142
Innovation launch event 145
In summary 147
References 148

06   Building innovation aptitude 149

Leadership – its criticality to success 151
Leaders need to build a compelling vision 153
Leading outwards 156
Why leaders need to engage HR 159
Identifying and engaging intrapreneurs 161
The structure to support innovation ecosystems 163

How will innovation be measured? 169
Deciding on relevant metrics 171
Designing your innovation process 174
In summary 176
References 177

07   Embedding a culture of innovation 179

Embedding change 180
Too short, too sharp, too shallow 183
Moving change forward 188
Early stage challenges 189
Innovation people 193
Hiring for cultural fit 195
Evolving innovation 197
In summary 198
References 199

08   Conclusion 201

Reference 206

Index 207

LIST OF FIGURES

FIGURE 1.1   The six-stage framework for building a culture
of innovation 2

FIGURE 1.2   Invention versus innovation 4

FIGURE 2.1   Cultural assessment 39

FIGURE 2.2   The 4×4 innovation maturity model 43

FIGURE 2.3   The sustainable innovation mix 51

FIGURE 2.4   The strategic innovation decision 52

FIGURE 2.5   The innovation gap 54

FIGURE 2.6   Translating strategy into behaviour 64

FIGURE 5.1   The 4Es methodology 122

FIGURE 5.2   Using i-agents to translate strategy into behaviour 129

FIGURE 5.3   Influencing change 143

FIGURE 6.1   The 3Is innovation process 175

ACKNOWLEDGEMENTS

W e would like to thank our families and the Culture Consultancy team for allowing us to take time out of our already busy lives to write the book. Special thanks goes to Alison Griffiths for her boundless encouragement and patience, and for generally keeping us on track.

We would also like to thank our clients, partners and entrepreneur networks for their unwavering support, trusting us to deliver the results they needed, and allowing us to share the case studies in this book.

Extra material

You can find more resources to go with this book including templates, worksheets and white papers at **www.cultureconsultancy.com/resources**

Introduction: So you think your organization innovates?

This book is the story of the way in which organizations can deliver longevity and profitability through truly differentiated products, services, business models and exceptional customer experiences. Drawing on industry best practices, allied to innovation and organizational cultural expertise, this book will help your organization join the ranks of those who have refused to accept the status quo and instead have tried to do something better, something different to enhance the business/customer relationship and generate long-term strength and agility along the way. How? By putting a culture of innovation at the very heart of what the organization does and how it does it.

In this introductory chapter we'll look at the basic premise that underpins the innovation culture imperative. We'll examine why organizations may believe that they are innovating but are in actuality just tinkering around the edges of invention. And we'll move on to discover some of the social and economic drivers which have resulted in innovation culture being not only a force within the business community but also being seen as a potential change solution for governments and quasi-governmental organizations.

In future chapters we will guide you on your innovation journey; working through a six-stage practical framework, which will enable you to define, develop, champion and embed a culture of innovation in your organization. And as we are talking about innovation, let's be clear that we are *not* going to give you a universal panacea or an ABC of prescriptive steps to follow that will always lead to a fixed conclusion. That's not what innovation is about, that's not what differentiation is about and that's not how culture

FIGURE 1.1 The six-stage framework for building a culture of innovation

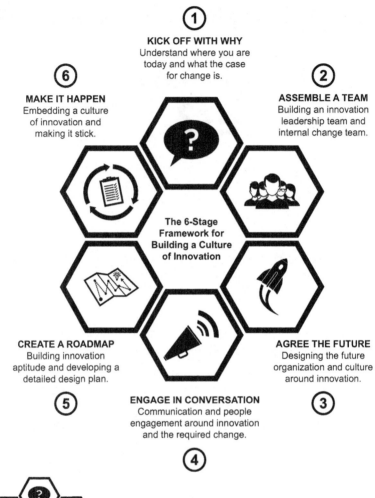

1

KICK OFF WITH WHY
Understand where you are today and what the case for change is.

6

MAKE IT HAPPEN
Embedding a culture of innovation and making it stick.

2

ASSEMBLE A TEAM
Building an innovation leadership team and internal change team.

The 6-Stage Framework for Building a Culture of Innovation

CREATE A ROADMAP
Building innovation aptitude and developing a detailed design plan.

5

AGREE THE FUTURE
Designing the future organization and culture around innovation.

3

ENGAGE IN CONVERSATION
Communication and people engagement around innovation and the required change.

4

Designing the future 04

Where am I?
Each chapter starts with a progress bar showing which stage you have reached in the 6-Stage Framework.

Unless you are skimming this book at random, by now your innovation journey has taken you from an appreciation of the importance of innovation in 21st-century business and onwards into developing an understanding of where your organization sits on the innovation spectrum today. Along the way we've taken in the sights and sounds of an organization change works. Rather, we aim to show you a pathway, which if followed, will lead you towards embedding a culture of innovation, thereby enabling you to discover and to realize the true potential of your organization.

Is adopting a culture of innovation a business imperative? We would say, unequivocally, yes – and the UK's Department for Business Innovation and Skills (BIS) Innovation Report 2014 would seem to agree, commenting that: 'Innovative businesses grow twice as fast as non-innovators and they are also less likely to fail.' (BIS, 2014)

Invention versus innovation

This book is not about the story of innovation, although we will touch on past histories from time to time as learning points. This book is more about innovating the future, about the ways in which businesses and organizations in general can transform themselves in order to transform the lives of their employees, their customers and even the wider world. So while we might touch upon the past our eyes are very much on the future: on changing attitudes, beliefs and behaviours in a profound way. But we need to start with a look back, with a nod to the past, which will help us to understand how profoundly game-changing innovation can be.

From the first time that man, instead of just sheltering under the tree, used leaves and branches to weave a shelter; from the first time that man looked at fire and wondered if food might be improved through heating it up; from the first time that man looked at a cave and wondered if it would make a good place to live, our development has been characterized by invention and innovation.

Essentially, invention and innovation are two sides of the same coin – the yin and the yang. They complement each other and build on each other, yet in some ways are incredibly different. For while invention seeks to build on existing knowledge, to make something new or different; innovation seeks to create lasting synergies and solutions. In other words, invention looks at the 'what,' innovation looks at the 'how'. Before we go any further let us make it clear that innovation is not just about 'patents for design' but about a profound change in the attitude and approach throughout an organization.

One of the first hurdles for business leaders to overcome therefore, is to stop seeing invention and innovation as the same thing. The two may, in some cases, be inextricably intertwined but the attitudes and processes are very different. When we want to invent, we task groups of experts to create a product or introduce a process for the first time. When we want to innovate, we involve

FIGURE 1.2   Invention versus innovation

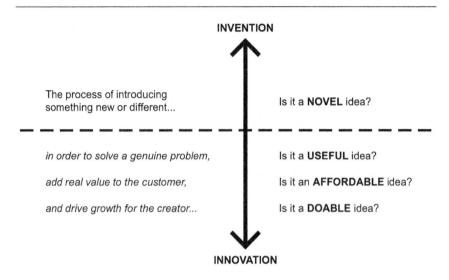

everyone in a drive to improve on products, processes, services or experiences or to create solutions to genuine problems. So invention looks for new ideas, new products, new things; innovation asks: What can we do differently; what can we change; how can we improve but more importantly, how do we implement; how do we get our 'solution' into the hands of those who need it?

The following diagram may help you communicate the difference between invention and innovation across your organization and provide a simple checklist by asking yourself is it *novel*? Is it *useful*? Is it *affordable*? And most importantly – as even the greatest idea is worthless if it sits on a shelf – is your idea *doable*?

The area above the dotted line, ie the process of introducing something new or different, is what would be generally considered as *invention*. The three elements below the line are the extra ingredients that are required to move invention towards *innovation*. So the prime consideration is whether a genuine problem exists. Where no problem exists then you may have designed something 'funky' but are generally in the field of invention; where finding a solution to an observed, identified, articulated or unarticulated problem is the aim, then you are more likely innovating. It is probably worth highlighting here that just because a problem is unarticulated, it may still require an innovative solution. For example, customers may not realize that a change in legislation or specification may result in future problems. Anticipating and providing a solution to those problems may well still fall under the heading of innovation.

Secondly, innovative solutions not only solve a problem but do so with the target market in mind. This means that the solution has to be accessible, ie affordable. However, don't confuse affordable with cheap: a genuinely affordable solution means that the cost is relative to the problem and to the size of the market. This means that some 'affordable' solutions may carry significant costs depending on the sector and on what the customer deems to be good value. It is also important here to remember that affordable doesn't always relate to pure cost. For example, a solution which saves the customer costs but leaves them having to spend extra time ploughing through a computer interface may not be an 'affordable' option.

Finally, all of the above is only worth doing if the organization is going to generate a return. Now, depending on what your organization does or what your strategy is the 'return' may not necessarily be financial. For example, strengthening customer loyalty or reputation may be seen as a successful outcome. For organizations that have a social contract, reducing or mitigating the effects of climate change or taking steps towards sustainability may also fall under the 'successful outcome' banner. But whatever the aim, the key is to consider whether the organization will benefit in the long term and therefore whether the time/cost-benefit makes it a doable idea.

Understanding the difference between invention and innovation is crucial if businesses are to create long-term differentiated propositions. Let's look at a couple of examples starting with a glimpse back to 3,500 BCE. When asked to name the top 10 inventions of all time, the invention of the wheel would probably appear high on many people's lists. However, the wheel itself is merely an object. It is how the wheel is used, the problems it solves and its continuing development which makes it an innovation. Moving forward through time the same is true for other inventions, such as the steam engine, batteries, non-stick surfaces or the microchip.

The microchip is a prime example of an invention which is then used in innovative ways. Apple, under the leadership of their late CEO Steve Jobs, is widely credited as being one of the most inventive and innovative organizations of all time. But if you take a moment to break down the Apple products an interesting pattern starts to emerge. At heart, all phones, computers and portable devices are a conglomeration of microchips, speakers, power transformers and so on. All of these had already been invented in one form or another when Apple hit the scene, so its accolade of being an inventive organization is perhaps questionable. What Apple managed to do was to take all of these disparate elements and combine them to produce computers, portable devices and smartphones which met the public's need for easy-to-use, secure, well-designed and multi-purpose devices and it's through the combination of those components and surrounding systems that it truly deserves the accolade for innovation.

Why innovation?

Now that we are starting to get to grips with the idea that innovation and invention are different, we have to stop and ask the question: Why innovation? The practical effects of Moore's Law, which says that the number of transistors in a dense integrated circuit doubles approximately every two years, result in the continual opening up of technological potential. So with this pace of technological change surely all businesses need to do is to invent, to improve on existing products or to take advantage of new programmes?

In fact, with all this inventive potential out there why bother with innovation? Well, there are two very strong reasons why invention is not enough. The first is that invention for invention's sake can easily result in products that simply don't resonate with the market. Go back a few generations and look at the way in which VHS soundly beat off its competition, Betamax, despite – in the eyes of the purists – Betamax providing a better-quality recording. Wind the clock further back to just after the Second World War and take a look at the Bristol Brabazon aeroplane. Designed as a luxury alternative to the passenger liner, its inventors thought it would take the market by storm. Instead, this airliner was rejected in favour of smaller, faster and more economical planes, which would pave the way for flying the masses across the globe.

These are just two examples of inventions which, in theory, were superior in terms of quality but failed to capture the mood of the time. Therein lies one of the fundamental problems of pure invention: no matter how superior the quality, no matter how technologically advanced the product, if it doesn't resonate with customers, if it doesn't solve a genuine problem or need, articulated or not, it won't succeed. This is particularly so when it comes to today's generation of consumers. Forged in the fires of recession, and with their awareness of the world shaped by 'always-on' internet access, today's customers and consumers are very different from previous generations who were more willing to accept the quasi-authority which emanated from established business. We'll come back to this later on in the chapter when we look at Generation Z, but it is worth noting that this change in consumer attitudes plays perfectly into the collaborative aspects of an innovation culture. Working with customers to establish their needs and then to co-create solutions with them not only strengthens customer loyalty, it strongly meets some of the key innovation criteria.

There is one further element to examine here and that is the way in which some items catch the public imagination or are adopted because people can see that they fill a void and others simply don't catch on. Why did the iPad take off while Google Glass was taken off the market? It can't have simply been down to concerns raised about privacy; it just seemed as though the public were ready for one product but not for the other. Nevertheless, even though Google Glass was withdrawn it is still under development and no doubt will appear again in different form in the future. This perfectly illustrates one of the key attributes of an innovation culture: that 'failure' is a learning point and that what does not work now may still be a stepping stone to the future.

Another key reason why pure invention is not sufficient to guarantee sales is down to the changing world order brought on by the internet. The world has moved on from the days in which a new invention, a fresh product, a slick advertising campaign or a new marketplace could deliver enough growth to keep an organization's shareholders happy. The advent of the global-digital age has levelled the playing field to a dramatic extent. The idea that certain products or services were the sole preserve of 'the big players', with smaller entities left to pick up the crumbs, has vanished.

We now live in an era of homogeneity, in which every business, large and small, potentially has the same level of access to products and technologies. A sole trader can advertise online and take part in social media interactions as easily as a larger organization. Technological breakthroughs are dissected and disseminated online in a short space of time and young entrepreneurs are seeing and acting on market opportunities on an international scale. In fact, smaller businesses and entrepreneurs have the ability to be faster and more agile than their longer-established competitors, as they don't have the legacy or the fear/risk-averse mentality. This is the marketplace challenge that larger organizations have to face if they are to secure future growth.

In some cases organizations are even sharing their new technologies online in the hope that their inventions will lead to marketplace changes. The internet has also led to the growth of a new phenomenon: turning to the power of the crowd to create fast solutions for global problems such as potential cures for disease.

This levelling of playing fields is challenging larger, more established organizations in ways that they would never have expected a few years ago. To meet these challenges, organizations have to reinvent themselves, to meet the entrepreneurs on level terms and to match them in the flexibility stakes. In other words they need to harness the power of *intrapreneurs*, creating a workforce as capable, agile, empowered and engaged as that seen in entrepreneurial businesses. And when the same levels of technology can be accessed by everyone then the differentiators are increasingly moving towards creating differentiated business models and customer experiences through innovation.

Apart from homogeneity there are two main drivers that have made a culture of innovation an imperative in modern business. They are the changing expectations of consumers, in particular, Generation Z and a new imperative from regulatory bodies worldwide.

The drivers of change – Generation Z

We've mentioned above that today's consumers are not willing to be as accepting of the authority of business as they might have been in previous times. This is partly a result of the recession and partly thanks to the successive scandals, such as mis-labelled meat products, London Interbank Offered Rate- (LIBOR) fixing, mis-selling mortgage-backed securities in the United States and Payment Protection Insurance (PPI) mis-selling in the UK, which have tainted the view of businesses as always being right. But far more than that the growth of the internet has given rise to a new breed of consumer and employee, and these individuals have a different world viewpoint from any seen before. They are the inheritors of change; they see technological and social change all around them and they are out to embrace the potential that this change brings. In a way they are the embodiment of the people to whom Eric Hoffer (1973) refers when he said: 'In a time of drastic change it is the learners who inherit the future. The learned usually find themselves equipped to live in a world that no longer exists.'

In the 18th century wealthy young men – and a few women – went on The Grand Tour; a journey through Europe that was designed to open their eyes to cultural heritage and other ways of living. But for the masses who stayed at home, the social and consumerist order was very much dictated by secular and religious leaders from the local community with local concerns far outweighing international affairs, unless a war intervened.

Gradually, with the advent of newspapers and then radio the worldview broadened. Those returning from war brought back tales of other ways of life, and following the Second World War the way became open for mass travel and our horizons broadened. International trade expanded, we no longer looked overseas for purely luxury items and businesses started to incorporate overseas suppliers in their 'best value' models for sourcing products.

But even then, the general viewpoint was one of parochialism first. Until, that is, the internet intervened and brought the grand tour and a world viewpoint to everyone's homes, businesses and smart devices. The first generation to grow up and enter the world of work in tandem with the rise of the internet was Generation Y. In 2014, those born at the end of Generation Y turned 18 but they have already had a profound effect on interactions within the workplace and on consumer habits.

But in a way Generation Y were merely the harbingers of what was to come, the ones who learnt about the internet but who were not fully steeped in its potential. So if you think that Generation Y's demands for a new way of business shook up the way we viewed the world, just wait until Generation Z hits the marketplace in force. Born around the turn of the century, this generation has already widely been recognized as the most diverse, technologically savvy generation we have ever seen.

Generation Z inhabitants have never known a time without fast access to broadband. According to an Ofcom report in August 2014, 6-year-olds have the same digital understanding as 45-year-olds and those aged 14 and 15 are way out in front when it comes to digital quotient scores. These are the young people for whom 94 per cent of their communication time is spent in social networking or instant communications at the expense of e-mail (2 per cent) and voice calls (3 per cent) (Ofcom, 2014). These are the always-on, connected, multi-tasking generation whose attention span may be just eight seconds but who also pack so much into those eight seconds that they put earlier generations to shame.

Organizations which cling to the old way of working, which believe product is only as important as the cheapest price point, that short-term profits are more important than long-term stability and that customers and employees are necessary nuisances are in for a profound and steep learning curve if they are to successfully interact with Generation Z. Even Next Generation Organizations – those which leverage Intelligence, Collaboration and Adaptability to create products and services that resonate with the changing marketplace – will have to stay on top of their game to meet the expectations and worldview of the post-millennial internet generation. We'll look at Next Generation Organizations in more depth later on in this chapter.

Make no mistake, over the next 10 years, as Generation Z matures, they will transform the business landscape. Out goes unthinking acceptance and passivity and in comes ownership and interaction. As a report on Generation Z from pluralthinking (2014) says: 'Gen Z have never been passive recipients of brand messages, users of products or choosers of ideas. They expect to be involved in a brand's creation and destiny.' If you take sports shoes as an example, we've been through the 'white plimsoll' generation, moved on into 'brand loyalty is all' and have now reached a time in which we can go online and design our own individual colour and style.

Not only does Generation Z expect their chosen brands to interact with them, they also expect them to reflect a more mature, ethical viewpoint. Growing up in the chaos of recession and unrest, Generation Z is a far more mature and caring generation than that which has gone before. A report from sparks & honey (2014) which looked at Generation Z in the United States revealed that Generation Z are:

- hyper-aware about their impact on the planet;
- more caring, with 60 per cent being keen to volunteer;
- more self-directed – being used to looking for answers online;
- more entrepreneurial, with 72 per cent wanting to start their own businesses.

They also think in 4D, are at home communicating with images and the report also suggests that Generation Z are far more spatially aware, being familiar with viewing and communicating shared images – including 360-degree video – online. In fact, the ease with which they multi-communicate has stepped them out of the team orientation of previous generations and towards a collective consciousness. So different are Generation Z from the preceding generations that it will take a concerted leap for organizations to successfully integrate them into the world of business, as customers or as employees.

As employees, with Generation Z being more caring, more mature and more tech-savvy, it stands to reason that the workplace needs to be a very different place. These future employees simply won't resonate with the silo-based hierarchical daily trudge. When these individuals hit the workplace they want to be involved, to use their multi-tasking creativity as a force for good. And don't forget, one of the key reasons for workplace diversity is for the employee mix to represent diversity within the organization's sphere of influence. This means that if you have Gen Z customers you need Gen Z employees who will help to design products and services, values and attitudes perfectly aligned to the customer base.

Adapting to Generation Z is a challenge in its own right. Employers will have to change their business models in order to attract, retain and reward the best and brightest of this generation. Flexible working, a blending of personal and business time and an embracing of inclusive collaboration will all have to enter the business lexicon, and that's without even having to face up to the innovation agenda.

From the business perspective Generation Z is just what is needed to transform the landscape. They don't need to have the benefits of an open, innovative, transparent business culture explained to them because they live it on a daily basis. This generation not only believes in inclusion and communication, it is part of their DNA. But woe betide any organization which seeks to pigeonhole these people into an existing hierarchical system or who thinks that paying lip service to corporate social responsibility is sufficient. The inhabitants of Generation Z will expect to see values such as social responsibility, inclusivity and sustainability demonstrated on an ongoing basis and if they aren't then they will be off, taking their talents to a more open and innovative business culture or to set up business on their own.

So responding to this new generation requires organizations to adapt to an innovative and agile methodology. Social media is not just an adjunct to marketing it is now an intrinsic part of the product itself. Selling is now less about the product and more about the experience. In a world in which interconnectedness is taken for granted, those seeking to stand out have to offer original experiences that bring a sense of ownership to the user.

There is one further change being imposed by Generation Z consumers and that is the idea of *hyperlocalism*. Because the world is their backyard, in their search for identity this generation is far more likely to embrace products and services which they can identify as having a personal or local meaning. This idea of providing a local slant to a global product will only grow in as Generation Z comes into its own. In fact, according to the Generation Z report from pluralthinking (2014), this rise in hyperlocalism has already seen McDonald's offering country-specific products such as Ebi Shrimp in Japan, while at the 2014 World Cup Brazilians turned out in force wearing locally made products.

In fact, when you think about it, hyperlocalism is one of the natural next steps to take in response to an increasingly homogenous world. When all can be the same then the differentiator increasingly has to have meaning. How we provide exceptional customer experiences is one aspect of this, as is involving the customer in the design of the product; but so is creating a product which speaks to and has a personal meaning for the customer.

The drivers of change – regulation

'Innovation-led growth can also provide the manoeuvrability that will make it easier for governments to address pressing social and global challenges, therefore being critical for facilitating the transition to greener economies.' (Angel Gurría, 2010)

Since the OECD (Organization for Economic Co-operation and Development) Secretary-General made these remarks in 2010, the imperative to boost global growth through innovation has gained fresh momentum. The fallout from the global financial crisis and from successive mis-selling scandals has led the world's regulators to see innovation as the solution both for driving growth and for creating a new business imperative which values the culture of doing things right over the culture of short-term profitability. Wherever you look, from international organizations such as the G20, the OECD and the European Union to individual countries and on down into business there is recognition that innovation-led growth is the only way forward.

In fact innovation is very much on the G20 agenda. G20 meetings in Australia in 2014 highlighted some 1,000 initiatives that have been identified as having the potential to boost global growth by 1.8 per cent. And this imperative has been taken up across the world. Selecting three articles from 2014 as examples there is a worldwide recognition that embracing an innovation culture can help to drive growth:

- 'If the Australian economy is to continue growing and living standards are to continue to rise, we must embrace innovation as a national imperative.' (*The Australian*, 2014)

- 'Future challenges for China include the transition of investment-led growth to innovation led-growth.' (National School of Development, Peking University, 2014)

- 'We need to make swift progress towards realizing South Africa's economic potential in an inclusive and sustainable manner. Innovation-led growth is essential to realizing this objective.' (Whelan, 2014)

The UK too is strongly in favour of the innovation imperative with, at the time of writing, the government sponsoring a Growth and Innovation fund, which is supporting employer-led projects to boost growth through innovation. UK regulators are not far behind with the Financial Conduct Authority announcing in 2014 that: 'Our commitment to fostering innovation in the interests of consumers is not a fad. It is now an important part of our regulatory philosophy.' (Wheatley, 2014)

This theme of developing organizational culture to meet changing dynamics was echoed by the Financial Reporting Council (FRC) at the beginning of 2015 when it announced that in 2015 it would continue to 'assess how effective boards are at establishing company culture and practices, and embedding good corporate behaviour.' (FRC, 2015)

The culture of innovation

Now that we have built an understanding of the difference between invention and innovation and examined some of the imperatives that are driving organizations to future-proof themselves by adopting a culture of innovation, it is time to develop our understanding of what an innovation culture actually is. We'll start with a look at organizational culture but it may be helpful to first have a quick look at a couple of definitions.

Our definition of culture: 'The combination of leadership style, values, behaviours, attitudes and working practices of an organization's people together with the formal and informal infrastructure which makes it stick (policies, processes, systems); it's visible not only to employees but also to customers, partners and suppliers.'

Our definition of innovation: 'The successful implementation of something new or different that is affordable, accessible, adds value to the customer by solving a real problem and drives growth for the creator.'

Let's start by looking at the basics of organizational culture. Every organization has a culture. It may be toxic, it may be nebulous, or it may be the one thing which drives business-changing synergies but whether recognized or not, it is there. An organization's culture starts to develop even before the organization is formed on paper. It is affected by the thoughts and actions of its leadership team and its employees; it can evolve over time and can be changed by a concerted effort (change programme) or by a change in leadership, merger with another organization, etc.

It is tempting for organizational leaders to believe that their culture is synonymous with their employee handbook, performance management process and workflows but in reality culture runs far deeper. It is less the things that are done and more the way in which things are done. It is the DNA of the organization and it ultimately guides the organization's engagement with its employees and its relationships with the wider world.

Organizational culture is essentially the collective beliefs, values, attitudes, behaviours and communication style of the people who work within an organization. Unless deliberately set, or re-set, by the current or previous leaders of the organization, the culture will have been built up and modified over time from every internal and external interaction. An organization with a strong culture will be more likely to have good relationships with its suppliers, have engaged employees, a loyal customer base, a positive online reputation and will attract investors and financial institutions that are happy to support the business with loans and other investments.

To help our understanding let's have a quick look at two hotels which sit side by side in the same town. They may have identical facilities and pricing but one is more popular than the other. The reason for this difference is likely to be due to differences in culture with one greeting and treating guests as valued friends while the other sees guests more as paying transactions. The hotel with the better culture sees a spiral improvement with delighted guests posting positive reviews online which encourage more guests to sign up and so on.

Or let's look at an organization which professes on its website or in its literature to put customers first or to provide an outstanding level of customer service. If the words are backed by actions with every person and every process geared towards customer excellence then the business will profit. However, if in reality employees are given targets for numbers of calls answered irrespective of outcome, if departmental leaders play a game of one-upmanship and if the leadership team value the bottom line over all else then clearly the words don't match the actions and the business will suffer.

Sadly, sometimes despite the best intentions at the top the message about an intended culture change is filtered through successive layers until the employees on the front line have no idea that they are supposed to be changing their behaviour or even how to change their behaviour. In effect the intended transformation of the marketing values hasn't been translated into tangible behaviours leading to employees who have not been educated, engaged or enabled to act.

Pausing for a moment to take the theoretical into real life let's have a quick look at Zappos. com. Widely held as one of the leading innovative organizations in the world, Zappos started as an online seller of shoes and clothing in the United States. But to simply describe Zappos as a seller of shoes would be somewhat akin to calling Michelangelo a painter and decorator. With 10 core values, which range from 'Deliver WOW through service' to 'Be humble', the Zappos way is widely cited as an example of outstanding company culture, innovation and employee engagement, so much so that Zappos has now expanded its offering to include 'boot camps,' showing other leaders how they can learn from the Zappos experience.

Some may point to the company as an anomaly, an organization whose whimsical weirdness could only work in the world of fashion. But while it is true that not every organization could run with the full Zappos model, it is equally true that every organization can learn from the way that Zappos has shaped its organization to meet its core mission of 'providing the best customer service possible'. This mission has resulted in a focus on employee engagement, on putting the customer first and on innovation. But despite all of the attention-grabbing headlines, creating a strongly innovative culture is not the same as creating anarchy. So while fun, weirdness and adventure sit within the core values, the code of conduct includes more traditional sections such as integrity, confidentiality and honesty.

But make no mistake; whether you fully embrace a culture of fun or seek to preserve a more staid image, the one thing that will differentiate your business from all the rest is the way in which you embrace innovation as a means to providing outstanding customer experiences. Some of the original Zappos ideas such as free returns and free delivery could easily be matched by any other sales organization but it is only when these are backed up by outstanding service allied to committed employees that a business can start to showcase *how* it delivers rather than *what* it delivers. And to make sure that the 'how' stands out, all new Zappos employees, no matter at what level, start with a four-week orientation process which includes manning the phones and dealing with sales and returns. At the end of that time, provided they have lasted the course, prospective employees are offered the alternatives of choosing a job or taking a cash sum to leave. This two-way process means that not only is Zappos hiring employees for cultural fit but the employees are choosing the company for the same reason.

Innovative, engaged, and holacratic; the Zappos way is not for everyone. But it has resulted in a low staff turnover rate, loyal customers and a fair amount of business arriving through recommendations. As CEO Tony Hsieh says, 'Your culture is your brand. Customer service shouldn't just be a department; it should be the entire company' (Zappos).

So if a strong culture results in good returns, why bother with taking the next step, which leads to a culture of innovation? Is a culture of innovation really a necessity or is it simply another fad which leaders can use to look good on the website? Quite simply, having a strong culture alone is not enough in a 24/7 homogenous world, making an innovation culture an imperative – so much so that an *Economist* Intelligence Unit Report in 2015 commented that: 'Most firms identify innovation as a strategic priority' (*The Economist*, 2015).

Just looking back over the last few years we have seen seemingly strong organizations fail simply because they have not been agile enough to change their offering in response to technological change, or else they failed to understand the changing requirements of their customers. Having a strong culture is no longer enough unless that culture embraces the triple innovation goals of intelligence, collaboration and adaptability.

Quite simply, an innovation culture is one in which the organization is geared up to deliver products and service levels which will enable it to stand out from its competitors. In effect, with an innovation culture driving the organization not only do we get game-changing products, we also get a whole new way of working which leads to game-changing levels of customer experience. But successful innovation cultures go one further. They understand that to really make a difference they have to not only respond to customer demand but also be at the forefront of the demand, shaping and creating markets, leading and driving the change.

Next Generation Organizations

There are three types of business in this world, those which failed to survive the recession, those which survived but have either plateaued or are in slow decline and those which will create the future. We call these last businesses *Next Generation Organizations*. Next Generation Organizations understand that the future will not be delivered through existing ways of working. They know that the game has moved on from 'what' to 'how' and that they need to master strategic innovation in order to deliver new business models and to deliver differentiated experiences. And to be a Next Generation Organization they need to focus on three core elements of innovation, namely Intelligence, Collaboration and Adaptability.

Why intelligence? Because despite the growing prevalence of 'big data', customer satisfaction indices still show a gulf between expectations and delivery. In fact, the UK Customer Satisfaction Index Report for January 2015 commented that: 'results reflect profound shifts in the market environment. Customers' expectations have evolved rapidly, leading to an ever-growing desire for convenience, speed and value.' (Institute of Customer Service, 2015)

Why collaboration? Because the marketplace has moved away from insular, siloed ways of working and towards a more open approach, which draws ideas in from everywhere. The Institute of Customer Service report mentioned above also commented that: 'in this new environment, those organizations that put service at the heart of their business models and collaborate to deliver the end-to-end experience will be the most successful.'

Why adaptability? Because 54 per cent of firms see creating new products and services as a top three priority in the next few years (*The Economist*, 2015). Businesses that are not geared up to adapt and bring products to market fast are going to be left behind by disruptors, some of which have not even been set up yet.

And these concerns aren't confined to the UK. The foreword to PricewaterhouseCoopers' 18th Annual Global CEO Survey (PwC, 2015) commented that: 'given the scale of the challenges and uncertainties that today's CEOs face in global markets, it's little wonder that the one "must have" attribute they point to for future success is adaptability.' The same report revealed that when it comes to collaboration, 51 per cent of Global CEOs are looking to enter into new strategic alliances or joint ventures in the forthcoming year, 69 per cent are either already collaborating or considering collaborating with suppliers and two thirds are either collaborating with or looking to collaborate with customers. Let's look at these attributes in a little more detail, starting with *intelligence*.

Where does your interaction with your customers begin? Is it when they see an advert in a paper or click on an e-mail? Perhaps it is when they browse the net for their next purchase; or does customer interaction start and end when they step over your threshold? If you think any of these things then your business is very much in trouble.

In truth, everything you do as an organization is part of the customer interaction process. More importantly, every decision, every action, every process should be carried out with the sole aim of providing an exceptional level of customer experience. But this begs the question: 'How well do you know your customer?' and more importantly: 'How well do you understand your customer?'

The trouble with living in an information age, when big data abound and surveys are only a mouse-click away, is that it is all too easy to confuse facts with understanding. You may know the average age, sex and spending patterns of your customer base. You may even have carried out some whizzy survey which shows how many newspapers your customer reads or whether they like indoor or outdoor pursuits. But do you really *know* them? How much do you really understand about the daily lives of your customers and how they interact with your product? More importantly how far does this translate into providing different products or services, which will go over and above meeting customer needs?

It's the age-old dilemma. Do you give people what they want or what they really need? Do you satisfy whims or enrich lives? Let's look at one theoretical example. Say you manufacture toothpaste and want to know more about your customers. You send out surveys, you run focus groups, you may even observe as customers brush their teeth in the mornings. But all of that activity only tells you about the time when your customers are actually using your product and thus is only ever likely to deliver incremental improvements. What happens over the rest of the day? What do they eat and drink, whom do they see, what environments are they in? Would gaining a true insight persuade you to look again and come up with a product, which your customers can use as an adjunct to their brushing schedule while they are on the move? Shock horror – you've just invented toothpaste chewing gum!

But gaining a true understanding of your customers requires a new approach. If you want to know more about the world and how to use it to create opportunities, shape markets and change the game then you need intelligence – an increased focus on insight and new approaches to gathering it from customers, consumers and markets. Technology has moved on to such an extent that every organization has access to information-gathering techniques which were unheard of only a few years ago. Store card use, monitoring web interactions, social media traffic: all have the potential to help businesses to really gain insight into their customer base. So why do 47 per cent of businesses say shifting customer expectations and demand (32 per cent) and customer empowerment (15 per cent) are among the trends most affecting their businesses today (illumiti, 2013)?

Perhaps it has something to do with the fact that organizations are still focusing on statistics, on measurable patterns rather than really trying to get under the skin of their customers. Statistics tell you what has happened in the past, intelligent innovation means predicting what will happen in the future. To succeed, organizations need to step out of their comfort zone and to use the services of experts who are better-placed to aid in predicting future trends. Let's look at an example. The supermarkets are well known to use the services of psychologists and behaviourists to help them to design store layouts to maximize impulse buys and to draw the eyes of shoppers to certain products. Yet supermarkets in general have been caught out by changing shopping patterns, which has resulted in the decline of the weekly or monthly shop in favour of daily purchases. A Food Standards Agency survey in 2014 revealed that just 57 per cent of households still relied on a weekly shop (Food Standards Agency, 2014) while other research revealed that at 4 pm, three in four people still hadn't planned what they were going to be eating for dinner that night.

Intelligent innovation requires businesses to use every different type of insight-gathering technique or resource they can on top of what they are already doing: from ethnography to using the services of subject matter experts, of psychologists and of futurologists to bring their knowledge of social shifts and of cultural changes to bear on predicting how current buying patterns will change in the future and then to change the business model to meet those fresh demands. It's this increased mix of activity and focus that shifts an organization from just gathering data or 'insight' to becoming more intelligence-based. And when you are gathering this intelligence don't ignore the tried-and-tested method of encouraging your people to interact with customers.

Building a deep understanding of the importance of intelligence, of truly understanding customers as opposed to knowing facts is the first step in designing a Next Generation Organization. Organizations which strive to be exceptional, to provide the highest levels of experiences in order to differentiate themselves from the marketplace have to embrace intelligence before they can move on to create experiences through collaboration and adaptability.

It's not easy. The old adage that you need to walk a mile in someone's shoes before you understand them is frankly unambitious. But the process starts with the desire to make a difference and with the realization that facts or a 'shed-load-of-data' won't help you to gain true understanding. If you want to make a difference and build a Next Generation Organization that puts its customers at the heart of innovation, start by getting to know them and the world better!

Once you have deeper understanding then you can move on to look at creating new pathways through collaboration. What does collaboration mean to you? If your instinctive answer is that collaboration means working together then you are not alone but forgive us if we come up with a supplementary question and ask what working together *really* means.

You see, for many, in business and in life, collaboration or working together is just another way of explaining task allocation. We need to paint the house so you wash the walls down while I go out and buy the paint. We need to come up with a great advert so you write the words while I source a picture. For many these would be good examples of collaboration and yet all they really are is a way of allocating tasks.

True collaboration is another level again. True collaboration means bouncing ideas off each other; true collaboration means leveraging individual talents and knowledge to enable groups to come up with something far greater than can be achieved by one person alone; in fact true collaboration means that the whole IS greater than the sum of the parts and once you move towards a collaborative model you will find that adaptability becomes so much easier. And let's be clear here; true collaboration doesn't mean setting groups of employees to work on a problem, true collaboration requires the business to draw in customers, consumers, industry experts, subject-matter experts, gurus, suppliers, partners, university research departments and sometimes even your competitors in a holistic search for innovative solutions.

It's time to learn the lessons which were bequeathed to us by organizations such as Comet, Blockbuster, Woolworths, and others – all seemingly rock-solid organizations that succumbed to the tsunami of recession and changed shopping patterns which swept across the globe. And the main lesson which we all need to take forward into this new period of growth is the need to be adaptable, to increase the focus on agility and to be able to execute change better and faster.

People have changed, shopping patterns have changed and will continue to change and businesses, which are not set up to change with them, are businesses which may learn the value of adaptability too late. In a world in which one picture, one thought, one tweet can go 'viral' in a few minutes, the only certainty is that there is no permanence. But by leveraging intelligence, by collaborating and by being agile, organizations can not only respond to trends but can drive change themselves, benefitting the organization, its investors and its customers.

We've already mentioned how some organizations are looking to collaborate with customers but even if this level of interaction has not yet been reached, the more innovative the organization, the more the customer benefits. Changing the focus to one that provides outstanding products alongside outstanding levels of service and experience is one which all businesses can benefit from. In a homogenous world it is the little touches, the attention to detail, the customer care, the responding to market trends and the attention to innovation which results in the exceptional levels of customer service which can feed into longevity, sustainability and profitability.

Pointing the way towards innovation

So far we've hopefully shown you why a culture of innovation is not only a 'nice-to-have' but is in fact an imperative which can transform, and save, organizations. But for those who are hanging on, reluctant to step into building a culture of innovation before they are forced to, what are the signs that tell you that the time for change is now?

The list below is not exhaustive but it does contain many of the more common scenarios. Some will also act as a warning that a general culture overhaul may be required but we make no apologies for including them here, as if a culture needs to change, it makes sense to move it forward to embrace innovation rather than tinkering at the edges of change.

- *The regulator tells you so* – Starting at the top, the clearest and most obvious sign that embracing a culture of innovation is a 'must-have' change is when the body regulating your particular business sphere sends out strong signals that it is looking for a culture of innovation. We've already had a look at this area under the 'drivers of change' section but it is worth touching on again in this section here, as it is a clear signal that change is required.

  Those within the financial services sector have perhaps received some of the highest-profile signals that the time for innovation is now, with the (Financial Conduct Authority) FCA commenting in 2014 that: 'We've committed to opening our doors to those – regulated and not – who come with new ideas about how to deliver financial services.' (Wheatley, 2014)

But innovation is not simply confined to this one sector. Water Services Regulation Authority, Ofwat's roadmap for 2015–16 for Wales includes a determination to 'drive innovation within the boundaries set by the Welsh Government to ensure improvements in efficiency' (Ofwat, 2014). Even the legal profession is not immune with the Solicitors Regulation Authority launching in December 2014 a research project to 'explore the reasons for innovation in business practice, such as in service delivery or business models, rather than legal practice innovation. It will investigate the impact of competition on the development of new business approaches, how well innovative change serves the needs of people using the services and the barriers to greater innovation.' (Solicitors Regulation Authority, 2014)

It's perhaps also worth highlighting here the fact that even when the regulator doesn't promote innovative behaviour, they may bring in changes that require innovative solutions. New legislation, a change in regulatory regimes, even a fresh approach to regulatory audit may be the catalyst for change.

While these examples are drawn from the UK, similar examples can be found across the globe. International reporting standards bodies, the European Central Bank, the United States Securities and Exchange Commission (SEC); regulators everywhere are looking for a new approach which moves away from the toxic practices which partly contributed to the recession.

Quite simply, if the regulator is looking for innovation then there is little choice if you want to avoid censure and being overtaken by those within your industry.

- *New entrants start taking market share* – There's nothing worse for an established organization than some upstart company coming in and taking market share away. But taking market share is what new businesses are all about. Be they dotcom companies taking share from high street retailers or 'instant cash' lenders taking share from the banking industry, start-ups come with none of the baggage of established businesses and are therefore geared to be more innovative and flexible. Muttering about traditional values won't bring back customers who have been attracted by choice, fast delivery or flexibility. And, to borrow a phrase from the financial services arena, past performance is no guarantee of future results. You may have served your customers well in the past and built up a measure of loyalty but that has no value unless you continue to deliver in today's marketplace.

- *Changing consumer expectations* – Even if new entrants into the marketplace aren't a threat, a change in consumer expectations or in buying patterns may well require innovative solutions. Towards the end of 2014 we started to see a fall-off in supermarket profitability with major players reporting a change in buying habits, away from the 'large' shop and towards a more as-and-when style of spending. So radical is the change that it prompted Waitrose Managing Director Mark Price to say that, 'This is a once in 50- to 60-year change. The last big change was the supermarket [in the 1950s]. I think what you are seeing now is as fundamental.'

- *Product homogeneity* – When my smart device looks like your smart device then the only differentiator is in how we sell the product and how we back up our sales with service and reputation. When someone working out of a garden shed can source IT products in China and sell them direct to consumers across the globe then why should we buy from an established company unless that company can offer something more than pure product? Homogeneity forces organizations to differentiate with exceptional customer experiences and that requires innovation.

- *Technological developments* – The fast pace of change means that organizations have to continually reinvent themselves and their products just to keep up. In fact, 75 per cent of CEOs say that fast-changing market conditions are forcing them to reinvent themselves faster than ever before (PwC, 2012). When traditional methodologies don't work the solution is to involve consumers, suppliers and the organization in an agile and collaborative drive towards new value creation.

- *Project delay* – There's an old saying within the building industry that all projects end up taking twice as long and costing twice as much as was originally envisaged. While we are not saying that that is universally true it is surprising how few projects, building or otherwise, manage to come in on time and within budget. Poor scoping at the outset, unrealistic estimates, deficient leadership, project creep; whatever the reason the result is the same. But when the pace of change is such that over-running projects have been themselves overtaken by events before they have been completed then the organization needs to take a hard look at a new and more innovative way.

- *Inter-departmental wrangling* – Perhaps initially seen as more of a culture problem, when departments start to in-fight then a radical solution is required. It doesn't matter whether the friction is caused by two leaders jockeying for the same promotion, by leaders who are so protective of their bonus that they refuse to allocate resource to help others out or simply because of a lack of understanding about the importance of differing roles. Whatever the reason, for the sake of the long-term good of the organization, it has to be sorted and the introduction of an innovation culture which looks away from silos and towards collaboration is an ideal solution.

- *Employee disengagement* – Countless surveys have pointed to the link between employee engagement and profitability. Quite simply, disengaged employees are more likely to leave, are more likely to take sick leave, create more wastage, don't care as much about professional outcomes and give less than their best to the job. When engagement levels fall then the culture needs an overhaul and introducing an innovation culture in which everyone has a stake in the direction of the business sends out a strong message about the way in which the organization values its employees.

- *Falling sales* – Creating new products and services may be a top-three priority for 54 per cent of corporations but a quick look at company reports reveals the extent to which organizations are still relying on fading revenue streams (*The Economist*, 2015). It is only when you look behind the statistics at the reason why revenue streams are fading that true pictures start to emerge. We've already touched on some of the reasons for falling sales, ie loss of market share to new entrants and changing consumer expectations, but there are many other reasons why sales may be falling. How about the product no longer being relevant in today's market, or product quality falling due to a problem with manufacture or sourcing? Are the sales and marketing departments working to their best or is there an element of disengagement creeping in? Are newer/better products taking market share or has a technological development rendered the product line obsolete? Whatever the apparent reason, the underlying truth is that the organization is either failing to leverage intelligence and/or adaptability in the right way or is simply not agile enough to keep up with changing trends.

- *Faltering reputation* – Time was when poor service may have been reported to a select group of friends but that was as far as it got. Now, poor service is broadcast across the world in seconds with social media, feedback forums and the like, all amplifying dissatisfaction. A single complaint can easily go viral and thereby give a wholly disproportionate view of the organization. Managing reputation is now a role in itself but why did the complaint arise in the first place? Is there a lack of understanding of the customer base? Did product failure come into play? Are targets skewed to sell rather than to provide exceptional levels of customer service? Has the organization lost touch with a focus on customer excellence?

- *Something just doesn't feel right* – Perhaps a bit of a catch-all here but leaders with their fingers on the pulse of the business often get a feeling that something is wrong long before it shows up in any statistics. Exceptional leaders know that when that feeling arrives it is time to act; to review the culture and engagement levels; to reconnect with suppliers and clients and to test the market.

Overcoming barriers to innovation

If you've been reading this chapter sequentially then by now you will have developed an understanding of innovation culture, its importance and the signs that may indicate that a change of culture is required in your business. In Chapter 2 we'll start looking at the first steps in a six-stage process which will lead you towards a fully scoped and embedded culture of innovation. But before we leap into the innovation stream there is one final element that we need to consider and that is the barriers which may arise on our journey.

'Be Prepared' is a motto that should hang over every change manager's door, particularly as failure to bring change in on time or on budget is often caused by the unexpected. Simply being aware at the outset of the barriers and pitfalls which may arise will enable you to either put steps in place to avoid the barriers or to swiftly deal with them when they arise. Let's start by looking at some of the barriers to innovation change.

- *The regulators won't approve* – Well actually, not only will they approve they are actively looking for business to transform, to move away from a hidebound, slow, process-driven, 'profit-is-all' mentality and towards something which delivers solutions for today's problems.

- *The investors won't back it* – Let's face facts; investors are looking for a return on their investment. They certainly won't back a business which consistently shows itself to be behind the curve and if the business goes under because it was not agile enough to adapt in response to changing appetites then the investors will place the blame squarely on the leadership team. The rise of crowdfunding, direct fundraising and peer-to-peer loans testifies to the public appetite for rewarding those who are prepared to challenge the status quo.

- *There is no public appetite* – Just look at the queues that develop outside shops across the globe when new models are released and then try and say that the public won't back change. Or look at the way in which online posts can go viral across the world thanks to near-universal adoption of social media technologies. How about the way in which online banking and shopping or working from home or from alternate sites have risen from nothing to being seen almost as a right in a few short years? These are all examples of the way in which the public are only too willing to accept change, provided it is presented in the right way. And don't forget the rise of Generation Z. They are actively looking for new models and want to be involved in co-creation.

- *Employee resistance* – It is a perennial challenge to balance the innate change-resistance within mankind with the explorer spirit which searches for new things. And: 'We've always done it this way', is hard to overcome, particularly if you are looking to replace hierarchical silos with a more collaborative way of working. But managing change and educating employees is a key element of any change programme and we'll cover this later on in the book. We'll also look at the associated challenges that come from creating ownership of the programme. And at the end of the day, if all else fails you can always borrow the 'if you don't like the change then leave' strategy adopted by Barclay's CEO Antony Jenkins when he brought in a sizeable culture change near the start of his tenure.

- *It's too risky* – Risk appetite is hard to overcome, as the fight-or-flight response is set within our genes. And when we talk about collaboration, flatter structures and innovation, which embraces failure as a learning point, then those with even mild risk-phobia can get twitchy. But innovation culture is not an unstructured free-for-all. Success is dependent on putting the right structures and goals in place and these manage risk far better than any tight control. Look at the financial services sector for example. The old regime under the then Financial Services Authority (FSA) imposed regulation after regulation and we still had mis-selling and malpractice. That's why the regulators are encouraging organizations to transform their cultures to ones which value care and ethics.

- *The technology isn't there* – Well, if you are losing market share to new entrants then the technology certainly *is* there. And if it isn't then it probably will be in a very short time. If you wait for technology to be in place then you will constantly chase the market, if you look to construct and to deliver then you can shape the market or create new ones.

- *It doesn't fit with our strategy* – As a CEO, you can't simply 'ask' for innovation, you have to move from talk to execution. Just like any other business imperative innovation requires a robust strategy that defines the course of action best suited to your organizational vision. We'll look at innovation strategy and alignment later on in this book.

- *It doesn't fit with the culture of the organization* – Well no, it probably doesn't at the start because otherwise you wouldn't be looking to build a new culture. Building and embedding a culture of innovation is only possible if you look at the change required in a holistic way. Your strategy and framework for innovation will depend on how much you are prepared to change your existing culture so that existing operations do not conflict and counteract the drivers that innovation requires. In almost every survey over 90 per cent of senior execs say people and culture are the most important factors for driving innovation! But the surveys also indicate that senior execs remain unconfident about how to approach embedding innovation. From that it's easy to see why the focus remains with capability and why that narrow focus rarely creates enough momentum to positively change culture.

- *Our people don't have the capability to be innovative* – What's commonly known as 'The Fuzzy Front End' is where most organizations start their innovation journey. However, the likelihood of anything more than incremental from the typical 'brainstorming' session is remote. In order to capitalize on your people's capacity for innovation, capability-building is key. You'll need to learn how to enhance idea generation and use design thinking to turn powerful ideas into commercially viable improvements, products or services quickly and consistently. This includes moving people way beyond the traditional 'brainstorming' sessions because in their current format, they just don't work! Innovation requires an organization-wide approach to the tools, techniques and processes that enable and enhance it. Create processes for gathering fresh, forward-thinking insight, genuine customer needs, wants, problems and tensions, ie intelligence. Then create a funnel for channelling ideas in the right direction towards implementation. Like anything else in business, if you don't have a process, your innovation efforts won't have consistency, won't be scalable and won't be efficient.

- *Our product is so similar to other businesses* – If your position is that the only thing you can do is compete on price so you can't afford to change then you might as well shut up shop now. When competitors' products are virtually identical then it is how organizations deliver the product that matters. Exceptional customer service and experience, strong reputation and even that word *trust* all come into play because the ultimate goal of innovation is as a driver of differentiation.

- *We don't know if what we do is working* – Generating lots of ideas is all well and good but more than ever we need those potential solutions to add value both internally and externally. Simply flooding an organization with large numbers of ideas is counterproductive and doesn't help the ongoing case for innovation when people don't see follow-through from their input. Measuring and gaining an understanding not only of the starting point but also of progress made is something which we will look at in depth in Chapter 2. Later on we will also look at the importance of generating some 'quick wins' to help to keep enthusiasm alive until such time as innovation is fully embedded in every individual and every process. As with any change programme, the better the communication the more easily it will be embraced.

CASE STUDY Identifying and overcoming barriers to innovation

Introduction

We've just been looking at some of the barriers to innovation change and starting to develop an understanding of the way in which the better prepared the leadership teams are, the easier it is to anticipate and overcome those barriers. But what does overcoming barriers actually mean in practice? We turned to Prudential to see how it successfully launched a new venture in Poland thanks to some strong leadership for innovation.

Situation

Following an analysis of the Polish marketplace, Prudential took the strategic decision to design, build and launch a new suite of products which were tailored to meet the needs of the Polish people. This meant not only taking into consideration the taxation and regulatory requirements which were specific to Poland, but also designing and implementing a business structure which would deliver expertise on a local level while maintaining the Prudential ethos. With the parent company sitting in the UK, product and sales methodologies would also have to satisfy UK regulators.

Although the leadership team were able to draw on their experience of operating in the UK and Asian marketplace, moving into a new territory brings its own challenges. Particularly so as CEO Abhishek Bhatia saw the opportunity to create a key market differentiator by taking the concept of a tablet application which was being used in Asia and integrating it into the Polish business model.

This app was planned to sit on sales agents' own devices ('bring your own device' – BYOD) and provide personalized customer illustrations as well as enabling electronic capture of customer data, leading to immediate processing of the policy (straight-through processing).

Approach

The benefits of the new app were clear to see in its use in Asia, with an improved customer sign-up rate allied to business efficiencies arising from electronic processing. In Poland, this was a completely new concept and Abhishek Bhatia could see that the app would differentiate Prudential from its competitors and assist with both recruitment of a sales force and promotion of products to customers. However, introducing such technological innovations to a self-employed sales force and to customers who were not used to such an approach potentially threw up a raft of business barriers including IT security and risk considerations.

The first challenge was to undertake an exercise which cut through rumour and generalities to identify the real potential barriers to change which those charged with introducing the new business would face. When involved in change management of any type, it can be all too easy to rely on the negative responses of a few change resistors, any of whom may come up with excuses to justify their internal reaction to change. Accordingly taking the time out to identify real threats will help to ensure that solutions will tackle real issues rather than smoke-and-mirror beliefs.

Following on from the initial exercise, the next step was to engage the people on the ground to take ownership of the project. Steps were taken to clarify roles and responsibilities, mapping out those who had ultimate ownership accountability and oversight responsibilities. Following on from this, Polish compliance and IT functions, as well as other key stakeholders were encouraged to buy into the project and to start not only to own the project but also to work with the leadership team towards providing solutions to perceived barriers.

One of those barriers related to the need to ensure secure access to client information on BYOD devices. The leadership team were aware that resolving this issue was key not only to the success of gaining general acceptance for the process but also to receiving regulatory approval. Accordingly, the leadership team engaged security architects to give guidance on possible solutions which included identifying optimum encryption levels and minimizing the amount of personal data which would be carried on external machines.

Once access and security had been mapped out the company followed rigorous penetration testing exercises to ensure robustness, and was ultimately able to satisfy both regulators and those concerned with risk governance of the security of the process.

While the technological barriers were relatively simple to overcome thanks to rigorous analysis and the creation of robust solutions, one of the biggest barriers which the project faced was the challenge of shifting peoples' mindsets. There was no 'burning platform', people couldn't visualize what it would be like or why it was so necessary to have the tablet app so their natural inclination to maintain the status quo came to the fore. This led to people talking about the solution in terms of risk rather than opportunity; but in reality risk was being used as a substitute for individual appetites for change.

This was where having a small group of people who were equally passionate about the idea was critical for success. Those within the group wouldn't give up, were driven and passionate about change but also felt supported by the leadership team. This support group were key to obtaining general acceptance on the ground but they would not have been able to do so without having strong leadership and sponsorship from the top. Identifying and drawing in those who would ultimately be responsible for the process at an early stage built a team of enthusiastic employees who were able to buy into and take ownership of the product, creating a momentum, which lead to a successful introduction.

With the leadership team being convinced that the tablet app was critical for success and championing this at every stage, the support group felt enabled to take the idea forward. As Abhishek Bhatia believes, the role of a change leader is to get more people to carry the dreams. He also believes strongly in the importance of maintaining momentum, delivering innovation in a short time-frame to avoid losing the initiative – having this small team in place to drive the idea and solution forward was key to success. In the spirit of this, and reflecting a wider innovation minimum viable product (MVP) ethos, 'sooner rather than perfect' was one of the key leadership messages which drove the project towards an on-time launch supported by rapid delivery of enhancements.

Conclusion

The success of the project was largely due to the innovation leadership provided by Abhishek Bhatia. He was clear about his vision, championed the products, methodologies and solutions, influencing and encouraging people to stretch beyond their comfort zones.

The new business using the tablet application was launched in 2013 with an initial product range and other products have since come on stream. On average, over 85 per cent of insurance applications are made on the tablet app and the majority of these proceed straight through to automatic underwriting. This means that the time it takes for the customer's policy to be issued is effectively halved, from eight days to four. Marketing surveys have consistently shown customers rating Prudential as a company that 'sets the trends' and 'is different to the competition', aspects that have an obvious connection to the innovative use of technology.

In the two years since launch, Prudential Poland has made significant inroads into the life insurance market, with brand awareness in the top 10 life insurance companies in Poland and rising. There are Prudential offices in 16 Polish cities and a sales force of over 600 agents, all of whom are equipped with tablets, and the company recently passed the 10,000 policy mark. The use of the tablet application has been a key factor in the company's success

In summary

In this chapter we've worked towards developing an understanding of the internal and external drivers which combine to make innovation a 21st-century imperative; not just for business but for other organizations as well. Along the way we've explored the difference between invention and innovation and shown how innovation can be used to provide solutions which add real value and drive growth.

This chapter contains a wealth of statistics which are designed both to be thought-provoking and to show the potential for change which is waiting for those who are prepared to grasp differentiated innovation. The key questions you now need to ask yourself are:

1 *Invention or innovation?* Do you want to just think of new things irrespective of whether they are genuinely useful or not or do you want to create customer-focused, game-changing solutions? Understanding where your organization sits on the invention/innovation spectrum will help you to concentrate resources at the most appropriate level.

2 *What are your key drivers of change?* In a heavily regulated environment your key drivers may be government or regulators. In other environments customers or social mores may lead the way. But whatever the drivers, however heavy the regulation there is still no excuse not to innovate.

3 *The clues are there* – Internal or external pressures, marketplace changes, new technologies; whatever the reason, the more you keep your finger on the pulse of your business the better you will know when the time for change has arrived. We'll come back to this in Chapter 2 when we look at cultural assessments.

4 *Surmounting the barriers* – Whether you are looking to adopt an innovation culture or simply change a process, anticipating potential barriers to change will enable you to negate potential barriers or to swiftly deal with them when they arise. As we'll see in later chapters being aware, planning and communication are the keys to success.

Key insights

- Innovation has moved from being a 'nice-to-have' to being a strategic imperative which transforms organizations and enables them to become market leaders and shapers of the future.

- Invention seeks to build on existing knowledge, to make something new or different; innovation seeks to create future-fit solutions to genuine problems and needs.

- Creating the future, becoming a Next Generation Organization, requires organizations to understand and embrace Intelligence, Collaboration and Adaptability.

References

BIS (2014) [accessed 13 January 2015] Innovation, research and growth, *Innovation Report 2014*, [Online] https://www.gov.uk/government/uploads/system/uploads/attachment_data/file/293635/bis-14-p188-innovation-report-2014-revised.pdf

Food Standards Agency (2014) [accessed 10 February 2015] The 2014 Food and You Survey, *Food Standards Agency* [Online] http://www.food.gov.uk/sites/default/files/food-and-you-2014-uk-bulletin-executive-summary_0.pdf

FRC (2015) [accessed 10 February 2015] FRC reports on better compliance with UK Corporate Governance Code and need for improved adherence to the UK Stewardship Code, *Financial Reporting Council* [Online] https://www.frc.org.uk/News-and-Events/FRC-Press/Press/2015/January/FRC-reports-on-better-compliance-with-UK-Corporate.aspx

Gurría, A (2010) [accessed 13 January 2015] Online OECD, 28 April 2010, http://www.oecd.org/economy/innovationandgreengrowthforajob-richrecovery.htm

Hoffer, E (1973) *Reflections on the Human Condition*, Harper & Row, New York

illumiti (2013) [accessed 13 May 2015] innovation and differentiation, [Online] http://www.illumiti.com/wp-content/uploads/2013/12/Oxford-Think-Piece-4-Innovation-and-Differentiation-document-55.pdf?submissionGuid=983c6926-2b7e-45f4-b846-dce3a56b9636

Institute of Customer Service (2015) [accessed 13 May 2015] [Online] http://www.instituteofcustomerservice.com/5629/UKCSI-executivesummaries.html

Ofcom (2014) [accessed 13 January 2015] The Communications Market Report, *Ofcom* [Online] http://stakeholders.ofcom.org.uk/market-data-research/market-data/communications-market-reports/cmr14/uk/

Ofwat (2014) [accessed 10 February 2015] Ofwat forward programme 2014-15, [Online] http://www.ofwat.gov.uk/aboutofwat/reports/forwardprogrammes/rpt_fwd201415print.pdf

Peking University's National School of Development (2014) [accessed 10 February 2015] National School of Development's Chief Economist Forum Successfully Held, [Online] http://en.nsd.edu.cn/article.asp?articleid=7441

pluralthinking (2014) [accessed 13 January 2015] Generation Z: The rise of the 8-second consumer, [Online] http://pluralthinking.com/2014/08/gen-z-the-rise-of-the-8-second-consumer/

Price, M (2014) [accessed 10 February 2015] Supermarkets are 20 years out of date, says Waitrose boss, *The Telegraph* [Online] http://www.telegraph.co.uk/finance/newsbysector/epic/tsco/11178281/Supermarkets-are-20-years-out-of-date-says-Waitrose-boss.html

PwC (2012) [accessed 10 February 2015] Innovation imperative, keeping your company relevant, [Online] http://www.pwc.com/en_GX/gx/consulting-services/innovation/assets/pwc-gyb-innovation-imperative-keeping-your-company-relevant.pdf

PwC (2015) [accessed 10 February 2015] 18th Annual Global CEO Survey, [Online] http://www.pwc.com/gx/en/ceo-survey/2015/assets/pwc-18th-annual -global-ceo-survey-jan-2015.pdf

Solicitors Regulation Authority (2014) [accessed 10 February 2015] New Research into Innovation, *Solicitors Regulation Authority* [Online] http://www.sra.org.uk/ sra/news/press/innovation-research.page

sparks & honey (2014) [accessed 13 January 2015] Meet Generation Z, *sparks & honey* [Online] http://www.slideshare.net/sparksandhoney/ generation-z-final-june-17

The Australian (2014) [accessed 13 January 2015] Growth Must be Innovation-Led: So what are we doing about it, [Online] http://www.theaustralian.com.au/ business/opinion/growth-must-be-innovationled-so-what-are-we-doing-about-it/ story-e6frg9if-1227079549633?nk=db4048f7c203fb991ad035c4e8bc7cb0

The Economist (2015) [accessed 10 February 2015] The Innovative Company, [Online] http://www.economistinsights.com/business-strategy/analysis/ innovative-company

Wheatley, M (2014) [accessed 10 February 2015] Competition in the interests of consumers, *Financial Conduct Authority* [Online] http://www.fca.org.uk/news/ competition-in-the-interests-of-consumers

Wheatley, M (2014) [accessed 10 February 2015] Innovation: The regulatory opportunity, *Financial Conduct Authority* [Online] http://www.fca.org.uk/news/ innovation-the-regulatory-opportunity

Whelan, C (2014) [accessed 10 February 2015] Innovation is SA's Potential Economic Killer App, *Mail & Guardian* [Online] http://mg.co.za/article/ 2014-09-16-innovation-is-sas-potential-economic-killer-app/

Zappos.com [accessed 13 January 2015] Your Culture is your brand, [online] http://blogs.zappos.com/blogs/ceo-and-coo-blog/2009/01/03/ your-culture-is-your-brand

Understanding where you are today

In Chapter 1 we looked at the background to innovation, examining the social and business drivers which make the adoption of a culture of innovation an imperative for organizations that seek to thrive in the post-recessionary marketplace. Now we are ready to move on, to set out on the first leg of our six-stage journey, which will lead us towards a fully scoped and embedded culture of innovation.

We start with a cautionary tale. Finding himself lost in the countryside, a driver spots someone leaning on a gate and stops to ask for directions. After a long silence and a thoughtful stare at the sky the answer finally arrives: 'Well, if I was going there I wouldn't be starting from here.'

Rural myth or not, the story perfectly sums up the way in which many businesses start their innovation journey. CEOs generally agree that innovation is an organizational imperative but all too often the approach used to integrate innovation into organizational culture is doomed to failure. Put simply, if you try to move to become an innovative organization by calling a meeting and demanding ideas you have lost before you start.

Changing an organization into one which lives and breathes innovation is not rocket science but it does demand careful planning, particularly if the leadership team want to engender enthusiasm in the concept of innovation by building in some early quick wins at the outset followed by further sequentially designed wins to keep enthusiasms fresh while the bigger culture change is under way. Starting the innovation journey in the right place, following the roadmap, is not a click your fingers and it's done solution but it can deliver quick wins along the way and it will lead to an organization that is transformed permanently and able to deliver consistently and continuously.

Admittedly while it's true that simply tasking the team to come up with 'something' may result in a few quick ideas, unless innovation has been incorporated into the organization's DNA, the impetus will soon fade to be replaced by cynicism and doubt. This in turn can lead to lowered levels of employee engagement as people start to see the move towards innovation as 'yet another fly-by-night idea' which costs them time and disrupts the norm. You will find that the topic of employee engagement comes up regularly throughout the book. Quite simply, however much time and effort is put into defining vision and strategy, unless employees are engaged in the process then it has little chance of succeeding. This is particularly true if employees are already jaded from previous failed projects. That is why it is so important for employee engagement levels to be considered not only at the outset but throughout any change project. This assessment should include an analysis of the general levels of employee engagement and why they are at current levels. In particular, the history of previous change programmes should be taken into account, whether these have led to 'change fatigue' and what barriers to change may have arisen as a result of previous programmes. This will enable the leadership team to put plans in place to learn the lessons of past culture change attempts and plan for success.

The only way to create lasting change is to tie it in with the vision and values of the organization and then engage employees in making it a reality. Remember, a new product or service can be copied really quickly by a competitor and be on the market instantly but what can't be copied is the workings of a culture where every single employee is innovation-ready and focused on making the vision a reality.

So this chapter is about understanding and defining the starting point, about making sure that when you embark on your innovation journey you do so with an awareness of the present guiding your steps towards the future. On this part of the journey we'll take in an assessment of the current organizational culture and examine how different levels of innovation maturity and employee engagement can affect planned innovation implementation. We will then move on to start to create the innovation strategy and to develop an understanding of the strategic mix which best suits differing organizations. Finally we will look at ownership of the innovation agenda and its alignment around the innovation strategy and primary Key Peformance Indicators (KPIs).

Why not simply buy innovation?

Before we really get going on developing an understanding of where we are today it is probably worth considering the merits, or otherwise, of simply buying in innovation. The rise of globalization allied with the pace of technological change seen in recent decades has resulted in a drive towards finding instant answers, instant solutions and that 'want it now' culture has resulted in an increasing trend for businesses to simply buy solutions from the marketplace. In Chapter 1 we touched on the way in which regulators, in response to public demand, are looking for a new way, one which values long-term growth over short-term profits and which looks towards the ethics of care and of doing it right. But for many organizations which have been steeped in the 'me-first, fast buck' culture of recent times, there is still a temptation to look for quick answers and quick solutions.

The simple and cost-effective answer is to gear the organization up to embrace agility as a by-product of innovation. The more an organization looks towards innovation, the more agile it becomes, resulting in a self-feeding drive towards incremental innovation on a daily basis. But with organizational cultures geared more towards 'easy' instant results the favoured approach to innovation, within the larger companies at least, has increasingly been to buy in innovation through mergers or acquisitions. Many have gone further, looking towards crowdsourcing and investing in start-ups to increase the inbound number of ideas and innovations.

The danger in this is that it not only disregards 'internal talent' or internal innovation capability, it can also create a divisive 'them and us' situation between different divisions of the organization. There is nothing wrong per se in buying in talent from outside and indeed when the parent organization is itself geared up for innovation then adding to the mix will only lead to long-term benefits. But when the internal innovation capability is not only undercapitalized but is actively suppressed and yet employees see energy, enthusiasm and funding being directed towards external innovators, the logical conclusion will be a fall in employee engagement levels alongside the development of a growing resentment towards the leadership team and the external organization.

It is perhaps appropriate here to mention Dan Pink's book *Drive* which examines human motivation. In the book Dan examines the three motivating factors, namely Purpose, Mastery and Autonomy. Give people a mission to believe in, allow them to become really good at whatever their role is and remove the red tape to allow them to innovate. Always buying from outside sends a message to staff that their ideas aren't valued or good enough. In effect it reinforces the notion that they are paid to process and follow orders rather than think for themselves and find better ways of doing things. This will disengage them. Conversely, engaging employees by involving them in what you are trying to achieve will pay dividends, as they get better at what they do and become more interested in doing better for the company.

So the more that you buy in innovation the more you will have to keep buying it in as people become more and more demotivated and disengaged. This then knocks on to another problem which can arise from simply buying in talent and that is that employees are the people on the front line. They are generally the closest to the problems and challenges that customers face, they may be at the bottom of the communication food chain or the most overburdened by internal bureaucracy. Consequently they are best placed to identify the challenges and to help devise the solutions, which will result in a better business model. Ignore them, fail to consider or even ask for their ideas and input and disengagement follows. It is therefore vital that employees throughout the organization have a voice. Include them once and if done properly you have instantly improved engagement levels and opened up the way towards innovation.

One of the characteristics of a fully developed innovation culture is that it looks outside itself to create solutions. Nothing is off-limits and those who are secure in their innovation capabilities will even draw in rival organizations alongside customers, suppliers and others to add to collaboration on innovation, better known as 'open-innovation'. So while looking outside the organization to enhance internal capabilities is a strong element of an innovation culture, doing so when the parent organization has yet to embrace innovation capacity can be a recipe for disaster.

The stark truth is that building a culture of innovation is a long-term initiative, as it should be when the end goal is long-term innovative gain. But for those who can become discouraged if immediate results are not forthcoming there are 'quick wins' to be had along the way and we will examine these in a later chapter.

Know thyself – the cultural assessment

Harking back to our rural myth of the lost driver, the first step on the road towards innovation capability is to know where you are starting from by carrying out an assessment of the current state of the organization's culture. This initial cultural assessment is effectively little different from the assessment which organizations should undertake when considering any cultural overhaul.

In fact, many of the steps to be taken on the innovation culture journey may be familiar to those who have studied the theory and practice of organizational cultural change. The difference here is that moving the organization towards an innovation culture requires a far more profound change than simply re-addressing the customer care charter, re-evaluating the sustainability policy or wanting to drive up engagement.

But whatever cultural change an organization faces, it will only succeed if it has a deep understanding of its starting point. With any culture change the golden rule is to measure–act–measure again and once an innovation culture has been adopted this pattern of continuous improvements becomes part of the organizational DNA. But in the first instance organizations are

FIGURE 2.1 Cultural assessment

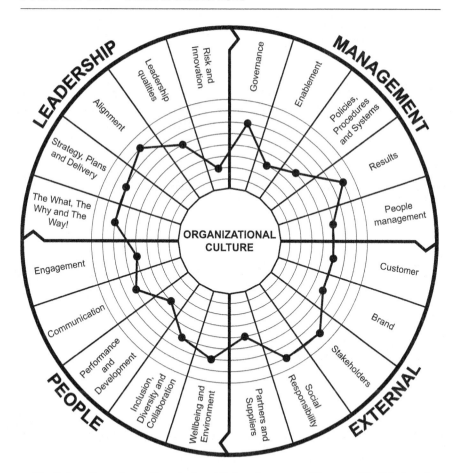

The Culture Consultancy Organizational Culture Assessment™ covers 20 attributes of organizational culture from 4 different perspectives (Leadership, Management, People and External). As an example, each ● above represents the score for each attribute which collectively show the overall picture of an organizations existing culture.

best advised to employ a suite of qualitative and quantative measurements which will enable the leadership team to develop an in-depth understanding of the current level of innovation maturity.

These measurements will vary from organization to organization but will generally include an employee engagement measurement alongside a review of leadership, management styles, behavioural norms, practices and HR metrics alongside customer, supplier and other external stakeholder feedback. We'll start with a quick look at a cultural-assessment diagram and then go on to examine some of the key areas on which those looking to move towards an innovation culture may wish to focus.

Breaking the cultural assessment down into leadership, management, people and external influences enables the leadership to focus more deeply on the factors which will drive or inhibit change. Depending on the nature of the organization, it may well be that sub-cultures come into play and therefore the results will differ across departments or divisions.

Understanding the enablers and inhibitors of the current culture will ensure that the leadership team can better understand the impact of 'the way things are done around here' on existing performance. Yes, the review may throw up factors which would need to be addressed in the short term, irrespective of any move towards an innovation culture but equally factors may come to light which are significantly driving a positive cultural dynamic. Care should be taken to ensure that these factors are retained or incorporated into the new vision to ensure that the organization doesn't lose a factor which is delivering a significant positive cultural influence.

When carrying out a cultural assessment, leaders should, wherever possible, strive for a holistic view rather than drilling down to uncover minutiae. Sampling the population and using as much existing data as possible will prevent early stages of the transformation becoming bogged down in data and will also reduce the burden on employees. With that in mind let's take a look at some aspects of the four key areas:

1 *Leadership* – Leading for innovation can be very different from leading a more traditional organizational culture. It requires leaders to be comfortable with empowerment and collaboration, with accepting failure as a learning point and with a new approach towards gaining insights. Knowing and understanding the leadership team's strengths, weaknesses and style at the outset will help to determine whether one of the first steps along the transformational path should be to work on leadership development.

    In particular we are looking here not just at the existing qualities of the leadership team but also at their propensity to embrace change. We'll see later on how important it is for the leadership teams to become fully aligned with the change. Identifying their risk appetite for change now, including whether they have the personal qualities which will embrace traits such as empowerment, delegation and collaboration, will make a measurable difference when it comes to defining and embedding change.

2 *Management* – Over-managed and under-led is not a practice which will work within an innovation culture. A cultural survey will help to pinpoint areas of strength which will help to drive the change forward as well as compliance and control areas which will require some changes. For example, if the permissioning system is overly prescriptive then changes will be required to bring it into line with a more flexible, outcome-oriented way of working.

3 *People* – It may come as a shock but this area encompasses far more than simply employee engagement. True, employee engagement is widely recognized as a key driver in the delivery of successful outcomes. Equally true is the fact that depending on the level of engagement seen at the outset, leaders may well have to build an employee engagement strengthening programme into the delivery mix to assure its success. In any event, a change of culture is a classic trigger for employee engagement levels to drop so understanding the starting point is vital if the organization is to take preventative measures and successfully align people with the new strategy and culture.

But the people area encompasses so much more. As you move through this book you'll encounter significant sections which are devoted to identifying innovation agents (i-agents), communicating change and the importance of diversity and people management. None of this is possible unless you understand the starting point and identify what the business and its employees need if change is to be successfully embedded.

4 *External* – An inclusive, innovative culture draws in not only employees but customers, suppliers and others. Taking account of social media at the outset can help the organization to gauge its current reputational strength as well as helping to define which social media/ focus group mix will maximize the chance of developing an innovative culture. Taking account of the level of innovation capability evidenced by third parties will help to form the basis of future collaborative dialogues. Taking account of the customer mix will help to drive any move towards greater diversity as well as forming the basis of the intelligence the organization will need as part of the innovation mix.

Incorporating self-assessment measurements into the mix at this early stage can bring twin benefits. Firstly, by comparing initial and subsequent results the leadership team can more easily keep track of the way in which the culture of innovation is diffusing throughout the organization, thereby acting as an early warning system should implementation slip at any stage. Secondly, and perhaps more importantly, by involving employees in assessments at an early stage the leadership team can send out a strong signal that they are serious about innovation and that they are actively looking for employee participation in the development of a culture of innovation. With one of the key planks of an innovation culture being open collaboration, the sooner employees are involved the more likely they are to be open to the idea of cultural change.

Innovation maturity

A key element of the cultural assessment is the identification of the current level of innovation maturity within the organization. It may be an old saying but 'you can't manage what you can't measure' is an important warning for leaders seeking to change culture around innovation.

Every company starting out on this journey will undoubtedly be at a different stage of 'innovation maturity' as by its very nature every organizational culture will be different and will work in a different (unique) way. Some will be reserved, some robotic, some will be creative, some will be toxic but whatever the nature of the culture it will have an effect on the level of innovation and hence 'maturity' at which an organization starts its journey as well as on the optimum pathway which an organization will need to follow. This is why it's impossible to look at Apple or Google or any of the usual 'they are amazingly innovative' suspects and copy their innovation strategy.

For a start, you'll never get any insight into what their real, full, detailed innovation strategy/approach is and even if you did, your culture is unique and you don't operate in the same way so simply implanting their 'way' into your organization will likely result in failure as their model is ousted by your corporate antibodies. Innovative or not, every organization's culture is unique. Culture redesign has to take into account past history, business sector, clientele, aims and strategies and a host of other factors, so copycat culture simply doesn't make business sense. You'll also be starting your innovation journey in a much less mature position than established innovators so it's important to define what we call 'the position of truth', ie just like a GPS or satellite navigation system can plot a route to your destination with absolute accuracy, it can only do so if it can pinpoint your starting location.

Innovation is like anything else: not only must you learn the basics first; your ability to learn will be considerably enhanced if you are realistic and open about your starting point. Borrowing from the martial arts vernacular, becoming a black belt is a journey that starts with no belt at all and requires fundamental techniques and methodology to be put in place in order to lay and set the foundations required. Defining innovation strategy, direction, approach, leadership, required culture/behaviour, tools, systems, processes etc, all takes time and needs to be tackled methodically, sequentially and pragmatically.

The model in Figure 2.2 will help you create a view of your current level of innovation maturity and help you define some of the things you'll need to do to increase your maturity level. This 4×4 innovation maturity model uses

FIGURE 2.2 The 4×4 innovation maturity model

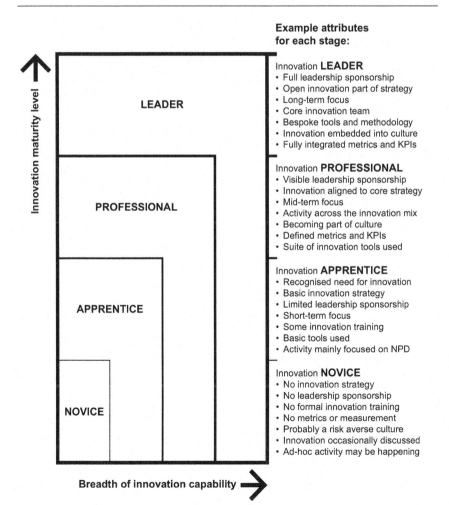

Example attributes for each stage:

Innovation **LEADER**
• Full leadership sponsorship
• Open innovation part of strategy
• Long-term focus
• Core innovation team
• Bespoke tools and methodology
• Innovation embedded into culture
• Fully integrated metrics and KPIs

Innovation **PROFESSIONAL**
• Visible leadership sponsorship
• Innovation aligned to core strategy
• Mid-term focus
• Activity across the innovation mix
• Becoming part of culture
• Defined metrics and KPIs
• Suite of innovation tools used

Innovation **APPRENTICE**
• Recognised need for innovation
• Basic innovation strategy
• Limited leadership sponsorship
• Short-term focus
• Some innovation training
• Basic tools used
• Activity mainly focused on NPD

Innovation **NOVICE**
• No innovation strategy
• No leadership sponsorship
• No formal innovation training
• No metrics or measurement
• Probably a risk averse culture
• Innovation occasionally discussed
• Ad-hoc activity may be happening

four stages of maturity from novice, apprentice, professional and ultimately leader assessed over four areas: strategy, leadership, culture and processes to build a picture of the current state of innovation and hence maturity in any organization.

Measuring innovation maturity

But measuring innovation maturity is only effective when the leadership team are clear about what they are measuring and when the measurements taken are appropriate and proportionate. So the key is to measure where and what helps you generate the type and area of innovation you need. We'll be looking at differing innovation models in more detail later on but one key mistake which leaders can all too easily make is to create a set of measurements which are too prescriptive.

For example, organizations may decide to follow the example of multi-national conglomerate 3M, which has prided itself on creating innovative solutions for more than 100 years and now boasts in excess of 55,000 products. 3M gives creative people the budget and freedom to innovate with Research and Development (R&D) receiving 6 per cent of revenue annually but it also gives all its people the freedom to explore and to innovate (3M, 2012). It would be easy to confine the measurement of success to patents filed and revenue generated as a result of the new inventions. However, while there is nothing wrong with this approach, it can silo innovation primarily with the 'men in white coats' and leave the rest of the organization out in the cold. That is why 3M also looks at areas such as business process, speed of getting products to market and intellectual property when measuring success.

This approach follows the contemporary and sustainable approach to innovation which moves it away from the province of the few and into the entire organization. With customers and consumers increasingly focusing away from product and on to experience, innovation expertise should respond by moving away from the few to become organization-wide. So focusing measurement on the few is self-defeating for an organization which seeks to develop a mature innovation culture across the board.

Part of the initial measurement of innovation maturity levels will come from the cultural assessment but on an ongoing basis it is also important to understand your innovation goals and to measure appropriately. The key is to fully understand what is required to deliver each different type of innovation as the ingredients will be different, ie what drives incremental innovation is very different to what delivers radical 'game-changing' breakthroughs. In other words, different inputs that deliver different outputs require different measurement. It is also important to develop an understanding of the type of people, skills and behaviour which will be needed to achieve your innovation goals as well as the optimum way to measure their performance.

In order to ensure that your innovation development is on track you need to build measurement and KPIs into the innovation process. This enables you to constantly measure and check along the way in real time at different stages of the process. Examples of measurements which track developmental pathways may include:

- numbers of problems unearthed or opportunities discovered;
- volume and quality of customer insight obtained during normal customer interactions;
- number of ideas about how to solve/capitalize on problems and opportunities;
- viable solutions, prototype development and refinement;
- revenue from new implemented ideas, ie Return on Investment (ROI);
- measuring the number of implemented innovations per person (IIPP).

Breaking down the process into incremental stages enables you to measure and understand if your innovation strategy as a whole is working and to identify where it may be improved.

One of the key lessons is not to measure too much. Innovation by its very nature is perceived initially (until it becomes part of 'how we do things around here') as additional work and adding measurement and criteria to the daily round only serves as a barrier to the progress which you are looking for. So while measurement is a vital tool in developing innovation, leaders need to be careful that measurement, or over-measurement, doesn't stifle any part of the innovation process.

Innovation maturity traps

An easy trap for leaders to fall into here is to over-rely on measuring innovation and to ignore other cultural indicators which allow innovation to happen. If you simply measure innovation then you have no idea what lies behind its success or otherwise. For example, innovative solutions may be flowing through because employees are fully engaged in the strategy of the organization or because you are offering a reward for ideas. Collaboration may be taking place because team leaders are encouraging it as an intrinsic part of an innovation culture or because the training is so poor that the only way employees have an idea about the product is if they ask other departments. Whatever the reason, the better idea the leadership team have about the underlying structure and culture of the organization, the more that they can develop it to deliver innovative transformations.

This is especially important in the first two developmental stages, ie the initial identification of problems, opportunities or gaps followed by the submission of ideas. It's very easy to unwittingly dismiss ideas because of measurements that are slightly outside the norm or are a little too radical or are slightly out of line with the typical product/service offered by the organization. It is also difficult to measure things that are somewhat 'adjacent' but in terms of differentiation through innovation it is adjacency that starts the journey to differentiation and competitive advantage.

Moving forward, measuring and re-measuring the whole innovation process gives you visibility of potential issues which may arise along the innovation journey. For example, if at some point the variety of ideas starts to decline it is likely that your ideas are starting to come from a smaller group of people. This provides an early warning that for some reason the innovation pipeline may have become siloed or that employees are becoming disengaged with the innovation imperative.

We mentioned before that the pathway towards a culture of innovation is similar in many respects to other culture change pathways and measuring the level of innovation maturity and development follows the same pattern. Defining and tracking innovation maturity isn't about reinventing the wheel and creating a whole new set of measurement surveys and systems. Rather it is about using what the organization already does, ie customer surveys, employee surveys, balanced scorecards etc, and tweaking them to cover the areas relating to innovation that you need to measure or understand. Adding a couple of focused questions to your existing processes may well be far more effective than issuing another separate survey/process.

Key = work with what you've got wherever possible.

Innovation maturity – accepting failure as a learning point

One of the key traits of an innovation culture is the acceptance of failure as a learning point and this applies to measuring innovation maturity as much as anything else. If what you measure isn't helping you get better at innovating – scrap it and figure out what you need to measure otherwise you waste enormous amounts of precious time and resources for no gain. Don't measure for measuring sake. Measuring should help you understand where to tweak and where to change in order to constantly improve your innovation engine. Like Formula 1 it's about constant development and refinement, with sometimes minute adjustments being the determining factor that delivers the podium.

But the acceptance of failure is not an easy concept to grasp, particularly in a heavily regulated sector such as law or finance. Perhaps here it is important to differentiate between making mistakes or malpractice and innovative failure. If a legal document is rendered invalid because the wrong case law was cited, if funds are incorrectly applied to the wrong account, if an employee deliberately misrepresents an outcome to gain a sale then the leadership team may well be justified in censuring those concerned. On the other hand, if time and effort was spent on trying to devise a new process which would speed up manufacturing and the project had to be shelved as the cost of re-tooling would not outweigh the predicted gain, then the project could still be seen as a valuable learning experience. What is important though is moving failures away from being a point of censure. If employees believe that their ideas and projects will be well received, then they will be encouraged to extend their efforts. Conversely, if they are censured for failure then they will stop trying.

Therefore, when devising an innovation strategy, one of the key elements for consideration is the level of risk which will be seen as acceptable in differing circumstances. Aligning this level of risk with a measure of value which will be acceptable to the organization, enables the leadership team to move away from a purely monetary 'x cost delivers y profit' model and towards one which incorporates a budgetary cost of failure within the overall mix. For example, acceptable value may be seen as equal to effort+attitude+output.

CASE STUDY The importance of the cultural assessment

Introduction

In this chapter we've been looking at the importance of understanding where you are now before you move off on your innovation journey. Carrying out a cultural assessment enables the organization's leaders to better understand the challenges which face them as well as helping to direct the shape of the cultural change.

To illustrate this idea more fully we turned to global multinational defence corporation QinetiQ to see how they succeeded in their culture change.

Situation

QinetiQ was formed in 2001 when the UK Ministry of Defence split its Defence Evaluation and Research Agency into two. The smaller portion remained as part of the MOD while the rest became QinetiQ, initially a public–private partnership before being floated on the London Stock Exchange.

When the new CEO took over QinetiQ, he could see that issues besieging the company were mostly due to its recent history of being part of a government agency but after two profit warnings there was no choice for the company other than to fundamentally change the way it operated. This meant shifting the culture away from a civil service mentality to a more commercialized, private-sector and innovation-focused culture.

The business was segmented into three areas: core, explore, test for value. Perfectly illustrating the way in which an organization may have a number of differing levels of innovation maturity within an overarching culture, each one of the three areas had its own sub-culture and each had a different way of measuring and rewarding performance. For example, the explore area already had a test and fail outlook.

Alongside the differing levels of innovation maturity, by their very nature the three areas also sat at different levels on the incremental/differentiated/radical innovation spectrum. The approach adopted by the business therefore had to take account of these variations to ensure that the potential for innovation momentum was maximized.

Approach

In an organization in which the status quo was seldom challenged and inertia was rife, it was deemed to be vital at the outset to assess the capability and appetite for change as well as identify where the greatest change effort needed to be focused. Accordingly a cultural assessment was conducted alongside a readiness for change review.

Areas for improvement that were identified in the assessment were to enhance leadership capability across the board, improve communication at all levels, break down silos and internal barriers and improve employee engagement.

A number of workshops were then held to determine the vision for the future and design the desired culture. This led to a high-level behaviours charter being implemented to identify to employees and others 'how we do things here' and a large employee voice initiative was launched called 'My Contribution'. This enabled and encouraged employees to drive innovation by submitting their own ideas for new products, services or improvements to working practices. The change in employee attitudes and behaviours was helped by a leadership 'upgrade' and the introduction of Lean processes.

Conclusion

At the time of writing over 9000 innovation projects are currently either active or proposed, driven by the employees for the benefit and future of QinetiQ. As a result of the 'self-help programmes' operating profit increased by 11 per cent and net debt was reduced by 75 per cent with some £75 million of identified savings having been made.

The strategic innovation decision

Once you have undertaken the cultural assessment and have developed an understanding of the level of innovation maturity within the organization the next stage is to start to develop your innovation strategy. We'll start with a thought.

When most organizations talk about needing to innovate they cite 'big', game-changing or radical as their requirement. The reality is that the 'big' stuff is a valid growth driver and genuine differentiator but few companies are really in the right place to pull it off. Most organizational cultures just aren't capable of radical, game-changing innovation. But they need to be!

In an ideal world innovation culture permeates the entire organization, drawing everyone together in a shared vision. But to expect to go from 0–100 in an instant is to invite innovation fatigue and burnout. We'll look at implementation strategies later on but for now it is important to understand the innovation mix and how it will impact the design of the optimal innovation strategy for organizations.

Just as innovation is about creating differentiated experiences, so too will innovation strategies vary from organization to organization. Creating long-term sustainable innovation requires what we call 'the innovation mix' and that means creating a balanced portfolio of activity across innovation areas and innovation types. The legacy of the recession and the immediate drive towards recovery has resulted in organizations and senior teams tending to favour short-term wins or returns over long-term gains. With sights being firmly set on the goal of being able to say 'yes, we're innovating' it is easy to get caught in the trap of incremental innovation to the exclusion of all else. Incremental innovation is a fundamental part of the mix but more often than not it focuses on internal improvements, tweaks and operational efficiencies ('lean' etc) rather than addressing the global picture and driving the organization forward.

Sustainable innovation therefore requires a mix of the following innovation types as illustrated in Figure 2.3:

- incremental – optimizing existing products, propositions and experiences and continuously improving internal business processes and efficiencies in order to stay as current as possible;
- differentiated – adapting existing products, propositions and experiences with a view to addressing real customer problems in order to drive additional business and short-term disruption;
- radical – developing breakthrough products, propositions and experiences for markets that don't exist yet in order to drive 'new to company' revenue streams and long-term disruption.

The key is to position some activity between incremental and radical. Our experience shows us that most organizations already practise incremental innovation; they just call it something else. So when the organization says that we need more innovation, the assumption is that it wants radical innovation as that's the only other type people know and talk about. Organizations need to position some innovation in the middle ground, in the place which we call the 'differentiated' innovation area. Whatever you call this area, the important thing is to create a stepping stone or sliding scale from incremental to radical. The biggest shift of the needle comes from activity in the middle!

The first thing an organization needs to do (once it has done the organizational assessment and it knows where it is) is decide how much it is willing to change in order to deliver its goals through innovation. This then requires the development of the innovation roadmap to deliver the organization's innovation aspirations and move up the innovation maturity scale. At this stage it is also important to understand the organization's readiness for change. This will include an assessment of the organizational capacity for change and take into account the history of change programmes within the organization. Questions will include why change has succeeded or failed in the past, what can be done to expedite the change this time and are there any other factors which will impact change such as existing programmes or recent reorganizations.

Change readiness assessments will of their nature vary depending on organizational size, structure and business sector. In general they will cover both subjective and objective criteria and will encompass both practical

FIGURE 2.3 The sustainable innovation mix

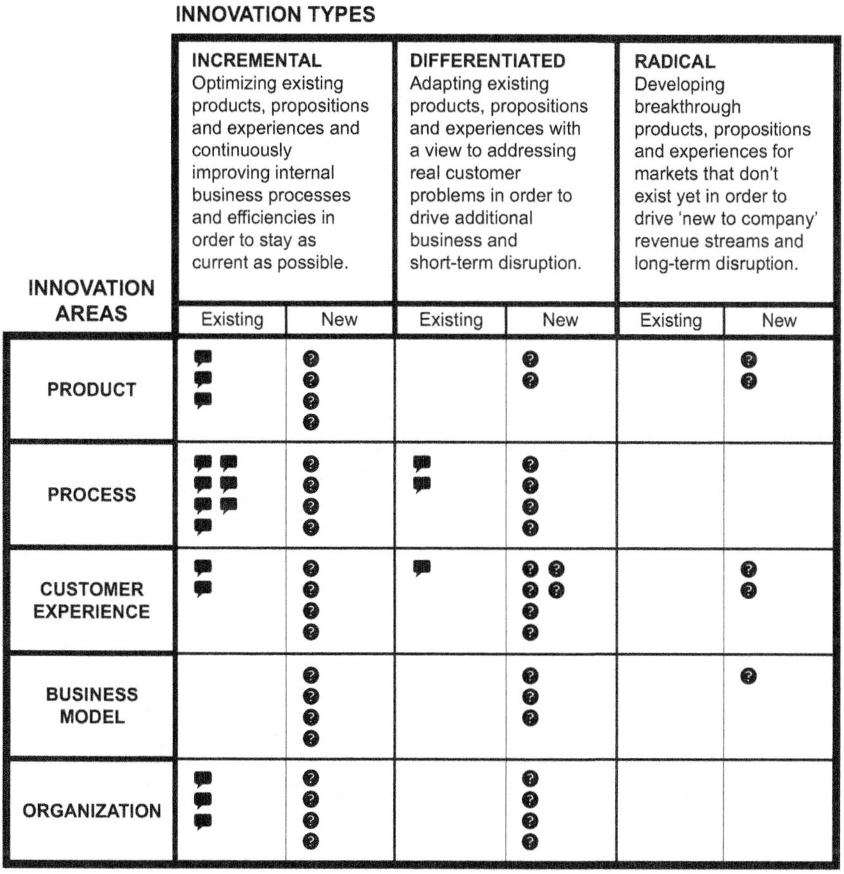

INNOVATION TYPES

INNOVATION AREAS	INCREMENTAL — Optimizing existing products, propositions and experiences and continuously improving internal business processes and efficiencies in order to stay as current as possible.		DIFFERENTIATED — Adapting existing products, propositions and experiences with a view to addressing real customer problems in order to drive additional business and short-term disruption.		RADICAL — Developing breakthrough products, propositions and experiences for markets that don't exist yet in order to drive 'new to company' revenue streams and long-term disruption.	
	Existing	New	Existing	New	Existing	New
PRODUCT	▪ ▪ ▪	? ? ? ?		? ?		? ?
PROCESS	▪ ▪ ▪ ▪ ▪ ▪ ▪	? ? ? ?	▪ ▪	? ? ? ?		
CUSTOMER EXPERIENCE	▪ ▪	? ? ? ?	▪	? ? ? ?		? ?
BUSINESS MODEL		? ? ? ?		? ? ?		?
ORGANIZATION	▪ ▪ ▪	? ? ? ?		? ? ? ?		

1. In addition to the 'Areas' listed above, add any area of your business that you could innovate in.
2. Fill in each section with the innovation activity that is currently going on inside your organization to map out your current innovation mix. (Each ▪ above represents an example of existing activity)
3. Now position new activity in each category in order to create the ideal innovation mix and put in place a process to identify and nurture high-potential ideas that will change the game in order to differentiate, disrupt and drive growth. (Each ? above represents an example of possible activity)

(process/equipment) and cultural (state of readiness) questions and observations. In general their usefulness largely derives from the care taken in scoping the assessment. Understanding what it is that you are going to measure, how to elicit the most meaningful responses and in what way you are going to interpret the data is key to a meaningful outcome.

One key question here is the extent to which you want/are prepared for your organization to change. This will partly depend on the results of your survey and partly on where you have decided your strategic journey will take you. This results/decision mix will be modified by the change appetite of the organization. For example, those who decide to adopt a low-key contextual cultural shift may lean towards an incremental culture change in which the emphasis is on a continuously improving culture where small steps forward happen every day.

For leaders who are more inclined towards a high-change structural innovation this incremental change may be integrated with radical innovation in a self-feeding mix in which a future-oriented, customer-centric culture seeks to push the boundaries by pushing innovation capability. On the other hand for those who prefer a more low-change model, incremental change as the base model may be structured to feed into a more dynamic and differentiated model which seeks to differentiate from competitors through how it does things.

FIGURE 2.4 The strategic innovation decision

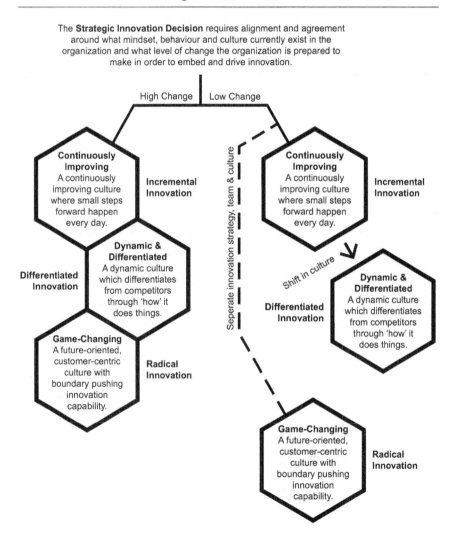

We'll come back to the innovation mix and the way in which strategic decisions impact the balance of incremental, differentiated and radical innovation at various times within this book as it impacts not only on the design of the initial roadmap but also on implementation and outcome. In the meantime the following diagram (Figure 2.4) may help to illustrate the strategic innovation decision facing organizational leaders and in particular the differing pathways which are open to leaders depending on the outcome of their discussions on the way forward.

We've mentioned the danger of becoming trapped in the incremental stage, tinkering with processes rather than driving change forward but there is also a danger that incremental innovation can become confined to one business area. For innovation to infuse the organization it has to span every area: product, service, brand, experience, organization and business model and the mix has to be appropriate for the organization in question.

For example a start-up business which is looking to be agile and innovative and break into markets fast may give a greater weight to the radical element than a more established organization with a strong customer base. One organization which is much quoted online is Coca-Cola, which openly acknowledges that an important part of its success is to do with its innovation strategy of investing about 70 per cent on the 'now' established and successful programmes; 20 per cent on 'new' or emerging trends which are starting to gain traction; and 10 per cent on 'next' ideas which are completely untested: horizons one, two and three respectively.

Coca-Cola isn't alone in this. In decision tree terms, 70/20/10 is as well known as 80/20 and has been applied successfully across a variety of business spheres. Whatever the mix the key consideration is to keep it balanced and in line with your organizational strategy. For example, directing 100 per cent of your efforts towards incremental innovation may in the short to medium term optimize the results to be gained from existing processes but will never result in the sort of differentiated or radical innovation which creates game-changing synergies. Similarly, concentrating 100 per cent of the effort on radical solutions is to ignore the gains to be had from incremental innovations. The exact mix will vary from organization to organization and across business sectors but to optimize results, the innovation mix should be just that, a mix of innovation types which delivers the defined strategic goals.

The following diagram (Figure 2.5) illustrates the importance of aligning innovation to the goals and strategy of the organization if they are to meet the identified growth gap which other currently forecastable activity and practices won't meet. In simplistic terms, let's say that the organization has been growing at a steady 5 per cent per year and is predicted to do so

FIGURE 2.5 The innovation gap

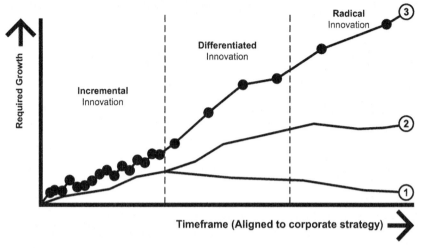

① Continuing to do the same thing i.e. the provision of existing products/services to existing markets.

② Forecast growth through updating existing products/services and 'business-as-usual' NPD (New Product Development). However, growth produced in one area could merely compensate for an inevitable decline in market share in another.

③ Required focus on innovation in order to meet the growth ambition of the organisation. (The Innovation Gap)

● An increase in activity across the innovation mix to create a balanced portfolio of activity. Ratio of innovations per innovation type i.e. 70/20/10 as an example.

ad infinitum if it carries on the current policies. If the leadership team are content with that level of growth and are in the happy position of being in a unique bubble in which there are no parameters which will affect the business then there is no point in even considering innovation. However, for businesses operating outside the bubble which will be affected by external events or which seek to grow market share then the first step is to look at the levels of current and adjacent activity which will go some way towards delivering that growth.

The innovation gap as illustrated in Figure 2.5 is defined as being the difference between the level of growth to be achieved through existing or adjacent activities and that which the business would like to achieve. Having defined the gap, the leadership team can then start to identify the innovation mix which is required to deliver the shortfall.

Real growth is likely to come from differentiated or radical innovation, sometimes also referred to as breakthrough or disruptive innovation. However, it is important to note that it's not just radical innovation that creates disruption, as differentiated innovation can also produce disruptive results. The key is to match your innovation strategy to the areas in which you think you need to set yourself apart from the competition and which you have established as delivering identified goals. For example, there may be an identified need for real market differentiation. Although this may not necessitate you doing anything truly groundbreaking or radical it definitely won't be achieved through a focus on incremental innovation or continuous improvement so the focus here will be on differentiated innovation.

The secret of identifying a successful innovation mix is to look at adjacencies in terms of products, solutions and applicable markets. And here we have a warning. New converts to innovation culture tend to become over-enthusiastic and talk about 'radical' and 'disruptive' innovation but the reality for most organizations is that taken in isolation it is simply too big and takes too long, costs too much and is too risky. That's not to say you shouldn't do it but it needs to be considered and aligned and relevant to what you want to achieve and in line with the organizational appetite for risk. We'll return to this topic again in Chapter 4 when we look at articulating the desired culture and defining the optimum innovation mix and strategy.

Owning the innovation agenda – engaging your people; developing enthusiasms

So far we have developed a high-level understanding of innovation maturity and culture within the organization and started to form an idea of the strategic mix which may best tie in with identified long-term strategic objectives. These themes will be developed in later chapters when we look in more depth at assembling a team and creating a roadmap which will define the journey towards innovation success. But in the meantime we have to pause and consider ownership of the innovation agenda.

By its very nature innovation is an inclusive process and the most innovative organizations position innovation at every level within the business as well as drawing customers, suppliers and even competitors into the innovation mix. So one of the hardest challenges for leaders is to decide not only who owns the innovation agenda but how that agenda is rolled out to a wider audience.

Building a culture of innovation is not rocket science but it does require careful stewardship as leaders and employees learn to step away from the comfort zone and into a world in which failure is treated as a learning point and in which empowerment and initiative are praised.

One of the key areas companies which try and embed innovation into culture get wrong is the way in which they encourage and inspire people to contribute to the innovation agenda. It's important that everyone in the organization understands the innovation strategy and how to contribute. That means there should be clarity on how to highlight problems, opportunities, threats, observations and so on as well as clear processes for submitting ideas to tackle identified problems. Further clarity is then required around how those initial ideas are progressed.

When looking at engendering enthusiasm the key is to be clear and focused on rewarding the behaviour you actually want, utilizing a balance of intrinsic and extrinsic rewards to motivate and to encourage people to willingly move out of their comfort zone and break free from the status quo. It is important here to foster inclusivity with the danger being that you actually breed a sense of division by unwittingly pigeonholing a certain type of innovation or activity within a select group and thereby alienate everyone else.

Owning the innovation agenda – the risk/reward mix

One of the main behaviours required by those adopting an innovation culture, and a must for reward, is that of defining the extent to which risk is acceptable. The key here is to be really clear about what kind of risk you want people to take, ie 'cavalier risk', or what we call 'smart risk' in which the consequences have been fully considered, reviewed and agreed. This risk appetite needs to be balanced carefully so that the process isn't too clumsy and therefore becomes a barrier to progress.

This requires clarity on what the boundaries are and how far they can be pushed so that people are willing to have a go. People will only be willing to put themselves on the line if they think the business is serious about ideas and more importantly is willing to listen to their ideas. Furthermore there has to be a clear understanding that there is a real process for evaluating and developing any ideas which are put forward. Ideas must therefore not only be valued but be seen to be valued and have the chance of successfully being implemented and that means the process must flow from identification to implementation. We will develop this theme later on when we look at the innovation process.

So clarity is needed on what is being measured and rewarded with employees being clear about whether the right behaviour will be rewarded even if it amounts to nothing or whether rewards will only be forthcoming if ideas increase the bottom line. In reality though, if the organization is only going to reward success then its attempts to inculcate a culture of innovation are going to stop far short of the ideal. Innovation runs hand in hand with the idea that failure should be treated as a learning point rather than a cause for censure. The consequence of this is that 'failure' should be removed from the company vernacular, to be replaced by the delivery of learning points or what we call 'learning episodes'. It is important here to be clear about the value which is placed on innovation and to the way in which the risk/reward matrix is formed. Yes, in the medium term the culture of innovation has to result in tangible improvements which add to the bottom line. Failure to do so will lead to a swift reversion to a command and control model which looks to buy in solutions. But looking at innovation from the outset in strict monetary terms will also lead to failure. For example, an innovative idea may result in an improvement in reputation. In the short term this may not add directly to profitability but as new customers are attracted by the growing reputation the business will start to benefit financially.

This leads on to another key reason for clarity around what is measured and rewarded, namely that employees have to be comfortable that their ideas will be recognized and rewarded even if they don't directly impact on the bottom line. This is important because if you only measure and reward around new products and getting them to market then you are pigeonholing, or siloing innovation within a select few in the organization and therefore alienating everyone else. It then becomes by default impossible to build an organization-wide culture of innovation.

Many organizations already have visible awards for ideas in place but they tend to be subjective and not part of a fully integrated innovation programme. This means that there is not only a question over how they are measured but also an unconscious bias towards ideas which impact the bottom line. Depending on the organization's level of innovation maturity that recognition/reward matrix will need to be flexed and reviewed to include ideas and solutions across the business. Ideas which lead to kudos, a published paper, industry awards or market recognition may not have a strict monetary value but they can benefit the organization in other ways.

When considering the suggestion and reward matrix the key factor is to distinguish between reward and recognition. Rewards can be financial – bonus, holidays, gifts etc – or can be less tangible like full public recognition, featured in the company magazine or newsletter, lunch with the boss etc along with the recognition and potential for advancement in the company the extra contribution generates.

So rewards don't have to always consist of financial recompense and in many instances having contributions openly acknowledged is better received than a monetary bonus. Simply saying 'thank you' is a key element of employee engagement and getting the idea/reward mix right can not only benefit the business but also help to strengthen employee engagement levels.

Essentially it's about the difference between extrinsic and intrinsic and the desire to do well and be seen to achieve and contribute, to be seen as an innovation champion. The recognition and visibility of innovation also helps others see that innovation is happening in the company and that their peers are doing stuff and getting noticed so helps breed alignment and push innovation further across and into the culture. Here again the importance of designing a unique culture and strategy which is right for your organization comes to the fore. The reward matrix will vary across organizations depending on the personality types of your employees and on the nature of their employment. What is seen as a valuable reward to one is akin to a slap in the face to another so it is vital that the strategy chosen matches with your employees.

Part of the innovation process should also deal with who decides who gets rewarded so that the process almost becomes automatic and hence not subjective and open to criticism or scepticism about why certain ideas have been progressed and rewarded.

Owning the innovation agenda – positioning ownership

One of the big barriers to innovation, and a major hurdle to embedding innovation into culture, is asking people for ideas then not doing anything with them; or not giving them feedback on what is happening with the submitted ideas and how they are doing, or indeed if they have been rejected and why. Particularly in the early stages it is a common failing for organizations to ask for ideas then find themselves unable to cope with the volume. So it is important when designing not only the roadmap but also when appointing innovation champions to ensure that from the start there is an innovation process in place to capture ideas, evaluate them and feedback/communicate what happens next (if anything) and why.

The issue with asking people to submit ideas is 'ideas about what?' Innovation is about solving problems or designing solutions to things that you uncover, unearth etc, so the process should really start with asking people to submit observations about those, with stage two being more about asking for ideas about solving specific challenges. This is done by issuing 'idea challenges' that have clear criteria about the context and parameters of the challenge and which can be seen to be aligned with the main corporate strategy. Remember, this process is as much about asking the right questions as it is about understanding the rationale behind the answers. Otherwise you can finish up in the scenario faced by Henry Ford when he commented that if he had asked people what they wanted they would have said 'a faster horse' rather than 'a car'.

Adopting this process in the early stages not only provides some 'quick wins' it can also start to generate enthusiasm and understanding for the innovation process. And it is this interest and encouragement which is not only key to the innovation ideal permeating the organization but also should act as a guide to defining ownership of the innovation agenda. Yes, eventually everyone will have a stake in innovation but in the meantime those who are tasked with ownership should be those who, by their role or personality, are best placed to take the agenda forward.

This means that ownership of the innovation implementation plan need not necessarily sit directly with the leadership team. However, that doesn't mean the leadership team can simply decide that in future 'we're going to be innovative' and then sit back. As with any culture change unless the leadership team are prepared to fully embrace the change then there is no point in even starting. And when the change is as profound as one in pursuit of innovation, the attitudes, beliefs and behaviours of the leadership team have to change for innovation to succeed.

We will be revisiting the subject of leading for innovation culture change in more depth in future chapters but at this point it may be appropriate to highlight some of the key elements. And we'll start with an obvious statement. Culture change won't happen unless the leadership team are 100 per cent behind it. It's surprising how many times leadership teams have an idea, launch it on the organization and then move on to the next big thing without ever having understood or committed to implementation. And when we talk about the leadership team here we mean that every individual has to be personally aligned and committed. If just one individual is not personally aligned then there is a real chance that you will be faced with disruption at the implementation phase.

Make no mistake; changing the culture to one in which innovation infuses every corner of the organization is worlds away from changing a reporting line or introducing new IT capabilities. The barriers to change will fight back at every round. Inertia, fear of change, bureaucracy, scepticism, traditionalists and those who simply don't understand will all consciously or unconsciously fight at every turn. 'Some cultural issues also featured prominently on the list of innovation obstacles, including the difficulty of implementing change (41 per cent) and the persistence of a one-time project mentality rather than viewing innovation as an ongoing capability (39 per cent)' (imaginatik, 2013).

So innovation culture change requires complete commitment from the leadership team. And more than that it requires the leadership team to define strategy, vision and values and then to deploy them using a three layered approach encompassing communication, delegation and mobilization. And this is another important point. Mobilization may require middle management to pick up the innovation ball and run with it but that doesn't mean that the leadership team can step back completely and move on to the next thing. To lead the change you have to be the change and that means changing your own behaviours not only as an example to others but also to set the tone for the organization.

Owning the innovation agenda – collaboration

But delegation and mobilization are also vital if the change is to succeed. For example, there is no point in moving the organization away from siloed departments and towards a more collaborative way of working if the leaders of those departments are still insisting on absolute autonomy. Similarly there is little use in moving customer service towards a model which embraces ownership of problems and ensures customer questions have been fully answered if the department leader is still targeting people on number of calls answered.

By its very nature innovation means collaboration and the first people who have to be seen to collaborate are the leadership team and higher-level departmental leaders. But that doesn't mean that the innovation agenda should necessarily be owned on an ongoing basis by the leadership team. They may initially devise strategy, values, beliefs and behaviours but with any culture change it is generally the emerging leaders who will translate that strategy into success. And when true innovation culture requires employees across the board to engage in innovative beliefs and behaviours it is important that innovation is not seen as simply another fad of the leadership team or something which had been taken up simply because it looks good in the accounts. The leadership team may therefore decide that once the initial phase is complete, ownership should sit at lower levels within the organization.

We'll come back to this theme in Chapter 3 when we look at assembling an innovation team but first we need to explore another aspect of innovation culture – that true innovation is not confined to the organization itself. With customers, suppliers and even rivals being drawn into the mix, businesses should consider whether external suppliers should be partially responsible for the innovation agenda. Naturally this would have to be carefully managed. No business wants to hand itself over to a third-party partner without first ensuring that its culture and values will be reflected in the work done by that organization.

Owning the innovation agenda – cultural due diligence

The answer therefore is to follow the cultural due diligence route which is recommended not only for mergers and acquisitions but also when looking to partner with a third party. Taking the time to carry out a full cultural review will not only highlight areas of synergy it can also help to pinpoint whether the external organization is in a strong position to drive forward your innovation plans.

When we appoint another organization to be our supplier or to provide advice or to take responsibility for back-up services such as IT or HR it is all too easy to choose price over context, delivery speed over culture. But in an interconnected world in which we are placing some of the responsibility for our business in outside hands we should be looking to carry out as full an assessment as possible. Third party/supply chain risk is increasingly creeping up the business continuity agenda and it should also be top of the innovation strategy agenda.

Cultural due diligence will help to identify synergies but it will also enable the leadership team to plan the communication, delegation and mobilization strategy which will enable third parties to assimilate the behaviours which arise from an innovation culture.

Naturally some outside organizations are more intrinsically suited to partake in the innovation mix and it may well be their level of innovation readiness which has attracted them to you in the first place. But for others you may have to build a measure of time/cost into your budget to help them to move towards an innovation culture which will reinforce your aims.

When you start to bring in third parties, this is where collaboration really comes into play. You start to place developments which will eventually help your customers into the hands of others. For example, you may task manufacturers or suppliers with improving products or supply chain; or you may work jointly with third parties to create the conditions which will inculcate innovation behaviours in employees, perhaps by sharing HR or training resources. Or perhaps it would be worth following the lead set by Toyota when it announced at the start of 2015 that it was throwing open some 6,000 patents for general free use in a bid to drive the development of hydrogen fuel cells forward. Speaking about the announcement Bob Carter, senior vice president of automotive operations at Toyota said, 'When good ideas are shared, great things can happen' (Toyota, 2015).

Owning the innovation agenda – sub-cultures

There is one other reason why the leadership team may not be the ideal choice to take ownership of the innovation culture and that is when a strategic decision is taken to position innovation within one business unit or subsidiary company. The existence of sub-cultures which sit under the umbrella of the group structure but are tweaked to take account of operational or local conditions is a fairly common practice within larger organizations.

For example, one element of the group culture may be to provide outstanding levels of customer service but client expectations will vary from country to country. History is littered with examples of organizations which tried to impose their business model across country boundaries and failed. In those instances, tweaking the culture to better represent local conditions can be far more effective.

Earlier in this chapter we examined the strategic mix, defining the optimum balance for an organization between incremental, differentiated and radical innovation. But although an organization may well have an optimum strategic mix for the whole, that mix may vary between different divisions. For example, customer service may already be well on the way towards an inclusive innovation culture, having adopted new working methodologies which look to provide a one-stop solution to queries. So for them, in the initial phase at least, incremental innovation may be most appropriate. On the other hand, the accounts or IT departments may have been constrained from developing due to financial or technological reasons and they may be far more ready for some differentiated or radical changes.

Defining the innovation mix for each department or division and helping those sectors of the organization to translate strategy into action is a task for the leadership team which they cannot afford to get wrong.

Instances in which organizations may opt to introduce innovation culture into one or more areas rather than across the group will include:

- Opening up in a new marketplace. With little or no history to act as a barrier to change, opening up a new division is the ideal time to introduce a culture of innovation.

- Acquiring a new subsidiary. That company will already be undergoing a time of flux as it is integrated within the parent organization so again leaders may take the decision to introduce innovation structures at the same time.

- Identified marketplace need. One division or product line may have been identified as being under threat from competition or from changing technologies. Countering that threat by introducing innovation matrices within that division may enable the organization to counter the threat without disrupting the rest of the business.

Owning the innovation agenda – aligning with innovation strategy

We're going to start here by stating the obvious: the organizational strategy is one thing, and the behaviours required to translate it into practice may well vary across the organization. Looking at a very high-level example, if the strategy was to provide customer-focused behaviours then for the IT team this may require learning a new set of code which would enable them to redesign the website to make it more customer friendly; for customer-facing employees it may require a change in metrics and approach to one which takes charge of the query and ensures a swift solution.

An important point to remember when designing an innovation implementation roadmap is that differing areas of an organization may have employees with very different personal aptitudes and will have to adapt in different ways but the end goal is the same for both. As illustrated in Figure 2.6, translating the new strategy into a set of behaviours which will deliver success may therefore require careful attention being paid to definition and communication in order that it can be understood in the relevant context for each employee.

Whether the organization opts for a complete transformation or simply to address the needs of one division with a culture of innovation; whether it decides to keep total ownership with the leadership team or outsource it to others, the key message for innovation owners is that the make-up of the innovation team and the roadmap which is subsequently designed to lead towards implementation must align with the identified strategy and core culture of the organization.

FIGURE 2.6 Translating strategy into behaviour

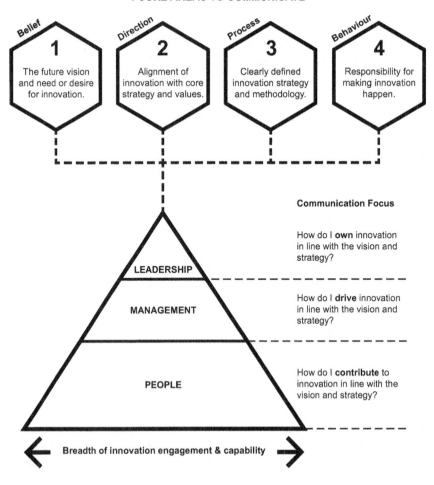

There must be organization-wide clarity around the innovation strategy so cascading understanding of the future vision, core values, processes and accountability for aligning personal behaviour and contributing to innovation is key.

4 CORE AREAS TO COMMUNICATE

Belief

1

The future vision and need or desire for innovation.

Direction

2

Alignment of innovation with core strategy and values.

Process

3

Clearly defined innovation strategy and methodology.

Behaviour

4

Responsibility for making innovation happen.

Communication Focus

How do I **own** innovation in line with the vision and strategy?

LEADERSHIP

How do I **drive** innovation in line with the vision and strategy?

MANAGEMENT

How do I **contribute** to innovation in line with the vision and strategy?

PEOPLE

Breadth of innovation engagement & capability

This means that those who take ownership of the innovation agenda have to be familiar with the strategy, vision and values of the organization and understand how these are affected by the outcome of the culture assessment. They also have to have a broad understanding of the innovation agenda including the opening level of innovation maturity. This means that while the leadership team may grant a certain level of autonomy to innovation owners they cannot simply leave them to plough merrily on without referring back to the core culture and strategy.

With any cultural change, communication is key and that works two ways. Communicating the change to employees in a way which engages their enthusiasm is vital but so is upward reference to ensure that change continues to meet and match up with identified strategy and KPIs. Mission creep is a perennial danger for any change within an organization and when that change is as radical as instilling an innovation culture, the chances of failure due to mission creep are high. In fact, in common with other culture changes, leaders and change owners should remain vigilant against the risk of failure due to:

- The leadership team launch the change project but then step back too far. Stepping back is one thing, retreating into the distance is another. It can be all too easy for the leadership team to move on to the next challenge and drop all involvement in the current initiative. This not only sends the wrong signals to both the implementation team and employees, but the lack of leadership buy-in can result in project failure as resources are diverted elsewhere.

- Mission creep. Unless the implementation team constantly check back against core strategy and identified KPIs, it can be all too easy for the project to start to drift off course or be hijacked by other agendas within the organization.

- Barriers to innovation. We looked at these in Chapter 1 but they include inertia, change resistance and lack of synergy between mission priorities and organizational processes.

In summary

Many of the ideas contained within this chapter will be revisited in later sections but the core message here is that unless the leadership teams take the time to fully understand the starting point then it can never be sure that the strategies which it puts in place to develop an innovation culture will be right or will actually work.

So the key elements for success here are:

- *How mature are you?* Make sure you're absolutely honest about your current level of innovation maturity. Only then will you be able to map out the change in line with your desired innovation ambition and how much you need to innovate according to your innovation gap.

- *How much are you prepared to change?* Be comfortable with your strategic innovation decision as the level of change you are prepared to make goes hand in hand with the level of innovation success. If you're not prepared to change your culture enough to drive the innovation you require then build your innovation capability as an autonomous unit. But be aware, doing nothing is not an option.

- *It's on the horizon...* Be prepared for the long haul if you want more than simply incremental innovation change. If you require deeper market impact then full innovation transformation will take time; so make sure the whole organization, especially c-suite (the chief executive layer of the organization), is comfortable with the long term and design some quick wins in the short term to keep enthusiasms alive.

- *Risk versus reward* – Innovation needs failure. Getting things wrong through experimentation and prototyping increases learning far better than anything else, so consider setting your KPIs around that. If you only target and reward success then your organization will never push boundaries. You'll merely become exceptional at being average!

- *It's all about communication* – The initial work behind the scenes to position innovation and determine how to move forward rarely encompasses input from the whole organization. Rightly or wrongly, culture-change definitions tend to sit within the remit of the senior teams, possibly with the collaboration of a number of people. But once the strategy and roadmap are in place the key is how well they are communicated so that it becomes everyone's innovation agenda, not just that of the c-suites. Communication around every part of the innovation strategy, agenda and activity on a daily basis is essential right from the start if employees, customers and others are to be engaged in the new culture.

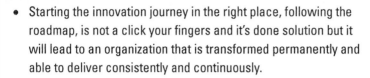

- Starting the innovation journey in the right place, following the roadmap, is not a click your fingers and it's done solution but it will lead to an organization that is transformed permanently and able to deliver consistently and continuously.

- The danger with 'buying in' innovation is that you never get the chance to grow your own internal capabilities and capitalize on the amazing talent, expertise and potential of your people.

- Failure should be treated as a learning point rather than a cause for censure so focus on taking 'smart risk' and evolve 'how' you do things through 'learning episodes'.

References

3M (2012) [accessed 14 January 2015] A Culture of Innovation, *3M* [Online] http://solutions.3m.com/3MContentRetrievalAPI/BlobServlet?lmd=1349327166 000&locale=en_WW&assetType=MMM_Image&assetId=1319209959040 &blobAttribute=ImageFile

imaginatik (2013) [accessed 13 May 2015] State of Global Innovation [Online] http://imaginatik.com/news/2013-state-global-innovation-report-shows -growing-corporate-focus-innovation

Toyota (2015) [accessed 14 January 2015] Toyota Makes 5,600 Fuel Cell and Related Patents Available [Webblog] blog.toyota.co.uk, January 5 2015, http:// blog.toyota.co.uk/toyota-makes-5600-fuel-cell-related-patents-available

Building an innovation leadership team

In Chapter 1 we worked on understanding the business and social drivers, which have resulted in innovation becoming not only a watchword for business differentiation but also a catalyst for national and international regeneration. Taking this knowledge forward, in Chapter 2 we moved from the general into the specific, looking at the importance of defining the current level of innovation maturity and using this information to identify the culture gap, which will need to be bridged.

Along the way we touched on cultural attitudes and behaviours as well as the barriers that may impede implementation. Now we are ready to move on, to take what is undoubtedly the most important step towards a successful cultural transformation. That step is to assemble a team that will define, shape and implement a game-changing cultural transformation to one of innovation.

We've already touched on the way in which innovation champions can, and should, be drawn from across the organizational spectrum and we will develop this theme further in this chapter. But no matter how far and wide the innovation implementation team net is spread, there is one indisputable fact and that is that:

If it's not on the top team's agenda, it's not going to be in the culture

Adopting a culture of innovation, or any other culture for that matter, is not simply a question of deciding to change the status quo, fiddling with a few processes and then moving on to the next project. Whether or not the leadership team have a significant presence on the implementation team, if innovation is to be embedded throughout the organization then the leadership team have to change their mindset so that they think innovation, live innovation and breathe innovation into every decision.

Put simply, a true culture of innovation permeates every aspect of the organization from the overall business structure to the way in which you interact with the outside world. The hiring process, employee expectations, how products, services and experiences are designed and developed, marketing, interactions with customers and suppliers, even IT support and accounts are drawn into the innovation mix. This means that for true innovation, every department and, by implication, every member of the leadership team has to embrace the innovation strategy if it is to succeed.

We'll come back to this theme later on in the chapter when we look at ways of ensuring that innovation is on the senior team's agenda and is then cascaded down to change champions and the implementation team. Before we do so, it is vital to develop an understanding of the importance of aligning the organization's strategy with the organization's appetite for innovation.

Aligning strategy with the organization's appetite for innovation

Working through Chapter 2 we started out on the road towards innovation by measuring the organization's current level of innovation maturity and the innovation gap. We also touched on the strategic innovation decision and the importance of defining an innovation mix that is right for the individual organization. Now we are moving on, looking to put real flesh on the bones of an innovation strategy that will deliver game-changing results for your organization. And while every organization will find a unique mix, which is right for them, we'll start with a universal truth:

If you are going to adopt an innovation culture then you have to adopt a 'venture capital' mindset. Some, or most, ideas won't come to fruition but by spreading the risk, those that do succeed will far outweigh those that don't.

Organizations which have traditionally demanded proof and costings as to the viability of projects before they even get off the ground may well find it difficult to adapt to an innovation mindset which accepts that not all projects will succeed. But changing the mindset is an intrinsic part of innovation success. Just as venture capital investors accept that not all of the companies in which they invest will prove to be equally successful, so too should innovation-seeking organizations accept that not all solutions will deliver the expected results.

But it is a rare failure which is a complete failure. Careful examination of projects will often glean learning points which can be used to create future successes either through later resurrection of the idea or through using the skills and methodologies developed in pursuing one project in future projects. These are the 'learning episodes' we mentioned earlier.

With that in mind, how should we shape the strategy? As we've already seen, the innovation strategy should be specific to the organization. It therefore must be grounded in reality both in terms of the organization's capability and its ability to execute and implement. It must clearly map out the journey from where the organization is today to where it desires to be in the future.

Innovation and building a culture of innovation is about momentum and momentum relies on small quick wins in order to reinforce the big picture and ensure that the ultimate goal is more than achievable. When you create that momentum you then start to create activity that naturally pushes past incremental innovation as people start to have bigger, more powerful, useful and/or commercially viable ideas.

With barriers to implementation in mind, the strategy must also be clear about the trials and tribulations that will be faced along the way. It must therefore be honest and congruent to what everyone in the organization believes is possible. When devising the strategy the leadership team therefore has to be open and clear about capabilities and buy-in. For example, there is little point in devising a strategy which relies heavily on IT capabilities if those capabilities simply aren't there or require funds which the organization simply doesn't have in order to bring them up to scratch.

Being open and honest (even if it means admitting failings) at this stage will help to ensure that the strategy that is signed off is a realistic blueprint for delivering the type of innovation and mix outlined previously. In other words it must be practical and pragmatic. It must be doable!

So what should the strategy contain? In essence the innovation strategy should be focused on strategic innovation, ie what problems, issues, opportunities, threats, trends, predictions and so on has the intelligence capability of the organization unearthed? Added to this the leadership team needs to understand how the collective capability of the organization's people will draw together to create powerful, differentiated solutions.

Yes, you must also allow people some freedom to come up with stuff outside of the core strategy. However, this freedom does not equate to anarchy. One myth about innovation is that it is about creative freedom and giving people the ability to create stuff free from constraints. Actually this is far from the truth. Innovation *is* about constraints but it is about the right use of constraints to create solutions within a free framework. It's not about letting people 'think outside the box'; rather, strategic innovation is about giving people the right box to think inside of! It's about creativity with direction and strategy, ie 'strategic creativity'!

In essence a well-rounded innovation strategy should plan and account for every piece of innovation activity that is going on in the organization at any given time from across the innovation mix. It's easy to undervalue the small things, the incremental innovations, in favour of the big prize-winning stuff. But in truth every bit of activity contributes to the right mix for any given organization; helping to consolidate the innovation agenda and bond everyone together to contribute in one aligned direction.

> Innovation strategies can be very different in approach from one organization to another. Apple pursues a top-down approach to innovation – often using skunk works. [A small group of people who are given virtual freedom to work on and develop a project in a perhaps unconventional way. The title originated in World War II from a project group set up by the Lockheed Corporation.] On the other end of the spectrum is W. L. Gore, which pursues a bottom-up innovation strategy based on exploiting core capabilities. Despite their radically different approaches and organizations, both expect people within the firm to understand the strategy and to innovate accordingly. (Kelley, 2010)

The key drivers of innovation

In Chapter 2 we developed an understanding of the innovation mix, looking at how incremental, differentiated and radical innovation could be combined to create sustainable innovation. Now we are adding to the framework by delving down into the three key components of innovation, those which are characteristic of Next Generation Organizations. We first met this concept in Chapter 1 when we examined the way in which organizations that have mastered strategic innovation are perfectly poised to create the future through a mix of Intelligence, Collaboration and Adaptability. Now we are going to examine how these three elements can help to define the strategic mix by asking ourselves some questions:

- **Does the leadership team know what the future will look like?**
  There's nothing like starting with an easy question! The pace of

technological change is such that when we look towards the future sometimes it seems as though the only certainty is that there is no certainty. However, the one solid fact that you can be sure of is that your sector is going to change and by really leveraging intelligence it is possible to make a fairly intelligent guess about the direction in which your organization needs to travel.

- **Do you know what will be successful in the future?** If there is one thing that internet crazes and viral posts have taught us it is that unless you're in the business of publishing cute pictures of baby animals then there is no certainty about what the public will buy into next. But you do know what works well now and with increased intelligence about the world you can make better, more informed decisions and predictions about what may work well in the future. In other words, use what you know now as your base level and leverage insights to 'best guess' the shape of future change. However, never lose sight of the fact that the world is changing daily so the insights which you gather should be on an ongoing basis if you want to avoid being caught out by change. And don't forget that innovation is all about solving real problems so if your intelligence points to problems in product, in integration with users, in sustainability, in 'greenness' or any other area then the chances are that by using informed creativity to provide solutions you are driving towards future success.

- **What trends are moving faster than your growth?** Again leveraging intelligence will help to provide part of the answer but to integrate fast-paced change into solution design will also require the organization to embrace adaptability. When the world is changing fast then permanence is not the solution. In fact, the challenge today is that leaders have to accept a measure of ambiguity, of knowing the preferred goal but not being certain what the end point actually looks like; resulting in the need to be adaptable and flexible without having a full understanding of the outcome. For example, implementing a new workforce planning system or internal sharing platform which meets current needs, but is not flexible enough to be easily scalable or adaptable to fit future business needs is a waste of funds in an ever-changing world. Using intelligence to 'best guess' the pace of change will enable the leadership team to develop a strategy that encompasses extrapolated areas of risk and to allocate resources accordingly.

- **Is there agreement on where to innovate and what to risk?** We'll be coming back to this theme later on in the chapter when we look at leadership team buy-in but this is a good place to start looking at collaboration. If the leadership team can't agree to work together to define innovation parameters then there isn't a lot of hope for innovation being embraced by the rest of the organization.

And collaborate they must. In a non-innovative organization there may be little overlap between the departments and where there are cross-departmental requirements they generally take the form of a transactional relationship which is limited in scope, shared knowledge and space for challenge. For example, accounts may require the IT department to service and maintain their accountancy programmes or marketing may need the HR department to draw up a contract for a new team member. But within an innovation culture there is frequent cross-departmental collaboration with employees drawing on ideas from multiple sources to create solutions. So agreeing on acceptable levels of risk and priority areas for innovation is the first step towards not only instilling a collaborative mentality within the organization but also demonstrating a collaborative attitude in front of employees.

- **How do you combine internal resource with external influence?** This follows on from collaboration within the leadership team. As the organization develops innovation maturity it will become apparent that collaboration is not purely confined to the business itself. Customers, suppliers, external organizations, research bodies, even rival businesses will all eventually form part of the innovation mix. As with other elements of the innovation strategy this external collaboration will develop over time but it is important at the outset to define acceptable levels of external collaborations.

- **Are your gambles on the future too safe?** The problem here is twofold. Firstly, the leadership team have to be in agreement about the level of risk which is acceptable and then devise a strategy which pushes the organization to achieve within those boundaries. We'll pass over the scenario that says that no level of risk is acceptable because in essence this equates to no innovation. But by leveraging intelligence and defining acceptable boundaries for external collaboration and adaptability the leadership team should be able to devise a strategy that will make optimal use of resources to deliver the required results.

However, there is a second element to this question and that is the way in which intelligence is extrapolated into 'best guesses' about the future. It can be all too easy to finish up with a very narrow focus on the shape of things to come. For example, at the time of writing driverless cars are about to undergo initial testing on public roads. Comments in the press tend towards factors of safety such as whether driverless cars can sense and prevent crashes or whether drivers will still need to be in a position to take control instantly should anything go wrong.

But looked at from an expanded viewpoint, will there be a need for personal car ownership as driverless cars could be called up as and when needed? What would that do for the finance and car trade sectors? With no personal car ownership, what effect would that have on the way in which houses and housing estates are designed? With the young, elderly and ill able to get on the roads in driverless cars what would that do for public transport and taxis? With crashes virtually eliminated would the insurance and car repair industry be decimated and would that create a knock-on effect on the police and other emergency services?

The more that the leadership team can play 'second guessing' at the outset the better they can devise a strategy which is adaptable enough to keep aligned with and even ahead of future change. Conversely, all the intelligence and collaboration in the world won't help if the strategy leads towards rigid 'business as usual' thinking.

CASE STUDY   Making the complex simple

Introduction

We've just been examining some of the most common scenarios which may indicate to leaders that it is time to adopt a culture of innovation. But we couldn't let this list pass without one further scenario, one in which individuals are so convinced that it is time for a change that they step out from an existing position to start up a business from scratch. This is the story behind Octopus Investments.

Situation

In 2000, the Octopus founders Simon Rogerson, Chris Hulatt and Guy Myles became convinced that there was another way to offer financial services; one which put the customer not only at the heart of the process but as the reason for the process. Leaving their positions at Mercury Asset Management they set off to create an organization which offered an innovative vision to 'delight our customers with innovative products and exceptional service'.

Starting a financial services organization from scratch is no mean feat. Even when potential investors have been persuaded to support the venture and regulatory approval has been received, there is still the matter of convincing potential clients to invest their money and their personal futures into a new business. The Octopus founders admit that they were the recipients of a certain amount of luck, with the Venture Capital Trust (VCT) tax rules change in 2004 leading to a quadrupling of the market in two years. Nevertheless the fact that at the time of writing the business has grown to a point at which it has £5 billion under management for 50,000 clients is testament to the vision and hard work of its people.

Approach

From the outset the Octopus founders had a strong vision of a future which put the customer at the heart of the business. They recognized that with a few variations, all financial services businesses essentially offered similar products so they set out to differentiate themselves by the way in which their product was structured and offered. Literature and sales aids were written in plain English, made to be as jargon free as possible with as little small print as possible. Financial advisers were coached to understand not only the products but how those products could help their clients and the products were designed to meet customer needs and also make a positive impact on society.

The focus was therefore not on getting sales by promising a significant return but on why the customer wanted and needed the product and how it would help them to meet their life goals. In the longer term the focus was also about providing solutions which would create strong and sustainable customer loyalty. These long-term goals were born out of the founders' belief that making an impact, putting the customer first and delivering service to customers was their prime objective. This moves profit flow firmly into being a side-benefit of the day-to-day approach rather than the reason for it.

Key to translating vision into reality has been the emphasis which Octopus has placed on taking on employees who share the values and attitudes of the founders. In fact the Octopus team sees maintaining the customer focus through employee attitude as an ongoing priority. As the business and its reputation grows there is no shortage of people looking for a place within the business but the leadership team are strongly determined only to take on those who will put customers before income. As one of the team says, they are not just looking for the best, they are looking for the best fit.

Conclusion

The entire Octopus model is one of innovation. From the original concept of creating a financial services firm which put customers first and treats profits as a beneficial consequence of providing great service, through to the emphasis on making the complex simple, the business is looking to be the disruptor which challenges more established and profit-driven cultures. Along the way the drive has been to forget the 'magic bullet' but instead try to make a difference in hundreds of little ways.

From phoning the first customer to say 'thank you' to an ongoing drive towards new markets and new products which will deliver difference, the Octopus way has resulted in numerous awards. But more than that, it has provided its growing band of loyal customers with a service which helps them to meet their life goals.

Innovation strategy examples

Now that we have started to gather intelligence, define required collaboration and acceptable risk parameters and embrace adaptability it is perhaps a opportune time to stop and look at a couple of innovation strategy examples. Although no two strategies are, or should be, the same, looking at ideas from other organizations may act as a catalyst for strategy change.

Example

First we'll take a quick look at the open innovation strategy adopted by consumer product company, Procter & Gamble (P&G). With beauty, personal care and prescription drugs included within their remit P&G are a great example to follow for those whose business is subject to the whims of fashion or the control of regulators. By their very nature P&G are in the business of continuous development and need not only to be current but to stay ahead of the game.

Embracing the interconnectedness of the world today, P&G have not only acknowledged the scientists, engineers and other firms which operate within their field, they have devised a strategy which embraces external collaboration. Called 'Connect + Develop', P&G's open innovation strategy seeks to tap into the potential of the marketplace to drive internal innovation. Commenting on the strategy, Bruce Brown, P&G's Chief Technology Officer, said: 'Connect + Develop Open Innovation has helped deliver some of P&G's leading innovations, and is critical in helping us deliver on our renewed growth strategy moving forward. Connect + Develop has proven to be a winning strategy, with still more room for growth.' (P&G, 2015)

Moving on from a company which is very much in the B2C marketplace to one which is more in the B2B field, we can take a look at Alcatel-Lucent.

Example

A global telecommunications company, Alcatel-Lucent is an IP networking, ultra-broadband access, and cloud technology specialist. Keeping up with the pace of development within the communication and broadband arena calls for an organization which lives innovation with its every breath. Staying at the forefront of the game takes determination and collaboration.

Alcatel-Lucent's innovation engine not only collaborates with scientists, researchers and engineers, it seeks to lead the innovation ideal throughout its business sector. Research helps it to devise and implement solutions that create significant competitive differentiation while incubating start-up projects helps to keep the business agile and innovative. Key to its success is the way in which this organization not only seeks to deliver innovative product ideas but also looks to 'anticipate, explore and de-risk technology evolutions'. (Alcatel-Lucent, 2015)

Making your innovation strategy and vision your own

What the two examples above perfectly illustrate is the way in which organizations create innovation strategies that are right for them but which also recognize the importance of interacting with the wider business environment.

The days of insular isolation are over and the innovative business that will succeed in tomorrow's world is the business which seeks to draw in and influence the whole marketplace. Collaborating to such an extent can lead some to fear that the end result will be a gradual decline towards convergence. Nothing could be further from the truth. When you innovate, when you look to create game-changing products, services, business models or experiences the end goal is still the longevity of your organization allied to customer excellence and investor confidence. This alone will differentiate your organization even were it not for the individuality of innovation strategies.

Think of it this way. Give 10 people a pencil and a sheet of paper, sit them in front of the same view and they will produce 10 completely different drawings. They have the same tools, the same input and even if they have chatted and exchanged hints along the way, the vision and approach which they all take will come from within and will result in differing outcomes.

The truth is there's no right or wrong answer to creating an innovation vision, roadmap and strategy but you can't simply take someone else's strategy and expect to apply it to your organization. 'Stealing with pride' is fine but every organization is completely unique in its culture, make-up and how it dynamically operates and so has to create its own way forward rather than try and follow others' footsteps. So using ideas as a catalyst is fine, trying an outright copy will only result in disaster; not the least because you will be at a very different stage of innovation maturity to any organization whose innovation strategy or approach you want to emulate.

Innovation visions and strategies, like any other business strategies, are also subject to required change in response to changes in the business world, in technology, in trends or in customer preference. The result is that strategies must be looked on as entities with a degree of fluidity. That's why adaptability is a key trait of the world's leading innovative companies and is a fundamental part of their innovation strategies. At any point where a degree of change or shift in direction or trajectory is then required in your innovation strategy and vision, how you are set up to meet this change with adaptability and how you communicate the change is absolutely key to success.

We'll look further into the importance of communication in Chapter 5 but at this stage we are going to touch on one aspect of defining the strategy which can trip up those who are used to a more linear method of working: the importance of positioning innovation for everyone.

Positioning innovation for everyone

Those who have grown up with a traditional (hierarchical) organization tend to have a fairly linear view of the business world. In essence, the leadership team devise the vision, values and strategy, the middle layers of management convey that strategy to their teams and the majority of employees get on with whatever their task is, as determined by the strategy. Employee engagement may come into the mix somewhere but here again the view is somewhat linear.

Adopting an innovation culture sweeps traditional boundaries aside. Cross-departmental collaboration, empowerment and the drive towards a solutions-based organization not only shakes up the structure once but continues to do so as challenges and solutions present themselves. Think of a child's kaleidoscope. The shapes within it remain unchanged but as you twist the toy around those unchanging shapes continually reset themselves into different patterns. There are set boundaries, the shapes themselves don't change and they operate within the confines of the tube but within those boundaries they respond to the outside influence of how the kaleidoscope is manipulated to produce different results.

The flatter, more interwoven structure created by the ever-changing nature of interactions can create challenges for the senior team when they are trying to devise a strategy that places innovation at the top of the agenda. This in turn can throw up issues of alignment between members of the senior team and can affect their ability to communicate a robust, pragmatic yet organization-pushing innovation strategy, which resonates across the organization.

This is where leadership through empowered decision making comes into its own. In the recession, empowerment suffered as decision making moved up the organization in order to increase control and manage risk. Now it is time for that movement to be reversed, to start the journey of empowerment again to support innovation. Committees and outdated processes quite simply won't provide the style of leadership which will lead to innovative solutions; for that you need agile thinking and practices. But this won't happen unless corporations actively gear themselves up to accept empowered decision making as a way of life.

The common language around innovation typically revolves around two types of innovation, namely incremental, which in essence can also be described as 'continuous improvement', and radical. In reality the majority of incremental innovation is typically focused internally on improvements to processes, systems, ways of working/operating and so on. However, sometimes it does manifest itself to small improvements in areas such as existing product lines or services, cost reductions or better value for customers. Internal changes of this nature tend to be more easily assimilated by the entire workforce.

The big issue comes with the next step, which is radical. This moves innovation away from the 'structural' context of incremental changes to the 'contextual' context of innovation around specific problems or strategic challenges. By default, contextual innovation largely embraces an external customer perspective or 'context'. More often than not creating solutions of this nature requires significant input into design, development, testing, investment and time to market. The challenge here when aiming to build a culture of innovation is that not everyone can contribute to innovation at this level; it's simply too big for the majority of employees.

So the solution is to create the addition of another stepping stone to slot in between incremental and radical innovation. We typically use 'differentiated innovation' as a simple-to-explain and position stepping stone but we would also encourage organizations to create their own definitions using language appropriate for them and their organization. However, for the purposes of explaining things further let's stick with 'differentiated' as the language. Differentiated innovation for us is about focusing attention externally, as there is often enough coverage of internal improvements through 'incremental' efforts. The external focus should solely be on 'how do we do things differently' for our customers.

Summing this up: Differentiated innovation is something more than incremental but not necessarily radical that absolutely differentiates you from your competitors. So, it should be enough to change how you and your customers behave through an increase in value and/or the creation of better, deeper, more aligned and more personal experiences. It's about you becoming the 'no brainer' choice for your customers.

Understanding whether innovation is incremental, differentiated or radical will help the leadership team to position the strategy in a way that will resonate best with the organization. Here again communication is key. Regardless of the innovation mix, the more the strategy has been devised to position innovation at an organization-wide level and the more employees are helped to gain a holistic viewpoint, the better the results. This puts the onus squarely on the top team to devise an inclusive strategy which will of itself be innovative and will have the full backing of the entire team.

Building leadership team agreement – are you ready?

In a moment we're going to move on to look at ownership and accountability but first it is time for a quick reality check and to ask yourself if you really know why you are looking to adopt an innovation culture. This is your 'read the book, seen the film, now it's time to wear the T-shirt' moment.

Quite simply, are you prepared to commit to rethinking your operating model so that it delivers the sort of differentiated innovation which will create lasting change? Are you prepared to increase your reliance on partnerships with customers, suppliers and others in order to speed up delivery to market? And are you fully prepared for your operating model to become more adaptable in order to be more agile and innovative?

You see, in some ways in this era of open communication it is all too easy to simply jump on the next bandwagon, to look on adopting the latest craze as a panacea for all your ills. You may not think of it like that. You may have been enthused by attending presentations, by reading up on innovation or by networking with directors who have themselves already travelled the innovation route. You may have read case studies which proved how innovation cultures are transforming organizations. Or you may have been influenced by publications from the EU or your sector regulators which encourage the adoption of an innovation culture as a way of driving forward growth. And you wouldn't be alone in assimilating the idea that innovation is the way forward. An Accenture report in 2013 revealed that 93 per cent of executives believed that long-term success was dependant on their ability to innovate (Accenture, 2013).

But whatever you have read, however deeply you have researched, are you really sure that you understand the specific case for change in your organization? The step from knowing something exists to actually being able to practise that skill can be immense. And even if you think you are ready to take the plunge, is your organization really geared up for change? As a 'starter for 10', ask yourself the following:

1 Is your approach focused on product or is the view that innovation applies to everything: brand, organization, business model, experiences etc; and all with customer focus very much in mind?

2 Is taking 'smart risk' not only tolerated but rewarded or are risks mitigated and chastised/frowned upon etc?

3 Is the focus on continuing to protect your existing business model and trying to gain a bigger share of the existing market or reinventing yourself for the future?

4 Is there a mix of innovation activity (a balanced innovation portfolio) across incremental, differentiated and radical innovation?

5 Are you prepared to completely change your culture or disrupt yourself in pursuit of an innovation-driven future?

6 Is there organization-wide tolerance for and exploration of disruptive, unconventional and controversial ideas?

7 If there's a strategic need to deploy resources for innovation outside the current organizational structure, is there a process for it?

8 Is there clear visibility of you and the senior team owning, sponsoring and taking accountability for driving innovation?

9 Are you prepared to sacrifice parts of the existing business in order to provide your innovation efforts with real-world environments in order to prototype new ideas, revenue streams and business models?

10 If necessary, are you prepared to completely reinvent your organization in pursuit of winning the new game through innovation?

Taken cumulatively the answers to these questions will indicate whether you are already well on the way to a culture of innovation or whether there is some tough work ahead in reshaping the business vision and ideals. Admittedly some of these are tough questions but unless the drivers for innovation are crystal clear then you won't be able to lead, to engage and to create an innovative scorecard. The questions also act as a handy checklist as you move through your innovation journey. For example, at the outset the answer to question six might be an unequivocal 'no' but as you move through your innovation programme, as departments or divisions gradually take on a more innovative mindset the way in which the answer changes will help you to track the way in which innovation is infusing the organization.

Building leadership team agreement – collaboration and risk

With the senior team fully focused on devising an inclusive strategy, one which will sit at every level of the organization, can we skip ahead to Chapter 4 and Designing the Future? Not quite. At the start of this chapter we highlighted the fact that if it's not on the top teams agenda then it's not going to be in the culture but there is one more significant barrier to cross and that is the unanimity, capability and resolve of the senior team.

Even if the design and implementation team draw in people from across the organization, the senior team must first be in absolute alignment about the innovation vision, strategic innovation decision and supporting strategy. If they aren't then they won't be able to clearly communicate how important innovation is to the future of the organization and more importantly what behaviour is required from individuals in order to drive innovation forward. This therefore requires there to be clear and visible ownership, sponsorship and accountability by the CEO and the senior leadership team in order to create an innovation movement at the heart of the organization. But this is not as simple as having an agreed risk appetite.

Put simply, the risk appetite of the organization is not the same as the risk appetite for individual elements of the business. For example, if an internal report is late then it is merely an annoyance; if a customer order is late then the reputation of the business suffers. But cohesion runs far deeper than risk appetite. Within the overall mix, each director will have their own targets, KPIs and pressure points and some of these will run counter to those held by other directors. When sales runs up against operations or marketing faces financial constraints, then directors generally work to agree an acceptable balance within the parameters of the business. But when innovation demands cross-department collaboration it is important for the top team to agree on the collective tension points (balanced scorecard) across the organization, including the risks, costs, reputation, service etc.

It is also important to understand where there can be flexibility in these pressure points, where a discussion or regrouping of thoughts is necessary to bring the organization back on track. Failure is an important element of an innovation culture but you can't let failure break your business. Accordingly the leadership team need to understand all the parameters and measurements, which will enable them to say 'yes, we can keep trying x, but only if y & z are in balance'. The challenge for leaders and the business is to fight the urge to pull away from the long-term view in favour of small wins today and meeting short-term targets. For example, short-term pressure on costs may take the focus away from the innovation goal but giving in to these short-term distractions doesn't move an organization forward and doesn't drive innovation-led growth.

Building leadership team agreement – personal acceptance

Even with apparent agreement amongst the leadership team, successful implementation requires deep personal commitment to the innovation ideal. By their very nature, agreement and consensus sit at the heart of boardroom life. True, there may be occasional disagreements on minor points but 'for the good of the organization' boards endeavour to show a united face to the outside world. So much so that in some boardrooms there is a danger that the desire to agree overwhelms the ability to question and to challenge.

Responding to this perceived danger, regulatory authorities across the globe have taken steps to increase board diversity and to encourage debate. For example, within the EU much has been made of measures taken to increase female representation on boards, but creating a gender balance on boards is only the tip of a wider diversity iceberg. Interestingly the 2014 Egon Zehnder Diversity Analysis report, which looked at the largest companies across Europe and the rest of the world, revealed that in Europe nearly 90 per cent of companies surveyed had at least one non-national board director and overall nearly a third of all EU board directors are non-nationals (Egon Zehnder, 2014).

This move towards diversity, not only as a means of better reflecting the wider population but also as a means of encouraging balanced debate may perhaps best be summed up by the UK FRC. (The Financial Reporting Council is the UK's independent regulator responsible for promoting high-quality corporate governance and reporting to foster investment.) Announcing an update to the UK Corporate Governance Code in September 2014, the FRC emphasized that 'key to the effective functioning of any board is a dialogue which is both constructive and challenging. One of the ways in which such debate can be encouraged is through having sufficient diversity on the board, including gender and race. Nevertheless, diverse board composition in these respects is not, on its own, a guarantee. Diversity can be just as much about difference of approach and experience.' (FRC, 2014)

Regardless of the level of debate and consensus, it is not enough for boards to present a united front; every member of the executive also has to assimilate the innovation ideal. Agreeing to move towards an innovation framework is not like any other board decision. If the board decides to open a new factory, close some branch offices, adopt a move towards new product lines then the collective decision may require action on the part of board directors but those actions are direct and tangible. So HR may have to draw up new contracts or start consultation processes, finance may need to source external funding and so on but the way in which they act needn't change.

However, when it comes to a cultural transformation, the way in which people think and act also has to change. It's not enough for the HR director or the FD to sign off on the policy and then carry on as before. 'Be the change you wish to see' means first understanding what the innovation agenda means personally and then working towards changing mindsets and behaviour models to lead the way. This may require some tough talking at the outset. If those who sit at the top table are not comfortable with innovation, perhaps seeing it as too fluid or ambiguous to deal with or feeling uncomfortable with perceived risk levels, then this discomfort needs to be dealt with right at the beginning. Failure to do so equates with an acceptance that the move towards innovation is only going to be fleeting. For example, you can't have the FD agreeing with the group but then suddenly pulling the plug because a project goes over budget or doesn't deliver instant returns.

Building leadership team agreement – ownership

This leads us on to ownership and accountability. We've already seen how important it is for every member of the top team to assimilate an innovation mindset into everyday thoughts, decisions and actions. But in general it would be unrealistic for the top team to collectively take ownership for the overall innovation programme, not least because innovation champions will eventually need to be drawn from every level of the organization. However, that doesn't mean that collectively the board members can step back too far and devolve ownership to a single individual. It's a tricky balancing act. Every team member must ensure that they have a well-defined role in creating the innovation culture but at the same time the overall strategy and direction needs to have a controlling force.

In a way this runs parallel to the drive by regulatory bodies, particularly those within the financial services sector, for increased levels of personal ownership and accountability as a means of curbing the excesses which led to some firms being brought to the brink of collapse. Under this new regime, while boards have overall accountability, approved persons are deemed to have personal accountability and liability for the sectors under their control. While this approved persons regime is best known as a measure adopted by UK financial services regulators, similar measures have been adopted in other business sectors and other countries.

With personal ownership and accountability running parallel to collective responsibility, the way in which innovation leadership is positioned within the organization is crucial to its success. Cast the net too widely and it is all too easy for every individual to assume that someone else is taking forward the transformation. Conversely, too narrow a focus can result in the rest of the top team sitting back and waiting for change to happen.

The 'best fit' will ultimately depend on the type of organization. However, one suggested model is for the leadership team to own the decisions and actions while the implementation team drives forward day-to-day change. This implementation team is generally led by one or two individuals who act as co-ordinators. Here we must add a warning.

The merits or otherwise of appointing a named Innovation Director have been the subject of great debate and in truth there is no one answer just as there is no one company structure. In some organizations therefore the role will effectively be filled by one or two individuals in existing positions of authority. But where a unique innovation director role is created the job holder has to have sufficient authority and seniority to create change within the organization. In other words, there is no point in appointing someone to take innovation forward if they are unable to interact on a regular basis with senior executives and are unable to influence process and culture change throughout the organization.

This can perhaps best be illustrated by a presentation given in 2010 to the European Economic and Social Committee (Ameel, 2010). The presentation entitled 'The Innovation Manager: Role, competencies and skills' highlights the importance of the innovation manager being able to interact and influence both at board level and operational level. For example, at board level the innovation manager has to champion innovation, build and maintain innovation capability and secure resources needed to innovate while at operational level the role includes leading the innovation process and working with individuals and teams to encourage and facilitate innovation.

Creating capability

So far we've concentrated on areas such as being prepared to embrace innovation cultures, taking ownership and accountability but there is one elephant in the room which we need to consider. That is the question of whether the top team are capable of driving change forward. Put simply, the leadership skills required for managing through change are different from those required for steady-state leadership and the leadership skills required for implementing an innovation culture are one step on again.

Earlier in this chapter we looked at whether the leadership team were ready to embrace and take ownership of innovation; now we need to assess personal and leadership skills with a view to ensuring the leadership team have the skills they require to drive change. There are a number of leadership assessment programmes available but for choice we would generally recommend the Leadership Practices Inventory™ (LPI). The LPI is one of the most widely used and trusted leadership assessment instruments and forms part of The Leadership Challenge™ programme.

Originally developed in 1983, The Leadership Challenge™ programme is based upon thousands of case studies which examined how leaders achieved extraordinary results. The research concluded that the majority of extraordinary leaders displayed five particular characteristics. They were:

1 Model the way.

2 Inspire a shared vision.

3 Challenge the process.

4 Enable others to act.

5 Encourage the heart.

Supporting these five practices are 10 commitments towards exemplary leadership, namely:

1 Find your voice by clarifying your personal values.

2 Set the example by aligning actions with shared values.

3 Envision the future by imagining exciting and enabling possibilities.

4 Enlist others in a common vision by appealing to shared aspirations.

5 Search for opportunities by seeking innovative ways to change, grow and improve.

6 Experiment and take risks by constantly generating small wins and learning from experience.

7 Foster collaboration by promoting co-operative goals and building trust.

8 Strengthen others by sharing power and direction.

9 Recognise contributions by showing appreciation for individual excellence.

10 Celebrate the values and victories by creating a spirit of community.

A 360-degree quantative review, the LPI psychometrically validated tool measures the frequency with which an individual leader and their observers witness these five practices in action. With the assessment helping leaders to understand their own individual style, the programme can then help leaders to develop their expertise with the aim of better leading innovation change.

Whether the LPI or any other programme is used, the leadership team should then be in a strong position to assimilate and drive forward change. But that doesn't mean that having completed the assessment or programme they should be instantly plunged back into isolation within the organization. Tapping into external expertise will help to get ideas flowing and to embed innovation into the culture so that it becomes a way of life. However, with collaboration being a strong element of innovation, the leadership team shouldn't be afraid to reach out to mentors or coaches to help them to keep their personal development flowing and the project on track.

Creating capability – managing resources

This leads us on to another question which the leadership team should consider early on in the process, that of sourcing and managing resources.

Programmes such as The Leadership Challenge™ can help with personal development but there are other areas which it is best to consider early on. Let's look at a few examples:

- *Digital capability* – How well do you understand your digital capabilities or the advantages which can be gained through leveraging digital potential? When you are looking to increase insights and collaboration then digital interactions are a must. From web design and search engine optimization to the use of social media and apps, the digital world is made for innovation. Taking the time out early on to assess and strengthen digital capability will help to ensure that when you need metrics, the information is already flowing. As an added bonus, taking the time to improve employees digital skills will send out an early signal about the way in which change and collaboration is on the way.

- *Existing partnerships* – When you go all-out to create innovative solutions, the last thing you want or need is for existing partners to create barriers to change. From external legal teams or auditors to suppliers and other support organizations your success depends on their cooperation. Some will willingly embrace change, some may already be ahead of you on the journey, but there will be occasions when you may need to seek out alternative progressive partners in order to ensure success.

- *Regulatory bodies* – We've touched on this before but it is worth repeating. If you are in a regulated industry then establishing an early dialogue with regulators will help to ensure that they are supportive of your development. Some may already have guidelines or supporting research which will help you to develop your new framework. Regulators don't have all the answers and may not formally approve plans at base product level but it is worth noting that leadership outside the business, such as that provided by regulators and industry bodies, may be just as important as internal leadership.

Leading through change

With support in the form of coaching in place and the top team collectively in agreement the way is open to design the future. There is, however, one more challenge which we are going to touch on here and that is the way in which the team is able to lead through change, ambiguity and uncertainty.

The team may be comfortable leading forward with vision and purpose but what about everyone else who works within the business? It is all too easy to be so fired up with zeal for change that you forget the people element of leading through change.

It is also all too easy to give too much weight to those who are most likely to resist change. In all organizations there are those whose preconceptions and adherence to the status quo won't let them see what is in front of them or even that there is another option available. These are the resistors, the people who will come up with all of the excuses or who will openly accept change but will then go back to business as usual. It is easy to see how the leadership team may feel that they need to concentrate on this group but in reality it is a false premise.

It is far better to spend time and resources on those of influence within the organization who will work with the senior team to lead change. They may sit at any level within the business but 'leaders without a title' are key to influencing change and making sure that it sticks. We will come back to this at a later stage when we look at appointing change champions and communicating change. We have already considered some aspects of this subject when we looked at overcoming barriers to change but for now let's start to map out some considerations.

First and foremost is the need to consider the way in which people instinctively react to change. The 'fight-or-flight' response to physical danger is well known but perhaps less well known is that people perceive social change in the same way. David Rock, an Australian researcher, described social pain within the business sphere using the acronym SCARF (Rock, 2008).

According to this model, when employees see change as threatening their 'move away' response is activated and change is resisted. However, when the employee perceives change as positive, their 'move towards' response is activated, which results in engagement and alignment. The acronym SCARF describes the type of social interaction that will strongly activate the 'move away from' response. The letters stand for Status, Certainty, Autonomy, Relatedness and Fairness. These factors, if mishandled, can trigger the brain's 'move away' response, creating resistance to change. Understanding and watching out for the five domains in the SCARF model will help leaders to manage change far more effectively. In general our top tips for leading through change are:

- *Be aware* – Being open to the possibility of change and resistance will help to anticipate and prevent problems arising. A quiet word now is much easier than departmental strife later.

- *Communicate* – One of the key planks of change management is to communicate early, communicate effectively and communicate often. Above all, don't wait for certainty before you start communicating. All this will mean is that rumour and speculation have had a chance to gain a foothold and then you have lost your best chance to gain enthusiasm and engagement in the change. We'll look at this in more detail in Chapter 5.

- *Listen* – Listen to what people are trying to say rather than the words which they are using. Use your eyes to read body language, be aware that emotions can lead to either over-hyped or under-played reactions. Stay calm and use open questions to elicit truths.

- *Clear and consistent* – With board unanimity this should be easier but the message which goes out has to be clear and consistent, not only from the top team but also in what is said to every person. And don't forget that 'don't do what I do, do what I say' has no place in change management. You have to lead the way by example.

- *Engagement* – Take the time to engage employees in the new culture. When you are looking to create game-changing customer experiences via an innovative and future-proof culture which delivers excellence for the business, shareholders, employees and the wider community then aligning employees with the business strategy means that they will stop being unwilling observers and start being active participants.

- *Quick wins* – Never underestimate the importance of quick wins for boosting morale.

- *Start with people who care* – Use the advocates you already have to help you build momentum around the change.

In summary

This is the time when the leadership team stop thinking of innovation as a theoretical exercise and start to put flesh on the bones of change. It is a time for asking tough questions and of committing fully to a new strategy which will be unlike any which has gone before. In the next chapter we will move on and start to shape the journey, clothing the strategy with vision, values and competencies. None of these will have any effect on the organization unless the leadership team have first assimilated the innovation ideal into their thoughts and behaviours.

So the key questions here are:

1 *Are you prepared to embed innovation into the top team's agenda?* Quite simply, if the leadership team are not prepared to change their mindset so that they think innovation, live innovation and breathe innovation into every decision then there is little point in going through the motions, only to have every attempt to move forward hauled back by inertia from the top.

2 *Are you prepared to create a strategy which is aligned with the organization's appetite for innovation?* Whatever the innovation mix the important message is that you have to adopt a 'venture capital' mindset. Some, or most, ideas won't come to fruition but by spreading the risk, those that do succeed will far outweigh those that don't.

3 *Are you prepared to move from a hierarchical leadership style to one which leads rather than manages and which empowers rather than controls?* The leadership team may find that they require some ongoing leadership training to help them to assimilate a more innovative and empowered style of leadership but all leadership is a journey and this is just the next stage which will lead to the future.

Key insights

- If it's not on the top team's agenda, building a true organization-wide culture of innovation is impossible.

- If you are going to adopt an innovation culture then you have to adopt a 'venture capital' mindset.

- The innovative business that will succeed in tomorrow's world isn't the one that competes in existing markets but the one which seeks to shape markets and even create new ones.

References

Accenture (2013) [accessed 3 April 2015] Why 'Low Risk' Innovation is Costly, [online] http://www. accenture. com/SiteCollectionDocuments/PDF/Accenture-Why-Low-Risk-Innovation-Costly.pdf

Alcatel-Lucent (2015) [accessed 3 April 2015] [online] http://www3.alcatel-lucent.com/wps/portal/!ut/p/

kcxml/04_Sj9SPykssy0xPLMnMz0vM0Y_QjzKLd4x3CvEASYGYRq6m-
pEoYgbxjgiRoJRUfV-P_NxUfW_9AP2C3NCIckdHRQBVX43d/delta/
base64xml/L3dJdyEvd0ZNQUFzQUMvNElVRS82X0FfQlRE

Ameel, D (2010) [accessed 3 April 2015] [online] http://www.slideshare.net/
EESCsocsection/the-innovation-manager-role-competencies-and-skills-the-
relevance-of-implementing-specific-positions-for-managers-creating-innovative-
organizations

Egon Zehnder (2014) [accessed 3 April 2015] [online] http://www.egonzehnder.
com/EBDA-2014-map

FRC (2014) [accessed 3 April 2015] [online] https://www.frc.org.uk/News-
and-Events/FRC-Press/Press/2014/September/FRC-updates-UK-Corporate-
Governance-Code.aspx

Kelley, B (2010) *Stoking Your Innovation Bonfire* (p 25), John Wiley & Sons,
London

P&G (2015) [accessed 3 April 2015] [online] http://www.pgconnectdevelop.com/
home/pg_open_innovation.html

Rock, D (2008) SCARF: A brain-based model for collaborating with and
influencing others, *Neuroleadership Journal*, 1 pp 1–9

Designing the future

04

U nless you are skimming this book at random, by now your innovation journey has taken you from an appreciation of the importance of innovation in 21st-century business and onwards into developing an understanding of where your organization sits on the innovation spectrum today. Along the way we've taken in the sights and sounds of an organization which is resistant to innovation, worked on focusing organizational energies to maximize results and delved into the attitudes and behaviours which are currently shaping your culture.

In Chapter 3 we worked through building leadership team agreement, creating a leadership team which will own, develop and promote innovation. In this chapter we are moving on, seeking to shake off the shackles of history and embrace the bright lights of innovation potential. We are going to look at shaping organizational visions and values and the way in which these values can be translated into competencies. In particular in this chapter we will look at the different approaches which can shape the innovation journey and the importance of aligning the team to step into the future.

In essence this chapter covers the initial design phase which will act as the bedrock for inculcating and embedding change. Those who have pursued change programmes in the past will already be familiar with the way in which the vision translates into values and competencies; working to create the attitudes and behaviours which will enable an innovation culture to take hold. Some, such as professionalism, may already be familiar elements of the existing culture; others such as empowerment may represent a complete change in the employer–employee relationship. But it is only when these elements have been mapped out that the leadership team can move on to start shaping the transformational journey and considering whether a dual operating system or gradual phasing in of change may be preferable alternatives to a 'big bang' introduction. Finally in this chapter we look at the importance of engaging your people in the required changes and looking at the supporting framework which underpins the innovation model.

We are going to start with a word of warning. For many organizations, this stage of the journey represents the tipping point, the moment in time in which the organization either slides back into the gloom or strides forward into the future. For this is the moment in which the organization needs to move out of its comfort zone, to put time and effort and resolve into designing a new, innovative, agile organization which provides exceptional customer experiences as a matter of course.

But with the rewards on offer, why is this stage of the journey so hard? Essentially we have arrived at the crunch point, the time when you know how you got to where you now are, when you understand on an intellectual level why changing your habits would be good for you but you suddenly realize that the change means hard work. So this moment is somewhat akin to the moment of truth for all those New Year resolutions. Yes, you need to get fitter, you understand why getting fitter would be good for your long-term health; but changing those habits which have crept in over the years takes resolve and drive and a clear vision or even a little pain to force the change.

But just as moving straight from a sedentary lifestyle into running a marathon is not generally considered to be a good idea, neither do you have to blast the innovation ideal out throughout the entire organization at the same time. Later on in this chapter we will be examining the benefits of introducing change via a dual operating system with innovation wrapping around core processes. Just as that can be phased in, so too can the innovation ideal be phased in across the business. As with the innovation mix, there is no one right answer for phasing in innovation. So businesses which are comparatively small or agile may decide to go all out for change, those which are larger or have more complex structures may decide to ease innovation into the organization with a phased introduction.

Shaping the vision

It is this need for a clear vision that we are going to examine first. In Chapter 2 we explored the importance of crafting a strategy which aligned with the organization's appetite for innovation. Now we need to take the next step, to shape the organization's vision and values so that they not only underpin innovative transformation but shape the organizational pathway going forward.

'Good business leaders create a vision, articulate the vision, passionately own the vision, and relentlessly drive it to completion.' (Welch, 1989)

Crafting a vision for the organization can be at the same time incredibly easy and fiendishly difficult. Somewhat akin to completing a cryptic cross-word, it's fairly easy to fill the blanks with words but quite another thing to make sure those words are the right ones. A good company vision has to speak to the heart, to inspire and to provide a goal which will challenge people to greatness. And don't forget that at every stage of the journey, the importance of customer experience and insight cannot be underestimated. When we look at the vision, when we move onwards into defining values and competencies they should all be aligned with customer outcomes. Harking back to Chapter 1 it is also important that future design anticipates the dif-fering requirements of the entire customer and employee base. For example, this may mean designing for different generations or for customers from multiple countries. Delivery will inevitably become more complex as you shake off the 'one size fits all' model but by correctly aligning the innovation mix, it is possible to provide a personal service for all.

When designing the future don't neglect the legacy of the past. There will inevitably be some processes or procedures which made sense in the past, for example multiple layers of sign-off as a means to control cost, which simply have no place in the future. Now is the time to sweep these aside if they are no longer required, to remove layers of governance which might act as barriers to collaborative innovations and to be clear on the impacts of decisions going forward. But there are other aspects of the past such as a deep commitment to customer service which may still fit in well with an innovation culture.

While there are almost as many definitions of a good company vision as there are management books, the common themes which define a good company vision include:

- *Brevity* – If you want to inspire hearts and minds the last thing you want to do is drop a 50-page tome on people's laps. Long rambling paragraphs only serve to disengage and won't help to articulate the vision.

- *Individuality* – We can all have a vision of our organization as 'the best in the field' but in a homogeneous world it is the way we do things which will differentiate us. Having an 'off the shelf' vision which we have pieced together from some examples on the internet or have copied from another organization says we have no intention of standing above the crowd. So the vision has to be right for our own organization, has to sit within our business sphere, and has to articulate the ways in which we intend to manipulate innovation culture to create a lasting, agile legacy.

- *Clarity* – Following on from brevity, the vision has to be clear, something tangible which can be used as the bedrock for norms, processes and behaviours and which will inspire belief, loyalty and trust.

- *Engaging* – The vision has to resonate with the team, enabling employees to believe in it and to align their hearts and minds with it.

If you are having trouble articulating the vision, then go back to basics. You already know your starting point from having undertaken the culture assessment and you have identified your innovation gap so you have a fair idea of what you do well, what you may need to improve on and where you would like to be. In Chapter 3 you took these ideas and started to devise your strategy, leveraging intelligence to make 'best guesses' about the shape of the future.

When articulating the vision therefore all you are essentially doing is combining these ideas to create a high-level roadmap which defines where the organization wants to be in the future. Thinking of this in terms of your GPS or satellite navigation system, you already have your starting point and now you are programming in your final destination and any stop-off points along the way. The actual shape of the journey, whether you use motorways or not and so on will come later on. Because we are still looking at a high-level strategy at this stage the sat-nav may only take us in the right direction, ie to the right town or suburb rather than to a precise address. As we further refine our strategy the destination will become more precise but there is still the chance that it may change shape, responding to circumstances which are encountered along the way. It is also worth remembering that our eventual destination is not fixed and may change because the world and the environment in which we operate continuously shifts and evolves.

We're now going to move on and start to look at the values which underpin the vision but before we do so it's probably worth taking a side trip to consider a 'new kid on the block', the cultural manifesto. The more that organizations start to delve into, and understand the importance of, their culture, the greater the realization that if that culture is to mean anything it has to be communicated in a way that resonates with employees, consumers and others.

The mission statement can be seen as a fairly bland statement of the vision; the cultural manifesto takes this to a new level, translation the vision into emotion and action. Apple's initial cultural manifesto talks about believing in deep collaboration and cross-pollination in order to innovate in a way others cannot while the Netflix cultural manifesto was hailed by the Facebook COO as the most important document ever to come out of Silicon Valley. When moving to an innovation-led culture the cultural manifesto may well be one key way of reaching and energizing hearts and minds in the change.

Defining the values

Moving on, we then need to look at the values which will underpin the vision. Some, such as honesty and integrity, may almost go without saying but it is important when defining values that every value is included if we are to avoid the hidden snare of assumption. In Chapter 2 we looked at the importance of taking the time to understand where you are today if you are to move forward with confidence. As a result of that analysis, the leadership team should have a thorough appreciation of the values that sit within the organization today, most of which may very well remain unchanged as the cultural drive moves onward.

But beware of the elephants in the room, the espoused values which will defeat every attempt to change unless they are tamed. They may appear in the form of an ingrained assumption of accuracy which means that every process and action is triple checked before it is signed off; or perhaps a respect for seniority which means that every diktat is followed without question; in multinational corporations it may be the assumption that every office will display the same responses to workflow and change which stifles innovation change. Whatever they are, espoused values can be the one factor which above all else can make or break the transformation. We will look at successfully overcoming rogue values later on when we visit leadership and communication.

Successfully defining values means determining what the organization should value most and making sure that that sits within the vision and strategy. And when you are trying to create an innovation-led organization, then your other values should not sit at odds with innovation. For example, an innovation culture means accepting failure as a learning point. If one of your values is 'accuracy at all costs' then innovation can never succeed.

As you move through your innovation journey, the importance attached to individual values may well move up and down the scale. The deeper you delve into innovation, the more you will find that values such as personal responsibility, trust, agility and initiative will come to the fore. Other values that may sit well within an innovation culture include collaboration, insight, communication and inclusiveness. The values you define at this stage, however, should not exclusively be confined to the innovation sphere. While the culture of innovation will drive your future development, other values such as integrity, accuracy or honesty will still be required to underpin the organization.

It is perhaps also worth reiterating here that some values may differ across organizational departments. Although core values will run throughout the business, in the same way as an organization may benefit from the added flexibility of operating with sub-cultures it may also operate with sub-values. For example, while your R&D teams may want to experiment with different models, the accounts department may wish to be more prescriptive when it comes to allocating items of expenditure across statutory accounts.

Depending on the type of organization, there may also be a requirement at this stage for a mission/purpose to be defined. When an organization has a clear mission that defines who and what they are and what they stand for, that mission sits above both vision and values as a constant reference point. But just because an organization has a mission, that doesn't mean that it has a divine right to carry on regardless, following the same pathways that have been laid down for decades. The world moves on and while the mission may only require the odd tweak, the way in which the mission is accomplished still has to evolve to take account of 21st-century methodologies. So while the mission may remain unchanged and virtually unchanging, that doesn't mean that the vision and values, which translate the mission into action, cannot be fundamentally altered to accommodate a culture of innovation.

In the same way that it is important for our vision to be clear, so too is clarity a vital component of values definition, not only in the values themselves but also in the way in which they will translate into everyday actions within the organization. We'll revisit this point in the next section of this chapter when we look at translating values into competencies but for now want to highlight another important aspect of values, namely the understanding of how each value sits both within the organization and alongside other values. For example, it is easy to list 'quality' among your values but what do you mean by quality and how is it affected by other values such as 'value for money', 'environmental responsibility' or 'sustainably sourced'?

If you don't take time to truly understand and articulate these inter-actions then you risk losing the trust of your customers and of your employees. This highlights another important aspect of shaping the vision and values: the need to be realistic, to tell it as it is. Not every organiza-tion can, or should, produce designer wear for the top of the market. Customers' requirements and budgets vary and organizations will find their own niche within the marketplace. If you are geared up to produc-ing bargain-bucket wear at sensible prices then there is nothing wrong in building brand values which match that reality. In other words, don't promise top quality if top quality can't be had within the price range of your customers.

This leads on to the importance of defining the specific purpose of inno-vation within your organization. In Chapter 1 we started to explore the triggers which lead organizations to recognize the need to build a culture of innovation but at this stage we thought it important to take time out to highlight the general and the specific purpose of innovation. As we high-lighted in Chapter 1 the biggest trap which organizations fall into is in co-mingling invention and innovation. If you want to invent you get a bunch of experts together and sit them in a room with acres of whiteboards or piles of laboratory equipment and you hope that they will come up with something new. In the meantime the business of the rest of the organization goes on around them.

Having an innovation-led culture means sitting on another plane entirely. Invention may result in innovation but true innovation culture permeates the entire organization, infusing everyone it touches with agil-ity, with flexibility and with the desire to create an exceptional level of customer service. In a world in which every organization has access to the same level of technology, in which the one-man band has the potential to ride the internet in the same way as a multi-country organization, in which technological changes are driving consuming habits to change at an incred-ible rate; in this world the 'what' has been superseded by the 'how'. This has resulted in organizations which are innovative and agile succeeding while others slip away.

Being blunt, if you want competitive advantage and growth then in a homogenous world a culture of innovation is the only answer. More than that, without a culture of innovation underpinning your other values, the organization is unlikely to succeed in its aims. This means that although innovation is a value in itself, all of the other values should be seen as a sub-set of innovation. And when you translate your values into competencies, you should do so with innovation in mind.

Translating values into competencies

This leads us on to the next section of this chapter which moves values on to the next stage, translating them into competencies. This defines the attitudes and behaviours which you want to see within your organization on a daily basis. The task of defining values and competencies may already seem very familiar, particularly if you have worked, or are working, in the personnel/ HR sphere. Competencies come up time and time again on job applications and when setting personal targets. But there is one major difference when setting the aptitudes which will drive an innovation culture and that is the collaborative and inclusive nature of innovation itself.

Traditionally competencies are aimed at encouraging behaviours which will drive internal targets. With innovation at the heart of the organization, the qualities required will veer more towards collaboration, customer experience and problem solving. That's why, when we talk about preferred attitudes, behaviours, management and communication styles in an innovation context we tend to use the phrase 'innovation aptitudes' in place of competencies.

Some values translate on a linear basis into innovation aptitudes. For example, the value of 'honesty' may simply translate into owning up to mistakes or not covering up errors. Other values may require a little more thought before they can become innovation aptitudes. Let's look at a few examples:

- *Professional excellence* – In truth professionalism has so many different connotations that it might be better sub-defined within values; but assuming that professionalism is a value in its own right then we have to ask what attitudes and behaviours are we going to expect to see if we are to live professional excellence on a daily basis. For example, we may require employees to look smart, to dress appropriately or to use appropriate language when interacting with others. Respect for clients and colleagues may also come into this arena but we also might require employees to apply a degree of diligence in their work or to take professional qualifications to further their knowledge.

- *Ownership and accountability* – This is very much an aptitude/value which sits well within the innovation sphere but unless there are some guidelines then initiative can equate to a free-for-all. Are you expecting employees to take ownership of problems, to be accountable, to look for solutions no matter what the cost or can they only do so within parameters.? How much collaboration is too much? Changing the mindset to embrace ownership, initiative and accountability is not easy for some. Accepting that the buck may stop with you is a far cry from doing only what you are instructed to do.

- *Collaboration and teamwork* – Again an area which is very closely linked to innovation. Gone are the days when individuals, teams and companies worked in their own bubbles, oblivious or uninterested in what other groups or entities were doing. With innovation comes a new definition of teamwork, one in which collaboration and free-wheeling interactions create solutions. Whether crowdsourcing or leveraging the advantages of open source technology, holding open meetings or simply being open for a chat, collaboration and teamwork is now about breaking down the artificial barriers, understanding the whole picture, connecting the dots, sharing information and finding ways to solve problems and create the future. And don't forget that collaboration and teamwork now extend beyond the confines of the organization, requiring additional communication and understanding skills.

- *Empowerment and Initiative* – In Chapter 3, we looked at empowerment and the way in which throughout the recession empowerment moved up the organizational hierarchy in a bid to manage risk. Empowerment though, is a key component of innovation but it should not be mistaken for a 'free-for-all' in which 'you can decide what actions or decisions you make, completely unchecked' or 'we'll back whatever decisions you make'. So when looking to define empowerment the business has to be careful that any limitations are clearly defined. When it comes to initiative, empowerment and so on the innovation aptitudes which you will expect people to display will need to be carefully linked to your innovation mix. You may want people to be empowered but you have to show them the way and set the direction.

  One of the keys to success here is to encourage people to be intrapreneurs, to 'think like a business owner' within the organization. We'll look further into intrapreneurship in Chapter 6 but behaviours may include using intuition to find out more from the customer, to explore an idea or to challenge the rules. The focus should be outward looking with listening and thinking skills to the fore.

We could equally talk here about adaptability, the need to have a broad range of skills and styles which people can flex depending on the situation.

Or we could talk about agility, being able to respond quickly to changing scenarios and in the process having a feel for when the rule book is important and when it should be rewritten. We could even talk about emotional intelligence, about understanding and empathy, about influencing rather than directing and about flexing communication styles to meet the audience's needs rather than your own.

Whatever behaviours you prioritize, when you are defining your innovation aptitudes, one area which should never be underestimated is the importance of the customer relationship. In an increasingly homogeneous world we are more and more defined not on results, but on how we achieve them. This places customer perception and interaction high on the values agenda. No more are customers simply users of products or 'things to be sold to'. Now customers, and in particular the customer experience, are the drivers of excellence.

We've previously mentioned how Generation Z are looking to become involved in co-creating solutions, in 'co-innovating' but this theme is worth reiterating as this new collaborative way of working turns organizational perceptions on their head. Businesses will now have to look to use customer experiences to drive innovation and use innovation to drive customer experiences in a self-feeding spiral of improvement.

Shaping the journey

With vision, values and innovation aptitudes under way it is time to move on, to look towards shaping the journey and taking the innovation ideal out from the top team and into the wider organizational sphere. The values set will also help to inform and shape external relationships, defining external partnerships which will help the business to drive the innovation ideal forward. This is where you really find out how on-board the leadership team are with the idea of innovation and how much they are prepared to change in order for the business model to move from the linear buy/make/sell option into one which looks to continuous improvement in the search for solutions.

'I'm really fired up about innovation but... I've just got to finish this project first... the IT system needs sorting... I'm in the middle of negotiations with an important customer...'

Whatever the excuse it can't be ignored. But neither should it be used as a reason to throw away all of the good work and scrap the innovation ideal. Investigation may show that the root cause is a fear of the unknown or of the potential effect of shaking up a comfortable organization into one which is far more dynamic. The control factor also plays an important part here. No matter where your leadership style sits on the control spectrum there is always a feeling of certainty, of knowing where the boundaries are and of being comfortable with those boundaries. Change inevitably moves the boundaries and this perceived loss of control can unconsciously throw up barriers to change.

In Chapter 3 we examined how the brain's protective mechanism reacts when it perceives threat. Even when the leadership team are the ones driving change, they can still perceive threats when confronted with change within their own sphere. Let's look quickly again at some of the SCARF trigger points:

- *Status and autonomy* – These are both fairly important trigger points where the leadership team are concerned. Moving from complete departmental control to a more collaborative way of working in which team members are empowered to act on their own initiative could trigger concerns about the loss of status and autonomy. Certainly innovation does require a different working style but that doesn't take away from the responsibility of the top team to shape the organizational values and the direction of the business. In a way it also places more responsibility on the top team to ensure that innovative working doesn't slip into a free-for-all. And in any event, if a member of the leadership team is solely in it for the status then they probably shouldn't be in the job in the first place.

- *Certainty* – Any change is going to shake up certainty and when the change is as dramatic as a move to a culture of innovation then change can be scary. The answer here is to take time out to review the benefits which can be achieved by getting the right design for your culture. We've covered some of these at the end of this chapter.

So even if the leadership team have bought into the idea of innovation as a cultural transformation it is quite possible that some qualms remain. With this in mind, what is the best way of shaping the transformation, moving from the now to a fully innovative model? Do you close your eyes, hope for the best and jump in, do you phase the change across divisions or departments, or do you adopt a dual operating model?

In truth there is no one right answer. This is where the leadership team's knowledge of the business and their expertise within their field come into play. It's crunch time when the leadership team links the strategic innovation decision with the innovation mix and risk appetite to decide which path they are going to follow.

While there is no hard and fast rule, in practice organizations that look towards an instant switchover tend to be those which are smaller in size or which already operate in naturally innovative fields such as marketing or design.

Organizations with comparatively few employees generally retain some of the start-up mentality. Collaboration and interaction is at a relatively high level with task and job sharing being more the norm. If on a Friday afternoon employees are regularly pulled away from their accounts or admin roles to help pack up a shipment or send out a mass-mailer then they naturally gain a more holistic view of the business, making collaboration and agility fairly easy concepts to assimilate.

Similarly, employees who work for organizations which operate in naturally collaborative arenas such as marketing or design are also more likely to be open to the idea of working with customers, suppliers and others to create solutions. For them it is a comparatively short step to take towards an innovation model.

Phasing changes across the organization so that some departments or divisions adopt an innovation model before others can be successful, but it can also be a disaster. Typically this model works best when divisions have relative autonomy or when they operate in a group leader/sub-company structure. Even then, unless there is complete separation between the divisions the leadership team will have to take steps to ensure that the more innovative model adopted by some doesn't impact adversely on the core business and vice-versa.

CASE STUDY   Building innovation capabilities

Introduction

This book takes you on a journey, moving you from a standing start through to building and embedding an innovation framework within your organization. However, while we can guide you on your journey the final building blocks, the 'what we do' tiles have to be individual to you. No two organizations or sectors are alike and therefore no two solutions will be identical.

As we have already shown, straight copying of ideas can never work as your organization will never be at the same level of innovation maturity as another.

This inevitably means that while we can act as a catalyst for ideas, ultimately the ideas have to come from your organization and its people. However, ideas gleaned from elsewhere can help to start you on your journey and we therefore turned to Cisco to see how they are managing their own internal innovation capabilities.

Situation

Operating across 165 countries and with more than 70,000 employees enhanced by some 30,000 contract and external staff, Cisco operates at the global leading edge of connectivity development and places innovation at the core of its activities. It has a multi-layer innovation approach which not only works to introduce innovation capabilities into the employee population, but also works to help customers to develop their own innovation programmes.

We are grateful to Matt Asman, Senior Manager, Global Services Innovation at Cisco for his invaluable assistance in providing this case study.

Approach

Within that global platform the business is split into differing sectors, each with its own innovation strategy and each with its own level of innovation maturity. This case study looks at the approach followed by the internally focused services innovation excellence centre (SIEC). Its three-fold mission is to enable ideas, to build skills culture and capabilities and to run innovation activities to drive business outcomes. We're not going to run through the entire process here as otherwise we could easily find ourselves adding a further chapter to the book but highlights include:

- A six-step process which guides internal innovators and provides end-to-end support for the development of ideas.

- Targeting internal innovation challenges around topics, otherwise known as 'swim lanes' (eg leadership strategy, people culture and so on). This includes facilitating crowd source solutions and allocating 'pipeline managers' who oversee end-to-end processes.

- An established framework which takes teams on a journey from awareness through competence to excellence.

- Running innovation activities and workshops which support initiatives. These include:

- a 'workshop in a box' which is packed with everything needed to run an innovation workshop;

- an innovation development box which contains items to help individuals to develop their ideas, including a primed Visa card which will enable them to source materials needed;

- a marketplace in which people can pitch their ideas and others are encouraged to join in and add expertise, time, skills or funding.

Conclusion

Within a holistic create and sustain framework, the Cisco approach encourages and rewards innovation at all levels. Careful attention is paid to measurement of outcome and results are fed back into the system to boost further initiatives. Success rests on leadership, the programmes employed and the strong communication links for which Cisco is globally renowned.

Dual operating system

One operating model which is increasingly resonating with business is the dual operating system proposed by Dr John Kotter. A thought leader in the fields of leadership and change, Kotter's book *Leading Change* is widely considered to be a transformational work in the field of change management (Kotter, 1996).

In his more recent work, *Accelerate,* Kotter propounded the idea of a dual operating system for organizations adopting innovation models (Kotter, 2014). In essence, the dual operating system enables organizations to gain the best of both worlds, to maintain business as usual while simultaneously benefiting from innovative activity. How? Quite simply by putting the thinking outside of the box. Kotter argues that by enabling the core business activity to carry on inside the box and then wrapping this box in another innovative box, businesses can be innovative without losing sight of the core objective. This means that while invoices are paid and orders are processed in the inner box, in the outer box innovative stuff is explored, rules are played with, people are free to challenge and try new stuff in pursuit of excellence and innovation.

The instinctive response when such a model is proposed is that it sounds very complex. How do you combine a traditional core structure which delivers business as usual with an agile network of people from across the organization? The simple answer is that it takes leadership as opposed to management with the innovation network and the core hierarchy being seen as interchangeable elements of the whole. The leadership team have to structure values and innovation aptitudes so that they manage the predictable and free the innovative.

'Where managing is about organising, coordinating and telling; leading is about inspiring and enabling and co-creating.' (Bradt and Davis, 2014)

With information, people and activities flowing between the traditional hierarchy and the change network, conditions are set for the organization to become more flexible and adaptive. Agility is boosted by the continual flow of information, with feedback on customer requirements or sector developments acting as a catalyst for change. As people move regularly between the traditional hierarchy and the change network, the shared knowledge base expands, creating enhanced awareness which feeds into further opportunities for change.

Some individuals by the nature of their roles or the way in which they embrace innovation may get labelled as change agents and end up in a 'change role' but ideally you want to extend the range of people immersed in a change initiative at any one time. People flowing back from the 'change world' back into the operational world will take a different perspective. Equally people taking time out from the operational world into the change network, will bring up-to-date customer insight/perspective as well as current operational challenges. So the key is, get the rotation of people, but appropriately support and develop them, don't just drop them into the change network.

For example, you may be working on a systems development using 'agile' methodology to deliver sprint design and builds. You may well have several 'sprints' with people rotating in and out as their aptitudes and the needs of the project require. Rotating individuals into and out of the project broadens the knowledge base, brings differing perspectives and enables a wider number of people to enhance their skills. In a similar way encouraging people from the customer service function to work on market insight/research activities will broaden their perspective as well as add a different perspective to the marketing team.

Over time the network serves as a continuous change function, one that accelerates momentum and agility because it never stops. This imparts a kind of strategic 'fitness'; the more the organization exercises its change muscle, the more adept it becomes at dealing with a very competitive environment. This does require strength of leadership to accommodate the dual model and an attention to training people to embrace the new methodology. So in the 'sprint' example above you would need to help people to develop an understanding of new working patterns, project documentation, communication and collaboration.

One model which rarely works is the deliberate splitting off of an innovative group to work separately from the main organization. Without the ebb and flow of information, the interactions with customers or the support structure of the main organization, splinter groups simply don't deliver progress in a way which will benefit the organization.

Example

In the late 1960s Xerox set up a sub-division with the remit of undertaking innovative research. Although PARC created some of the most exciting technological innovations of the time including the mouse, GUI and the Ethernet, its separation from the parent organization resulted in a disconnect between PARC and Xerox. With the parent company's management failing to appreciate the worth of some of the inventions and with PARC not always creating innovations which could directly benefit its parent, the parent company benefited little from PARC inventions.

This example doesn't mean that you can't have splinter groups within the main framework of the organization. The existence of splinter groups or fast discovery teams may help to accelerate progress but only where they are an integral part of the innovation layer and can therefore benefit from regular interactions and cross-boundary feedback. The essence of the change is that you move away from a tightly scripted 'change function' approach and towards a more freewheeling and agile 'change leadership' style in which people act as catalysts for driving change forward. This can throw up barriers to change as people who are more used to working in a traditional hierarchy look for a logical career progression which includes spending time in the change network before moving on. Now we are looking for a wider network of change people who move into and out of projects as need dictates.

This leads us on neatly to building the supporting framework and mapping out the high level roadmap which will take us from where we are now towards an innovation-led future. But before we do so we are going to pause for a moment and take a look at employee engagement.

Employee engagement

So far, the majority of the work has been contained within the leadership team. Creating the vision, devising the future shape of the organization, even shaping the journey are largely theoretical exercises. But we are now moving onwards into implementation territory and that means cascading new beliefs and behaviours through i-agents and into the employee layers. In Chapter 5 we'll look towards communicating change but before we do so it is important to understand not only the effect which this may have on employees but the way in which taking the time to engage employees in the new structure and values will dramatically affect the chances of success.

So what is employee engagement? Employee engagement comes about when people align with business strategy. This means that your employees not only understand their role, they embrace the organization's aims and values and work constantly with them in mind. So work attitude, relationships with colleagues and third parties and approach to tasks are all carried out to the benefit of the organization.

Employee engagement comes when you stop treating employees as just another asset. Through embracing individuality, making the most of talents and providing a sense of autonomy and worth, employees will come to align their aims with that of the organization and work to its benefit.

Employee engagement is not just a fluffy way of making people happier in the workplace. It leads to increased productivity, reduced wastage, improved margins and improved relationships with clients and suppliers. While one of the side benefits of an employee engagement programme is that employees are motivated and ready to put themselves into their work, engagement impacts every aspect of your operation. With engaged and empowered employees constantly looking to further the aims of the organization you may well find:

- *Improved relationships with suppliers* – means that you are more likely to receive priority treatment, advanced notice of new products, better discounts. With a strong relationship built by engaged employees suppliers are also more likely to collaborate with you on the innovation agenda.
- *Improved relationships with customers/clients* – means that clients stay loyal, increase their purchasing, recommend you to others and are more willing to help co-create and co-innovate with you.
- *Improved reputation* – means that it is easier to attract new customers and good-quality employees and be seen as a leading

organization within your field. A good reputation also opens up access to lines of finance and investment which may help fund more radical innovation projects.

- *Improved process flows* – leading to quicker turnaround times, less wastage, improved margins and ultimately increased adaptability and agility.

In addition engaged employees will:

- *be happier and less stressed*, leading to reduced absence levels and more focused working;
- *actively look to benefit the company*, leading to greater productivity and a constant desire to improve processes and generate new ideas;
- *want to stay with the company*, meaning lower staff turnover rates, less cost in training new employees and a more highly skilled workforce;
- *act as ambassadors for the organization*, leading to improved external relations thereby strengthening the brand image and reducing complaints.

Without engagement, there is little chance of successfully integrating an innovation matrix. If your employees aren't proactive they won't look for solutions. If they don't take personal pride in the organization then they won't seek to create strong relationships with clients and suppliers. If they don't see organizational goals as being interchangeable with their own goals then they won't look to create synergies.

Quite simply, innovation cultures require a 'get-to' mindset not a 'have-to' one. The actions and interactions which drive innovation come both from the head and the heart. Employees must be engaged in what they are doing and how they are doing it. So how do we create that level of engagement? Well, for a start you won't create it by lecturing, nor will you create engagement simply by providing a pool table and free food in the canteen. When you engage you build a relationship which the employees buy into and that requires using multiple channels and regular reinforcement. This means that engagement is personal, both to the business and to the employee mix but there are a few common areas including:

- *Listening* – If you want employees to feel valued then they need to know that their voice is heard. There are all sorts of ways to listen, from one-to-ones to group discussions and from company intranets to staff surveys, and internal social media like Facebook or Yammer. But whatever methods are used the important thing is to show that the voices have been heard. You may not like what you hear, it may be a totally impractical suggestion, but by taking a few moments to feed back a response you are showing that you value creative input.

- *Taking time* – No matter how busy you are, scheduling time to interact again shows that you value opinion and therefore value the employee and are creating time for innovation.

- *Saying thanks* – 'Thanks cost nothing' may be a cliché but saying thank you or recognizing contributions is a simple way of acknowledging the contributions made by employees. And don't confine your appreciation to those who have participated in successful projects; ideas, solutions, collaboration or even just the willingness to share knowledge are all valuable elements of an innovation mindset.

- *Sharing* – What are your plans, what exciting new project has the business embarked on, what is happening in the industry which may impact the business? If you want employees to have a holistic view of the business and to feel involved in its success then the more you share the more they are involved. This is particularly important within an innovation-driven culture. Sharing news and innovation updates is an important way of drawing people into the innovation programme and you never know, the one piece of news you share may trigger a thought in someone unrelated to the project which could lead to further iterations, improvements or breakthroughs.

- *Involving* – Engagement isn't just something which the top table impose on the business; rather it requires buy-in from everyone. So why not encourage employees to take some responsibility for their own engagement? Help them to set their own targets, to reach their own milestones and to create their own successes. Taking responsibility for their own engagement will also help them to develop innovative traits such as acting on their own initiative, problem solving and collaboration.

Creating alignment

Keeping employee engagement firmly to the front of the agenda will help to create a successful alignment protocol. In theory, alignment is simply a matter of taking your newly set vision and values and translating them into behaviour, attitudes and working styles which can easily be understood by every employee. However, it is all too easy to become sidetracked when moving from theory to implementation.

It is therefore vital that organizations keep the reason for wanting to build innovation capability clearly at the forefront of the planning process. This will include regular checks back to the innovation gap and vision and a continuing focus on maintaining a balanced implementation model.

But beware: if the model is skewed then you won't necessarily get the results you were looking for. Too far one way and you may finish up with incremental innovation but more radical and differentiated innovations won't see the light of day. Too far the other way and while some employees may be indulging themselves in creating new concepts, the support structure won't be there to ensure that what is being created will meet operational needs. The middle ground is where the 'glue' is; creating differentiated innovation that draws on the best of both sides, thereby eliminating polarization and creating real improvements.

It is at this stage that the high-level roadmap starts to form in earnest. The senior team have done their job in setting the direction for the future and understanding what the impetus for innovation is at a strategic level. Now that has been defined, the innovation roadmap can start to be built in a much more organization-wide and collaborative way with more people being able to contribute and play a part in developing the momentum which will drive the organization towards the identified goal.

Innovation agents (i-agents), HR, employee engagement and change teams can all now be brought to the table to start to build a cohesive and pragmatic plan for moving the company from where it is today towards the future-oriented, innovation-led and innovation-mature organization it wants to be. The innovation maturity level plays a big part here when combined with the growth position the organization wants to achieve as that in essence sets out what needs to be done to deliver the strategy and goals the organization has set. That then means that the appropriate people, departments and teams can be assigned their relevant tasks along the way.

When shaping the innovation team take time out to look at abilities and attitude rather than position. The obvious choices may not be the right people to lead change. Those with titles on their doors may simply be too resistant to champion change. Later on in the process you will need to consider i-agents who will speak positively and influence for change. These individuals will sit at all levels of the organization and it may benefit the implementation team to have some of them on board from this point onwards.

Success requires the change leaders to assimilate and be aligned with the end goal. Yes you have to have someone with HR experience on the team to shape future HR policy but it needn't necessarily be one of the HR team leaders. Especially if you are looking to operate the dual system within each department you will generally find that you finish up with some who initially maintain the status quo while others adopt a more innovative position. It is these others who you should encourage to join the implementation team.

As with any other team, don't overlook the importance of balancing skills and perspective to optimize results. You need planners and doers, communicators and influencers.

It is also at this stage that the organization needs to start to build its 'intelligence framework'. This will provide a continuing flow of information which will help the organization to ensure that its ongoing development is providing real game-changing solutions. In Chapter 1 we examined how Next Generation Organizations, those which will create the future, depend on intelligence, collaboration and adaptability to create success. It is worth reiterating here the importance of setting up and maintaining an intelligence framework which will help to ensure success. Remember, in this context intelligence is not just knowing that your customer tends to buy grapes on a Friday and apples every second week.

True intelligence looks behind the raw figures in an attempt to understand why the customer choice is as it is, what lifestyle and other choices define purchase decisions and what the customer would ideally like to see in the future. True intelligence doesn't simply identify that a customer who used to purchase a particular product has stopped doing so and therefore prompt you to offer an incentive to do so again. True intelligence looks to understand why the customer stopped purchasing in the first place and prompts you to design a product which meets changing requirements. In other words, true intelligence enables you to translate unseen needs into innovations.

Benefits of change

You've done all of the hard work and you have identified the top-level roadmap which is going to take you forward to success. In the next chapter we'll look at identifying i-agents who will work within the business to promote change and on communicating change to the wider business. You now stand on the brink of success and it can be a scary place. So before you wobble it is time for a reminder of the benefits to be gained from getting the right future design for your culture.

First and foremost is the reason why you looked to adopt an innovation model in the first place. There may have been some failing within the organization or you may have been overtaken by competitors. Perhaps technology had changed the face of your business sector or perhaps customer appetites had changed. Whatever the reason, you identified the innovation model as the way forward and you would have been right to do so.

Secondly, there is the collateral benefit which comes from engaging employees in a new system. With increased engagement come numerous benefits including longevity of employees, reduced wastage, an increased focus on customer experiences and a can-do attitude.

This then translates into a change in the leadership model. Leading people is much easier if you give them strong direction and something to believe in. Through innovation and engagement the leadership team can move away from a management model in which they spend most of their time dictating structure and process and towards a more open leadership style. Empowerment, encouraging the heart and delegation take the high ground and with everyone heading in the same direction it is easier to steer course changes as strategy and the market changes. The result is that the organization becomes more agile and proactive. In effect, with engaged employees looking for solutions the culture and the approach is virtually self-regulating.

Then there are the 'minor' benefits which come from being a proactive market leader. Good financial results allied to a strong reputation will not only attract customers but potential investors as well. Suppliers are also more likely to give preferential terms as they are drawn into the collaborative innovation mix.

In summary

Moving from strategy to vision, values and innovation aptitudes can seem somewhat daunting but by taking each step in order the design quickly falls into place. The Human Resources team will be invaluable here as they already have expertise in value and competency design.

The key point to remember, particularly for larger organizations, is that you don't have to introduce innovation across the entire organization in one hit. Phasing the introduction will mean that each step acts as a learning point for the next; and as successive departments or divisions see the wins coming out of those which have already switched momentum quickly builds.

Key insights

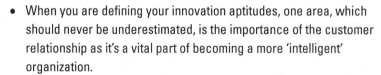

- A good company vision has to speak to the heart, to inspire and to provide a goal, which will challenge people to greatness; you have to 'innovate with purpose'.

- When you are defining your innovation aptitudes, one area, which should never be underestimated, is the importance of the customer relationship as it's a vital part of becoming a more 'intelligent' organization.

- Keeping employee engagement firmly at the front of the agenda will help to create a more successful and aligned shift towards embedding innovation capability.

References

Bradt, G and Davis, G (2014) *First-Time Leader: Foundational tools for inspiring and enabling your new team*, Wiley, London

Kotter, J (1996) *Leading Change*, Harvard Business School Press, Boston

Kotter, J (2014) *Accelerate*, Harvard Business Review Press, Boston

Welch, J (1989) [accessed 04 March 2015] [online] https://hbr.org/1989/09/speed-simplicity-self-confidence-an-interview-with-jack-welch

Communication and people engagement

C ongratulations, you've done all the hard work and it's now just a case of the easy run down to the finish. Or is it? Let's just pause for a moment and look at the journey so far. Starting with a feeling that something had to change but not really being sure why, we've now reached a point at which we have designed the framework for the future shape of the organization. Along the way we've taken time to assess and define the culture gap, worked on agreeing an innovation mix that will best suit the organization and its future plans and aligned the top team's values with the new strategy.

So what's missing? Why can't we just snap our fingers and let the plan fall into place? There's one simple reason and that is that so far the strategy, the vision and the values are all firmly sitting at the top of the organization. That's great for the top team; they have had time to think about the change, to assimilate the ideas and to work on what they personally have to do to bring the change into their own attitudes and working methodologies. But, what about the rest of the organization? It sounds trite but for the organization to change, everyone connected with the organization has to change. And that means that the leadership team now have to take the organization on the journey which they themselves have just completed.

Of course, in some ways the journey will be simpler the second time around. Having already completed the course the leaders know where the pitfalls are and can guide people around those tricky sticking points, which could confound those who are completing the journey for the first time. Barriers have been anticipated and solutions sought; the leadership team is in agreement and the brave new world has already been mapped out so there is clarity for everyone about the future direction and ambition.

However, with the organization moving towards a future in which collaboration and empowerment are the name of the game then the change cannot be imposed, the journey cannot be mapped out in the finest detail without collaborative input. Rightly, the leadership team have designed the high-level culture, the vision and the values. Now it is time to present these to employees and encourage them to define and develop the cultural manifesto which we introduced in Chapter 4.

In a way this is just the next stage in the journey. The leadership team have already engaged employees in providing feedback about the current state of the organization. Now it is time for employees to provide their thoughts, views and opinions on how the vision can come alive and how this will translate into actions and behaviours. The more that you engage people at this stage the more engaged they will be in driving forward the future shape of the organization. After all, culture change is not about the shiny new values on the lobby wall, it is about what you do with them to make the vision come alive; and where a culture of innovation is concerned, collaboration and empowerment cannot start too soon.

In essence, when translating vision into reality the CEO and the leadership team have to be leaders, rallying the troops, engaging hearts and mobilizing resources. Successful strategy is embedded strategy with all resources, from people to technology, aligned to that purpose. And here we don't just mean those who work directly within the organization; a true culture of innovation works best within an extended organizational framework, drawing direct workers, suppliers, customers and others together. And the key to successfully rolling out the plan across the extended organization is communication and engagement.

In this chapter we are therefore going to be delving into the communication matrix: examining some of the key elements of a good communications plan, as well as looking at different engagement techniques. We'll be examining some of the communication channels that can be used to deliver a communication and engagement mix that is right for your organization. We'll also look at i-agents, individuals throughout the organization who can help to support and spread the message throughout the organization. Finally we'll touch on the launch event, a key time which can make or break acceptance.

Developing engagement

It doesn't matter whether you run a bakery or a bank, a supermarket chain or a shoe manufacturer: the strict order and structure which was once seen in business has changed and is changing in tandem with the wider world. Equality and diversity are driving a new way of working, one that values contribution over hierarchical structure. For example, in Chapter 1 we examined the way in which successive generations, and in particular Generation Z, are driving a new way of working: one which perfectly suits the innovation model, but which moves away from autocracy and towards consensus. This puts the onus on leaders to change the way in which they interact with people, both within the organization and throughout the extended landscape.

Modern leaders are not only expected to be visionaries but to be able to communicate that vision in a way which engages hearts and minds and inspires actions. The result is that leaders need to be able to effectively communicate through multiple channels, both in person and via digital tools; failure to do so will result in discord. This places communication and engagement front and centre of the next step in embedding a culture of innovation within the organization and this is why we are devoting an entire chapter to communications and the engagement plan. Engagement may only be one work stream within an overall design and implementation plan but it is one which acts as a conduit for so much of the rest of the plan, carrying the message across the extended organization and delivering key elements.

We took a brief look at employee engagement in Chapter 4 but it bears repeating that unless attention is paid to aligning employee and company values then any seeming acceptance will fail. We would generally recommend working to develop employees using our *4Es Methodology*.

Firstly, you need to **Educate** your people as to what the changes are you are asking of them and show them why change is important to them, the business and the market as a whole. However, it is a mistake to simply concentrate on just the business angle. When making the case for change, people and the emotional 'why' are as important, if not more so, than any pure business case. Don't forget, in the past you have condoned, even encouraged one set of behaviours and now you are asking people to change their mindset, their outlook and their attitudes. Education works best when it is delivered in tandem with a perceived leadership change from the line manager.

You also need to **Engage** your people in the change that's required – culture change is no longer something that's done *to* people, it's very much something that's done alongside them, in collaboration with them, with their input – factoring their observations, concerns and experiences. Besides, you need their input – as the people on the front line, who are most probably closest to the client/customer and to the daily processes, policies and working practices, they have much to contribute.

Next, you need to **Empower** your people to act – to appropriately delegate accountability and allow your people to use their judgment to make sound

FIGURE 5.1 The 4Es methodology

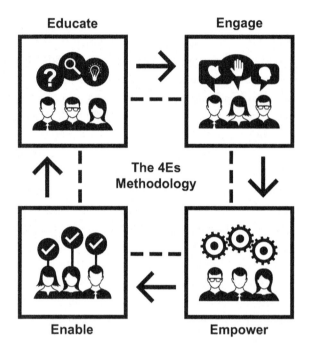

The 4Es Methodology starts with educating your people...

Educate

Engage

The 4Es Methodology

Enable

Empower

decisions, in line with the desired culture. If you've educated, engaged and put the right controls and governance in place then this should be achievable.

Finally, you need to **Enable** people to act. This is particularly important when it comes to an innovation-led culture. The more supportive you can make these programmes and the less 'tick-box and tell off' from HR and Compliance, the better they will be received and more receptive to the changes they will be. So, boosting soft skills such as communication and interpersonal skills, time and self-management skills, decision making and taking responsibility may be on the agenda.

Employee engagement is a book in itself but there is one other aspect which we think is worth highlighting here and that is that employee engagement doesn't have to be a top-down programme. There are other alternatives and one which is rapidly gaining popularity is the notion of employees taking charge of and responsibility for their own engagement pathways.

Employee-led engagement programmes

When it comes to innovation engagement, how you act is often as important as what you do. This is one of the reasons why best practice is moving away from employer-led engagement programmes and towards an employee-led engagement solution. This turns employee engagement into a self-managed motivational journey and the very fact of its adoption can be a strong signal to employees that the business not only cares about their development and welfare but is also sincere about building a culture of innovation.

Standing up and preaching to employees is never going to create engagement. Offering a self-managed programme which is driven by individuals in conjunction with their work colleagues can help to transform the attitude and work ethos of individuals, teams and leaders. Typically, self-managed engagement programmes will include elements such as surveys, development resources and action programmes alongside the ability to set goals and review progress, either individually or in conjunction with a team leader.

One of the benefits of self-managed programmes is that they tend to be partly or wholly online, cost effective and can be delivered in bite-sized chunks. With finances still tight following the recession, it is perhaps not surprising that a significant majority of businesses claim that budget constraints are one of the key barriers to improving engagement. Employee-led programmes make an ideal low-cost solution. And because these programmes contain a strong element of self-determination it means that employees and their immediate team leaders can drive the engagement process.

Another benefit of employee-led engagement programmes is that by their nature they tend to lend themselves to a continuing cycle of review and improvement. The traditional method for measuring engagement is to conduct a survey once every year or so, wait for results, discuss findings in focus groups and then start to act. By this time any benefit gained from conducting the survey has dissipated. Moving to a system in which employee engagement is an ongoing, real-time metric not only ties it in more closely with other management and innovation information it also keeps the idea of engagement as a priority at the forefront of the organization. Similarly, devolving the action planning process from purely central to a mix of central and localized action planning has been shown to significantly increase satisfaction levels.

Typically these self-managed programmes are systems supported with employees working either individually or in teams to input, track and monitor personal or team goals. Data are available in real time to line managers and others who can monitor progress and provide feedback. By tracking data the leadership are able to quickly gauge the results of any initiatives or to ensure that appropriate training is put in place where a need is identified.

Another benefit of employee-led engagement is that it helps to foster the ideals of empowerment and initiative which are a feature of innovation-focused cultures. The more employees are encouraged to think for themselves, to work on their own initiative, to identify problems and create solutions, the better they will be able to 'live' innovation. This is an important message to remember when creating the engagement plan and it is this that we are going to turn to next.

The engagement plan

As with employee-led engagement, the creation of an engagement plan as a top-down cascade of information which is confined to the few is not going to work in an innovation culture which seeks to truly engage people across the board. Yes, you need to set the tone 'from the top' but the final culture is the one that evolves from this point to be a more collaborative effort, incorporating the view from the front line and the buy-in of middle management.

If never before, this is the point at which employees have to stop being numbers or costs on the bottom line and become valued contributors to future success. 'Know your people' has never been more important than when you are looking for them to engage with change. And one of the most important lessons for the leadership team to assimilate is that 'your people' are not all the same. To create success you have to understand the internal drivers and tailor the communication and engagement plan to your internal audience. This means adapting the plan not only for leaders, managers and frontline staff but also by divisions, departments and teams.

The challenge for the leadership team is not only to recognize each group as having particular engagement needs but not to give mixed messages or be seen to be favouring or discriminating against any particular group. This can require a tricky balancing act, especially when some of the population can carry far more weight in the early stages than others. Let's look at some of these 'influencer' groups in a little more detail:

- *The intrapreneurs* – These are the people who sit at any level within the organization and who already display many of the qualities which the organization is looking to move towards. Intrapreneurs are the idea creators, the builders and risk-takers who are willing to try something new or different. They are aware of the risks but are also aware of the rewards which can follow success. Generally these people will form the core of the innovation agents, i-agents: the people who sit at all levels of the organization and who will drive the change. We'll look at i-agents in more depth later on in this chapter and will examine the role of intrapreneurs in more depth in Chapter 6.

- *The high influencers* – This group consists of highly regarded individuals. They may have long tenure, be leaders of large departments or be technical experts. In effect they are the group who are in a strong position to influence change. Some will do so for good and will become part of the i-agent population; others may be serial resistors who seek to strongly resist or actively block change. Either way they are a population whom the leadership team cannot afford to ignore.

- *New managers* – This is a very important subset of the management population. Inexperienced or junior managers can be keener to impress and more open to external support. At the start of their managerial journey they are less likely to have preconceived ideas and entrenched methodologies. They therefore can be quick to grasp new ideas and willing to carry them forward into their teams. In fact, the main danger from these people is that they are over-keen and may drive too far too fast without having the experience to know when brakes should be applied.

For every one individual within the above population who works to promote and apply change the chance of successful adoption and engagement amongst the general employee population is enhanced. But there is one other group who will bear a lot of the day-to-day change burden – the middle managers. Taken together with intrapreneurs and selected high influencers and new managers, the middle managers will form the 'coalition' of i-agents who will play a strong role in communicating, engaging and embedding change. Yes there may well be people outside these groups who are really passionate about innovation but the likelihood is that if they are they will probably already be in one of these groups. The focus should then be on finding/identifying the *real* intrapreneurs within each of these groups as they are the most powerful asset in the pursuit of innovation and building it into culture.

Before we look in depth at i-agents, let's take a closer look at middle managers. These individuals are the gatekeepers of innovation; they have the ability to lock or unlock, to open or close, the gateway to the future. Those who sit in the middle layers of management do not have an easy task. As Barry Oshry says in his book *In the Middle* (1994) these people have a tough job, sandwiched in between top and bottom. Moreover, they are rarely one unified team and unless the organizational mentoring structure is strong these individuals can feel isolated and powerless. We'll pass over the chance that they may be more likely to be competing against each other than supporting each other because if this is the case then the leadership team have a lot of work to do on organizational culture before they even think of moving towards innovation.

With this in mind, what do the leadership team have to do in order to support their middle management team? Firstly, there has to be an appreciation of where these individuals are in their home and career lives. The demographic of this population means that they are more likely to have external circumstances which can affect their work lives. Children, mortgages, elderly parents; whatever the call on their time outside work, it is likely to impact on their energy levels and hence on their appetite for risk and likelihood of embracing the innovation agenda. Even without these external pressures, within work these individuals are on a leadership learning curve and are more likely to bear a significant workload. Adding to the pressure by introducing change is only going to exacerbate stress levels unless the introduction is managed in a structured way.

The top priority therefore, is to engage middle managers in the change as early on in the process as possible. Having time to get used to an idea, to assimilate it into thought and behaviour patterns and, more importantly, to influence the shape of the idea will make a measurable difference to acceptance levels. On an ongoing basis the leadership team, in tandem with the HR department, need to work with individuals to assess and support their development needs. This will help them to increase their leadership abilities and to gain a greater appreciation of the way in which they can help the organization to achieve its goals.

We mentioned above that those in middle management are rarely a unified team but this stage in the process gives the leadership team the perfect opportunity to start to unify this group. When innovation culture infuses the organization, those in the position of leadership at every level will be working together to foster collaboration and strong outcomes. Starting the process now, perhaps with something as simple as a managers' forum, will pay dividends later on down the line.

Innovation agents (i-agents)

Now that we have had a quick look at some of the groups who will play a vital role in engaging and communicating the message, let's move on to those who will play the pivotal role in change, the i-agents. We admit that bringing others into the mix is going to require additional work but don't ever think of 'going it alone', particularly if you are looking to move towards a more empowered and collaborative culture.

Yes, in the first instance you are responsible for communication and engagement but also remember that if you keep all of the fun to yourself then no one else is going to buy in to the change. Every leader needs a messenger and, particularly when the nature of the change which is sought involves collaboration and a more free-wheeling structure, keeping lines of communication close to your chest is only going to send out the wrong message. Most of these individuals will come from the groups outlined above. We've called these individuals champions and messengers, intrapreneurs or innovation agents (i-agents), but you should choose terminology which is appropriate to your own organization, perhaps even have a competition to choose a name as part of the introduction of the innovation ideal.

It's a fine line, deciding when the lead should come from the top table and when it should sit further down but if you choose wisely then you can make a much greater impact in the long run. A great analogy is the restaurant industry, especially those with a Michelin star rating. Leading the way is the head chef. It is they who design the menu, define the ethos and theme for the restaurant and create the signature dishes. But if they were the only ones doing the cooking then they would be serving a very select clientele indeed and the business would have no scale. So they carefully select and train their team in the values and techniques required to take their genius out to a wider audience. No matter what happens the head chef still leads the way, overseeing, refining and ensuring the restaurant stays on course but the actual day-to-day translation of the ideals into the provision of exceptional food and service is in the hands of others.

So it is with culture change. The leadership team have created the high-level culture and values with more detailed design work involving people from across the organization but now it is time for the vision to be cascaded across the entire organization. And the people who will do this best, who will help to ensure that the change ideal not only touches the organization but also becomes embedded in it are the i-agents. Quite simply, people are more likely to change their behaviours when the message not only comes from the top but also from direct managers, peer colleagues, and most of all from someone they respect. But that doesn't mean the leadership team can then sit back and do nothing. To borrow from Gandhi, to communicate the change, leaders have to be the change and that means assimilating the change into their behaviour, outlook and actions as well as teaching others how they can also change in turn.

So who are these i-agents? In truth they could be drawn from any area of the business and even from outside the business as collaboration with third parties becomes the norm. Most importantly, i-agents are not simply team and department leaders. The change team may include some of these but equally we can think of some team leaders who would be the last people we would choose to embody the change ideal! And don't forget, if the dual operating system model discussed in Chapter 4 is chosen, there may be some teams and departments which run largely untouched, at least at first, while innovation wraps itself around them.

So i-agents are not simply team leaders but in a way they are a virtually self-selecting group. Stop and think for a moment about the people in your organization. There are some who stand out, who through their personalities and energies naturally affect those around them. Whether it is in their attitude to work, the way in which they approach a problem or the way they interact with customers and others, these individuals can affect the approach and behaviour of those around them. They may not have formal leadership roles or they may be at a very junior level indeed but whoever they are, these 'leaders without a title' are the people who will help to ensure that the desired change is successfully embedded within the organization and that employee engagement is strengthened in the process.

Apart from the observation that the top team can't, and shouldn't, do everything there are two very strong reasons for appointing i-agents at every level within the organization. The first is the need to focus the innovation strategy differently at every level of the organization. We encountered this idea in Chapter 2 when we illustrated how the high-level innovation strategy can become too complicated and confusing, the further you move down the organization. The result is that unless innovation implementation is focused with a clear explanation of the vision and strategy being structured to meet the needs of each group then employees may struggle to fully understand how they can contribute to change and what behaviours are required from them in order to drive innovation.

Simply by appointing i-agents at every level, leaders can help to ensure that the message is focused at every level and that feedback is received from every level.

The second reason for appointing a wide mix of people to take on the i-agent role is to ensure that the message is personal to everyone. Within a diverse, multi-country, multi-generational, multi-cultural organization a message which speaks to one person may not resonate with another. Actually the same is true even without the diversity angle as hooks which appeal to some departments may not appeal in the same way to others. There is a reason why some people become accountants and some go into sales and it is as much about the way in which certain occupations appeal to certain personality types as it is about any other factor. So the vision and values may be

FIGURE 5.2   Using i-agents to translate strategy into behaviour

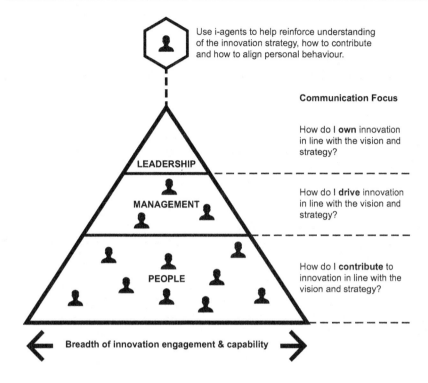

the same across the organization but application and implementation may vary between different divisions and departments. This is even more important when innovation inclusivity is spread away from the core business and into the wider supplier/customer world.

That's not to say that we should cynically choose our i-agents so that one comes from each diverse group or personality type. But by choosing those natural influencers and leaders from across the organization we can help to ensure that differing groups are more likely to find someone who speaks to their hearts. There is another reason why i-agents should be drawn from across the sectors. Individually, they can make a strong contribution to change; collectively they can become an extremely powerful force. Sharing successes, drawing on experiences or ideas from one sector to act as a catalyst for change in another, working together to surmount barriers to change; the i-agent force can be a true game-changer.

It is probably also worth mentioning here the value of stories to help emotional engagement and adoption of ideas. Storytelling at any time can be a powerful medium but when the stories relate to the immediate organization then they can act as a powerful catalyst for change.

We said there were two main reasons for appointing a mix of i-agents but there is a further reason, which may apply in some organizations, particularly those which are suffering from 'change fatigue'. There are some sectors where change for change's sake has been seen as a universal panacea for decades. Rather than looking inwards to provide exceptional levels of customer service and to create stability, leaders have looked outwards and embraced new working methodologies and approaches on a regular basis. Closed offices, open-plan customer areas, 'hot desking', centralizing and then devolving control – it has almost been possible to see the barometer swing back and forth across the globe as ideas took hold, were shared and then dropped.

For employees working in these sectors the relentless drive towards change for change's sake has resulted in a type of 'change fatigue': a feeling that no matter what is espoused by the leadership, something else will come along to supplant it within a short space of time. Feeling constantly battle-worn, these employees have developed a coping mechanism in which an outward display of acceptance conceals a 'business-as-usual' inner shell. If the leadership simply announce yet another change programme then this coping mechanism will swing into play. If i-agents are also seen to take up the cause then there is a far greater chance that a new optimism and acceptance may start to infuse the employee base.

Developing i-agents

Having identified our i-agents what next? Well, identifying them is one thing, taking them through the journey is another! This is where all of your preparation for change starts to come into play: identifying and overcoming barriers, developing the innovation strategy, the focus on employee engagement and so forth. Much of the actual communication methods used will be similar to those used in communicating change to the wider business so we don't propose to run through them in great detail here. However, we will just include one thought and that is the importance of identifying the 'hook', which will glue the i-agents to the programme. Some will simply embrace the idea and be glad to be recognized as influencers but when choosing and enthusing your i-agent team don't neglect the 'what's in it for me' angle; whether that be future personal development, more challenging work or something else.

In fact you may find that as the programme develops, you are communicating similar ideas to the i-agents as to the rest of the business, albeit some time in advance of the main communication run. But there are a few areas which it would be worth highlighting here. Firstly, just as no two areas of the business are alike, so the approach used to enthuse your i-agents won't be identical. Some may be brought in at the outset, others at a later stage in the project as it moves towards their area of expertise. For example, if you decide to phase in innovation starting with one division or subsidiary then engaging i-agents from other divisions too early in the process may work against you. However, that is not to say that you should completely ignore the other divisions and you certainly shouldn't leave suppliers and third parties out in the cold. To do so would be to create intense levels of negativity, which will lead to 'us and them' scenarios at the very least. To avoid this, let people know what is happening and why, reassure them that their time will come and even 'drip through' some innovation challenges. This will help to ensure that when the change is rolled out, people will be more ready to embrace it.

Then there is the way in which the idea of innovation culture is shared. We've already touched on this idea above, but it is worth repeating that different people have different hooks and it is important to modify your approach depending on personality type. This is particularly important when it comes to enthusing the i-agents and initially you may find that a virtually one-to-one approach is required. You may even find that this can be done simply and effectively by engaging them in the process, asking for their views and listening to them.

Finally, it is vital that your champions are not simply informed about the new ethos and then left to get on with it. They'll require help to develop the tools to act as change ambassadors and they will need a measure of understanding if they move away from a concentrated focus on their immediate tasks while they spread the word. In this, the support and understanding of the HR and training departments as well as of line managers is vital.

For example, if the i-agent is late back from a coffee break because they have been talking about the gains to be had from innovation then it should be an occasion for praise rather than for censure. Similarly, targets and work schedules may need to be adjusted to take account of the time taken in attending change meetings.

Depending on the business mix, much of the i-agent's influence may be seen to be in their day-to-day approach or actions rather than in formal meetings but nevertheless, the more you can help to enhance their personal skills the better they will be able to act to promote the new ethos and the more the business leaders can demonstrate how serious they are about inculcating change. This will be an ongoing process in which the more that the business can help to promote the idea of empowerment and initiative, the better the i-agents will be able to assimilate and promote the innovation ideal. So get their feedback and insights, get them to identify issues and blockers, give them the ownership of what the role of i-agent really is and support them in their journey.

The skills required will depend on the individuals and their roles but may include communication, influencing, overcoming objections, and emotional intelligence. Similar skills boosts may also be required by the top table as they seek to initiate change. Other key skills which the HR team may need to help i-agents to develop include:

- *Questioning techniques and listening skills* – These will help to ensure that they are driving a two-way approach rather than a one-way cascade.

- *Gathering feedback, and delivering that feedback up the line* – i-agents are an important conduit for feedback and can help to influence the future shape of the programme.

- *Influencing skills* – The i-agents may have been chosen for their natural leadership and influencing abilities but that doesn't mean that they won't need help in learning to overcome objections or to think laterally to solve a communication problem. Similarly, they have to be helped to develop the confidence to influence upwards as well as downwards or the feedback gathered will be wasted.

All of these may require the HR team to put a structured support mechanism in place to help i-agents to develop their leadership and change management skills. This may include bespoke blended learning programmes and support and challenge reviews.

Starting to communicate

You have your team in place and your i-agents are ready to go. The next stage is to bring the message to the organization and, potentially, to third parties. Later on we'll look at some communication pathways, putting together a communication and engagement plan which will act as the catalyst for change. Before we go charging off on this path it is probably worth having a quick refresher on the fundamentals of good communication. Whether communicating verbally or electronically, good communicators aim to be clear, concise, consistent, continuous and congruent. Let's have a quick look at these five key communication ideals:

- *Clear communication* starts by being clear in your own mind on the vision which you are communicating. The message should be open and honest and, as far as possible, free from slang or jargon. When communicating, pitch your message at a level which will be best understood by recipients, taking care not to go over their heads or to talk down to listeners. Remember at this stage that you have already gone through the change journey and therefore you are likely to have some built-in assumptions which your audience will not have at this stage. It's therefore important to ensure that the *entire* message is communicated, not just that which seems obvious to you at the time. And, as we said at the beginning of this section, the message should be carefully pitched and varied to ensure that each section of the organizational population receives a message which is appropriate for them.

- *Concise communication* happens when messages are kept short and to the point. Too much, or too little, information can lead to confusion and questions in the minds of recipients. You are taking your audience on a journey so, deliver the information in ways which will help your audience to assimilate the change rather than confusing them with a 'big bang' approach. Here we are back to the GPS or sat-nav analogy. It's good to know that when we come to the next roundabout we are going to take the third exit. That helps us to structure our approach and to choose the most appropriate lane. Telling us that after that we are going to go three miles down the road, take the first right, the second left, the fourth exit at the next roundabout... Well, you get the picture. Too much information delivered at once will only serve to confuse, overwhelm and engender panic. So while an initial 'We have a dream' speech may be the right approach to kick-start employees into envisioning possibilities, giving all the detail at the start will simply overwhelm. We'll come back to this theme later in the chapter.

- *Consistent communication* engenders trust; inconsistent messages will destroy any chance of success quicker than anything else. Initial communications should therefore, if necessary, be backed up by repeat messages across different media. More than that, this is the time when all of the effort which you put into building leadership team agreement comes home to roost. As we highlighted in Chapter 3, this is the leadership team's 'wear the T-shirt' moment: the time when everyone has not only to have assimilated the change into their own mindset but also be seen to espouse change through every action and decision.

- *Continuous communications* lead recipients to believe that you are hiding nothing and that the message can be relied upon. For example, don't start a weekly update blog and then stop after a few weeks. If you do then employees may start to believe that this is another bandwagon, launched with enthusiasm and then dropped as the next fad sweeps across the world of business. But continuous communication has another benefit. Carefully planned, the continuous communication schedule can help employees to assimilate the change; to take bite-sized chunks of the plan into their everyday actions and to truly believe in the change. Remember, you are looking for a permanent and lasting change and that is not going to come about if you simply communicate, tick the 'done' box and move on.

- *Congruent communications* simply means delivering the message in an authentic manner and in line with your normal style. Being yourself, delivering messages that you are aligned with is far more likely to lead to a general level of acceptance than putting on a false show which may lead to questions and concerns being raised. Here again, choose the most appropriate delivery method for each group of recipients.

Overarching the clear, concise, consistent, continuous and congruent message are the prime requirements for all communicators, namely: know your audience, communicate appropriately and check understanding. It may or may not have been Bernard Shaw who said, 'The single biggest problem in communication is the illusion that it has taken place,' but irrespective of the originator, the words are a reminder to all communicators about the importance, not only of shaping the message, but also of ensuring that it has been received.

The communication and engagement plan

Sadly all of the hard work and preparation can go to nought if the method of engagement is not appropriate for the organization or targeted subset of the population. No one likes to be the recipient of what feels like a 'To All' e-mail which doesn't speak to your specific needs/situation. We've seen far too many cases where the leadership team leave this key moment to a bald announcement and a couple of Q&A leaflets. In doing so they have signalled that their understanding of employee engagement, communication and what a culture of innovation is all about is somewhat lacking. In truth, the exact communication plan will vary depending on the size and structure of the organization, the innovation mix chosen and the implementation plan.

Let's run through some of the communication and engagement options which are available to us. As we do so, let's not forget that communication is a two-way process. Whether you hold meetings or focus groups, put specific feedback programmes in place or simply listen to the water-cooler chat, soliciting, receiving and acting on feedback is a valuable tool when shaping future stages within the plan. You will disengage people if you don't ask, if you ask but don't act or if you ask people to behave in one way but force them to behave another way by not putting in place the supporting infrastructure. We return to this theme in Chapter 7 when we look at embedding the change.

Before we move on to developing the plan itself we are taking a look at some of the communication and engagement options which organizational leaders can bring to bear in sharing and communicating change. We've split these roughly into communication options and engagement options, although in reality the two are interchangeable. Every communication is an opportunity to engage and every move towards enhancing engagement brings an opportunity to share and communicate. With that in mind, let's look at a few of the communication options.

Communication plan – verbal communications

Open meetings and focus groups, discussion forums and even water cooler moments: there is no shortage of opportunities for verbal communication to take place within an organization. Some will be structured and pre-arranged, others will be more impromptu but when trying to convey the message, nothing should be ruled in or out. Sometimes a quick word or two in the corridor can be as effective as a lengthy scheduled meeting. So what are the do's and don'ts of verbal communications?

With any communication the key to success is planning. Whether you are taking a large group off site for a major presentation or having a quick chat in passing, the message should be focused and targeted to the individual. Yes, the chat may be impromptu but that doesn't mean that leaders and i-agents haven't already spent some time thinking about the messages which they want to convey and to whom.

Think carefully here about the position and seniority of the people delivering the message. When is it appropriate to have the CEO leading the way and when would it be better to have the division head or department manager? This question is particularly appropriate when it comes to widening the scope outside the core business. For example, when looking to engage suppliers or other third parties in the innovation mix, having their known and immediate contacts on hand can help to enhance the message.

Breaking the announcement down to division or office level can also be an effective method of communication, but only if those who are giving the briefing are well coached. On the plus side, this coaching will help to generate enthusiasm in the new culture; on the negative side, it is vital that those who are giving the briefing are all good communicators and able to give out a consistent message.

Finally, never underestimate the benefits of open forums and water cooler moments. In a culture which values interaction and collaboration, these are ideal breeding grounds for the ideas of the future. The more that water cooler moments are encouraged, the more likely that employees will interact in future. There is also a side benefit in that i-agents can use water cooler moments to pick up employee sentiment, thus enabling the leadership team to refocus their approach and circumvent future barriers to change.

Communication plan – social media and collaboration tools

Whether you run internal chat rooms or intranets or piggyback on existing social media such as Facebook, Twitter or LinkedIn doesn't really matter. The important thing is that you encourage and enable a forum which will allow people to express themselves and to share. Naturally, if an external medium is used then there are the usual caveats about confidentiality and organizational reputation to consider but in general, encouraging social media will encourage buy-in to the new culture. And don't forget that the end goal for innovation is a collaborative culture which draws in customers and others from outside the organization, so the more that employees are encouraged to interact across team boundaries the better.

In fact, this is one area in which the lines between communication and engagement become truly blurred. We'll come back to this when we move on to engagement options but for now, take a look at the following case study, which illustrates how collaboration tools can not only enhance interactions but can also result in the development of some innovative new ideas.

CASE STUDY Innovation collaboration

Introduction

It is one thing to talk about external collaboration, quite another to actually create the conditions which enable and encourage interactive and 'open' innovation to take place. The mindset may be willing but if the infrastructure is not in place then collaborations and the sharing of ideas may not flow. We turned to Siemens AG to see how they had solved the collaboration conundrum.

Situation

Siemens AG (Berlin and Munich) is a global technology powerhouse that has stood for engineering excellence, innovation, quality, and reliability for 170 years. The company is active in more than 200 countries, focusing on the areas of electrification, automation and digitalization. With more than 29,000 R&D employees and over $4 billion invested in R&D in 2013 alone, Siemens considers innovation 'its lifeblood'.

Given the size and scope of the R&D department Siemens took the decision to source a platform which would not only enable individual business units to monitor and drive forward innovation but which could also be used to co-ordinate innovation, both within the organization and externally. As Ben Collar, Director of R&D, Siemens Mobility, Intelligent Traffic Systems said: 'We understand that innovation shouldn't happen only inside our walls, but is best cultivated when we can gather ideas from the bright minds of today and tomorrow.'

Approach

Siemens took the decision to deploy Mindjet's SpigitEngage to meet their innovation collaboration requirements. Designed to enable innovation at scale, SpigitEngage drives crowd participation and engagement as well as providing full process transparency and workflow. The value of SpigitEngage was demonstrated when Siemens decided to launch a Mobility IDEA Contest to provide solutions for some of the toughest challenges facing those tasked with managing traffic infrastructure. Aside from environmental concerns, the estimated annual impact of gridlock in the UK alone amounts to £4.4 billion.

Rather than sourcing solutions internally, Siemens launched the contest to draw in ideas from the crowd, aiming specifically at university students and professionals as well as looking for input from the public at large. A global contest requires global solutions and in this SpigitEngage proved its worth being both easy to use and having an interface which was familiar to many users. One of the key features of the platform was the way in which it enabled users to post suggestions for improving ideas that had already been submitted, and to vote on those ideas.

This led to a final selection of seven projects which were then pitched to a judging panel with the top three ideas being awarded a prize. The winning project involved the use of a quadcopter to identify empty parking spaces and to interact with drivers via an app to direct them to the nearest space.

Conclusion

Not only did the platform prove its worth in enabling Siemens to take its challenges out to a global audience, its ease of use contributed to the wealth of ideas which were submitted. Commenting on the success of the project Ben Collar said, 'It was a great experience interacting with the public in this way. We've been in contact with people from around the globe and learned about some of the specific problems that people face – many problems we weren't even aware of.'

One point to note here is that the success of the contest was only possible thanks to the innovation culture, which was already alive within Siemens. We have commented elsewhere about the danger of ignoring the internal culture when looking externally but the issue here develops this theme further in that the organizational culture has to be innovation-led enough to cope with integrating a platform such as SpigitEngage.

Communication plan – other platforms

In truth we could fill up a whole book with the communication platforms and methods available to organizational leaders. We have highlighted SpigitEngage above as one online method of enabling teams to collaborate on projects but there are plenty of others around. Look at Yammer for example, which also enables team collaboration, or pulseCHECKER, which offers a real-time survey, mostly used during change projects, and which provides a temperature check of the 'mood' of the company. We'll be touching on more of these when we move on to look at engagement options but for now, we'll just touch on three other methods of communication which organizations regularly call upon:

- *E-mails* – See them as a force for good or as a time-wasting system clogger, used appropriately e-mails can be a great way of sharing up-to-date progress with the launch. They don't need to be long and clumsy but they do need to be completely 'on message', so don't devolve responsibility to someone who is neither fully up to date with the programme or has a stilted writing style. Simple 'Since the last communication, we've done x,' or: 'Well done to the sales team who've had a great chat with one of our clients', or even: 'Thanks for all the hard work you've put in' messages can help to reinforce the idea that change is ongoing and that the top team value the way in which employees are embracing change. A word of caution: if your e-mail system is already overburdened with e-mails then rather than adding to the burden, look for other ways to share progress. In fact, with 'death by e-mail' strangling so many organizations, perhaps tackling the e-mail system may be one innovation which heads towards the top of the list. When you have to phone someone to tell them you have sent an e-mail that you want a reply to or wait to be chased before you even look at an e-mail you've been copied in on then there is a definite e-mail problem in the organization.

- *Alerts* – Phone, SMS text, e-mails: no matter what the medium don't ignore the wave of positivity which you can engender through issuing alerts — at least if you use them sparingly enough. Quick and cheerful messages such as: 'We've reached this milestone', or: 'Great news!' can help to keep the project at the forefront of employees' minds. Even negative: 'Sorry this has been put back by a day' messages are helping to reinforce the idea of communication and inclusivity.

- *Newsletters* – Sent out by e-mail or even in hard-copy form, newsletters which are issued on a regular basis can really give the impression that the project is rolling along. Once customers and outside suppliers are also drawn in to the project, newsletters can help to boost the impression that they are being drawn into the team and that their opinions count. Pack the newsletter with short articles, views 'from the front' and the odd quiz or task challenge for variety. If you link the newsletter to a social media site or to a bespoke innovation area on the website then you can boost the newsletter with the addition of periodic blogs and articles online.

As we move on to examine some of the engagement options available to organizations there is one art which, in tandem with the interconnectedness of communication and engagement, binds the two areas together. That is the art of *listening*. You may be looking to communicate your initial thoughts, to engage your people and to move the plan onwards to success but unless you also listen then your words and actions could be completely missing their target.

Verbal or written signals, body language or even the way in which attitudes to work change will all help to convey thoughts, reactions, views and concerns. So as we move onwards and look at engagement options, remember that communication is a two-way street and that however good you are at expressing your thoughts, unless you listen you are never going to know if your words are powerful forces for change or empty mumblings in the dark.

Engagement plan — surveys, feedback and engagement platforms

If you want to know how things are going, just ask. Surveys and feedback forms will not only help you to gauge sentiment they will also help to boost engagement. In fact, if you have adopted self-managed engagement programmes then monitoring and receiving feedback from these sources can lead to a continuing improvement loop when it comes to inculcating change.

The traditional method for measuring engagement is to conduct a survey once every year or so, wait for results, discuss findings in focus groups and then start to act. By this time any benefit gained from conducting the survey has dissipated. Adopting a system in which employee engagement is an ongoing real-time metric not only more closely ties it in with other management information such as sales results and budgets as well as culture change, it also keeps the idea of engagement as a priority at the forefront of the organization.

Interestingly, just 4 per cent of organizations operate a system of continual feedback and yet for these organizations staff satisfaction at engagement efforts sits at 90 per cent, compared with 59 per cent for those who are surveyed once a year. Similarly, devolving the action planning process from purely central to a mix of central and localized action planning increases satisfaction levels by 47 per cent (Smith & Henderson, 2014).

In the case study which we covered earlier in this chapter we saw how technology and online collaboration enabled the creation and sharing of innovative ideas. In that instance Siemens used the technology to gather ideas from outside but it could as easily have used the programme to foster collaborative working amongst its employees. Similarly, organizations across the globe are using the power of collaborative technology to monitor, measure and boost employee engagement. Solutions provided by companies such as TINYpulse, breatheHR and Jostle enable team participation, feedback and peer-to-peer recognition – in the process simplifying project flow and boosting engagement.

Engagement plan – immersive engagement

Going one step further, Wellevue brings game theory to corporate culture: creating missions or challenges for employees to complete; along the way boosting engagement, health and safety, company cultural or other values. The idea of immersing employees and third parties in the culture and engagement mix is rapidly gaining ground. Once upon a time, team-bonding activities might have consisted of hauling the group out to a rocky mountainside and seeing how they survived. Nowadays, although that method is still in use, the combination of technology and innovation has widened the scope immensely. Let's look at a few examples:

- **Culture Hack**^{TM} – This is a one day, technology enhanced, team-based activity in which a group of experts* facilitate a deep-dive discussion to develop and gain understanding of the steps required to move to the next level of the culture manifesto. It is suitable for any team but can be particularly useful for the leadership team, middle management or i-agents to review the high level plan, tackle any issues that have arisen and collaborate (at speed) to resolve and design the next stage.

- **Immersion Zone** – Highly interactive events which immerse people in an element of the desired culture and thus boost engagement. It uses a mix of storytelling, coaching and facilitated discussions to make the participants truly feel that they are experiencing the desired or non-desired culture eg excellent customer experience, diversity or what a culture where whistleblowing is prevalent might look like.

- **'*Innovateur*' *Dramatics*** – Educating and engaging through the use of actors and drama-based methods. One side benefit of this approach is that the leadership team and i-agents can use their contact time with the presenters to boost their individual presentation skills. Expanding

---

*Experts will be innovation culture experts but can also vary depending on sector, seniority, regulation etc.

on this theme, organizations could also consider an innovative way of getting people to identify and confront issues. Taking the form of live debates, impromptu plays or live simulated television shows, people are encouraged to think on their feet and to work together to find a solution. This can boost engagement, create collaborations or help implementation teams to devise optimum strategies for success.

- **In the Limelight** – This is an exciting and high-energy team problem-solving challenge which gets your people on top of the big issues facing your organization. It involves staging a bespoke series of live interviews focusing on each team's issues with employees playing a variety of roles to solve current and future challenges by enabling them to approach the issues from different viewpoints. This is a great way to boost engagement, enhance collaboration and solve real problems.

One of the common themes which runs through the above, is that they are all innovative: drawing on technological improvements to deliver something which is immersive, collaborative and engaging. The result is that while you are boosting engagement you are also starting to generate the idea that an innovation culture is different, is expressive and draws in experiences from outside. Other ideas which we could have covered here include co-creation master classes to draw customers or third parties into the mix, gamified learning experiences and the development of innovation aptitudes. We'll come back to this last idea in Chapter 6 but first we are going to move on to creating the communication plan.

Creating the communication plan

We've just seen how there are no shortage of ways in which to get the message across, so with that in mind let's look at developing the communication plan itself. And the first thing to say is that while the following section indicates some of the main areas, there is no single right way. The key to success is to choose an approach which best fits with organizational needs and speaks to employee attitudes.

In essence a communication plan is simple if you keep referring back to three key questions, namely:

1 Who is your audience?

2 What is your message?

3 What is the best channel and timing for your communication?

FIGURE 5.3 Influencing change

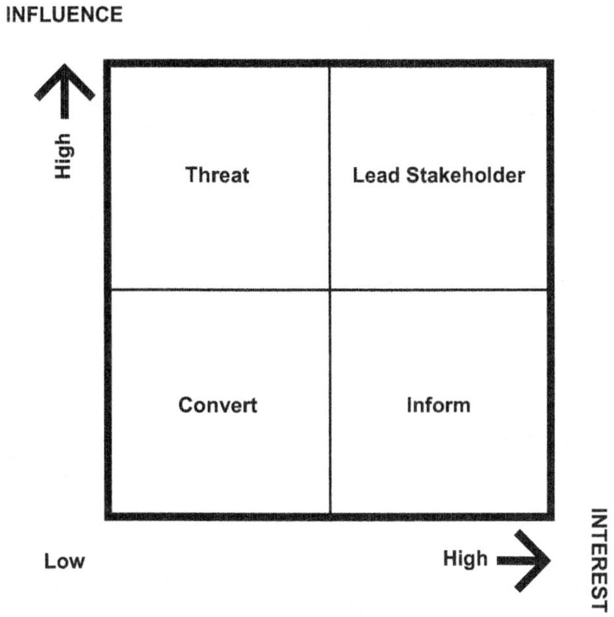

INFLUENCE

As we start to look at the communication plan, it may be worth reminding ourselves of a standard model which can be used to highlight those who are likely to have the greatest interest and influence in the change process.

What this Figure 5.3 is illustrating is that:

- Those with high influence and low interest are a potential threat. Care should be taken to nullify that threat as quickly as possible, preferably by giving them a greater interest, thereby making them advocates for change.

- It's easy to say that those with low influence and low interest can be ignored but as these are generally going to be the great bulk of your employees at the start of the programme, here again the task is to give them a greater interest in the project, converting them gradually into i-agents who not only have a high interest in the project but through their enthusiasm also have a high influence on its future success.

- Those with a high interest and low influence will generally be people who have become enthused by the new ethos but have yet to step up to deliver consistent results. The more that these individuals are kept informed the quicker they can be converted to a leading role.

● Finally, those which a high level of influence and interest are the lead stakeholders in the culture change. Initially this group may be confined to the top leadership team but as the innovation influence spreads across the organization this group will grow.

Although the example above refers primarily to key stakeholders within the organization, external influencers will also have their part to play, especially as the organization becomes more collaborative. Customers, suppliers and investors all instantly spring to mind but so do industry regulators, professional advisers such as solicitors or accountants and competing businesses. They will all have their part to play as innovation takes hold.

The first task in developing your plan is to identify and analyse stakeholders and to identify where they sit on the influence/interest scale. This will enable you to identify who needs to know about the forthcoming culture change and what level of information they should receive.

Once your stakeholder analysis is in place you can move on to creating your communication matrix, working out which is the best method to use to engage with each group and when. One method which works well here is to overlay your culture change timeline with one which covers communications. This helps to ensure that vital communication steps aren't missed and that the change is not held up while employees are trained in communication or while the marketing team develop an innovation-focused website integration.

Running alongside this timeline it can be helpful to have a schedule of aims, media and content, which will add flesh to the bones of the schedule. For example, the aim of briefing key stakeholders may be to gain their buy-in to the change so that they can use their influence to promote awareness. The media used may be a face-to-face interview or a teleconference and the content may be initial impression of the change and an idea of the likely implementation schedule.

The communication matrices outlined above are little different from those which you may use for any change programme, or indeed any project. But when you are moving towards a culture of innovation there is one key difference and that is in the frequency and content of your updates. When agile, collaborative working is the name of the game then the more that you can draw employees into a cohesive whole the better. Taking control of the communication matrix as a vehicle for providing a holistic viewpoint is a perfect way to start to prove to employees that this change is one which you are determined to succeed with. And that leads us on to the best chance you have of making an instant impact: launching the innovation programme.

Innovation launch event

You get one chance to make a first impression and the innovation launch event is your one chance to really engender enthusiasm in the new culture. We're not going to tell you to fill a hall with champagne and cheerleaders or to decamp the entire workforce to a local beauty spot for a picnic. You know your workforce; you have a strong idea of your existing culture and engagement levels and therefore you are in the perfect place to choose a launch event which will resonate with your people.

Whatever you do choose, it has to shake up ingrained perceptions, to make employees sit up and take notice and it has to be memorable. There will be times ahead when doubts creep in and it is the initial launch, backed up by strong communications, which will carry you through. This leads on to the golden rule for a successful launch: planning and preparation.

It is a rare business, which has not, from time to time, organized an event for employees or others, but none of these compare with the task you are facing now. So whether you rely on the office junior or call in an events company, you simply can't afford to hand over all the preparation to them. For your organizer(s) to launch your new culture, they have to buy into your new culture. So by all means use an outside firm but brief them, talk with them, co-ordinate with them to ensure that they are as 'on message' as you are.

And that goes for all of the senior team as well. There may only be two of you giving a presentation but the entire team have to be seen to have bought into the change. So before you even think about launching take the time out to run through expected questions and answers, to thoroughly understand the timetable, and to be prepared to face up to and overcome objections. And, if you can bring some of your i-agents into the mix so much the better. Oh, and collaboration, a changed ethos, fresh new approaches don't just start with the launch. If the attitude and behaviours of the senior team can be seen to change before the launch so much the better; it will act as an added springboard to build momentum.

You are now ready to step off into the future. In Chapter 7 we will examine how you can take the momentum forward and really make a culture of innovation part of the DNA of the organization. Before that, in Chapter 6 we're going to look in more detail at the roadmap to the future, examining how you can translate behaviours, analysis and frameworks into a strong structure which will support ongoing innovation. But we are going to end with another case study, illustrating how one organization leveraged communication expertise to draw their customers into an innovative system change.

CASE STUDY Launching innovation projects

Introduction

One of the key innovation messages which runs through this book is that the seeds of an innovation culture may start to flourish first in one corner of an organization but eventually the culture will grow to encompass not only the business itself but its customers, its suppliers and third parties. But how do you take your culture outside of your employee base and engender a buy-in from others? We turned to customer feedback experts Feefo to see how they had drawn their customers into an innovative system change.

Situation

Feefo is a trusted facilitator of customer feedback. By positioning its proposition firmly on delivering feedback only from customers who have actually bought products, feedback reviews are trusted both by consumers and by the search engines. As a result, using Feefo to manage customer feedback is seen by a growing number of businesses as a way of showing how much they care about creating genuine rapport with existing and potential customers.

Feefo's original data platform had stood the company in good stead for a number of years but the decision was made to take advantage of technological improvements and migrate the platform onto an innovative open-source data system; thus bringing additional functionality for their customers as well as 'future proofing' the system against future change.

With their platform closely linked to customer sites and internal programmes, it was imperative that users were comfortable with the new system and that any legacy issues were solved before the new platform was in place.

Approach

From the outset the Feefo team identified that communication was key to success. Drawing up a communication plan which included telephone conversations with key stakeholders, update e-mail briefings, workshops and presentations helped to create a two-way dialogue which drove development and installation of the programme. So successful was this dialogue that when Feefo asked its users for volunteers to test the new system it was overwhelmed by the positive response.

One initiative which proved particularly successful was the series of workshops which were delivered to employees, stakeholders and users. These provided opportunities for the new system to be demonstrated and for constructive feedback to be incorporated into the overall plan. The workshops were backed up with a succession of communications which updated stakeholders on the progress of the project and prepared them for their next milestone activity. As data migration approached, employees and stakeholders were also invited to take part in open conference calls which provided further information on progress and sought to iron out any areas of concern.

With communication playing such a vital part in the success of this innovative project, key individuals were coached on communication, influencing, and networking skills to help them strengthen relationships, both within the business and with stakeholders. This coaching not only equipped the individuals with skills in relation to this project, but also with new beliefs and behaviours which would support improved performance in their other daily responsibilities.

Conclusion

Whether engendering enthusiasm within an organization or seeking to draw customers and others into the innovation mix, the value of communication cannot be underestimated. Thanks to a strong focus on communication, the Feefo team received a strong level of buy-in from their users and this led to a successful implementation of their innovative new programme.

In summary

If you want to successfully deliver your change plan then communication is the key to defeating the four horsemen of doom, namely: lies, rumour, speculation and gossip. How you communicate and what you communicate will vary from organization to organization but in every case the communication plan has to be well thought out, clear and targeted.

Appointing i-agents will help to spread the message throughout the organization and into the wider population as third parties, suppliers and even clients become drawn in to the innovation mix. I-agents can act as forces for good: spreading positive messages, helping others to assimilate change and acting as feedback conduits. Above all else, the key message is that communication is not a one-off exercise. If you want collaboration, if you want agility and intelligence – above all, if you want *engagement* — then communication leads the way.

Key insights

- Culture change is not about the shiny new values on the lobby wall, it is about what you do with them, your actual actions and behaviour in order to make the innovation vision come alive.

- Every leader needs a messenger (i-agent) and the way those messengers are chosen, engaged and empowered has a direct correlation to the success of the pursuit of innovation.

- Communication means changing how you present things depending on the audience and creating the conditions for listening and feedback as well as sharing the message outwards.

References

Oshry, B (1994) *In the Middle*, Power & Systems Inc., Boston

Smith & Henderson (2014) The state of employee engagement [accessed 24 May 2015] [online] http://www.smithhenderson.com/state-of-employee-engagement-guide/

Building innovation aptitude

06

In the earlier chapters we examined changes which organizations will have to make when building a culture of innovation and why innovation is now considered to be an intrinsic element of future success.

Chapter 5 was devoted to one of the most crucial elements of cultural transformations, namely the way in which the culture change is communicated across the organization and in Chapter 7 we'll be looking at the future, discovering what actions and attitudes we need to adopt to ensure that the organization's culture permanently incorporates the innovation ideal.

So what's left? Well, in Chapter 4 we looked at defining the high-level roadmap, starting to structure the way in which the leadership team can guide the organization from where it is now towards a more innovative future. Now we are going to delve more deeply; looking at how systems and metrics, as well as people, can aid in the transformation. In essence this chapter is about what leaders need to do, what managers need to do and how to get the right behaviours selected, trained and 'live' in the organization.

Some of the ideas/measurements within this chapter may seem familiar, either because you have encountered them in earlier chapters of this book or have already come across them in the course of your business life. We make no apology for this. A good idea is a good idea but it is how you link good ideas together, connecting things that on the face of it may not seem to go together, that is one of the core building blocks of innovation, and it's that ability that creates the change which you are looking for. So whether we have already touched on some of these concepts or whether they already sit in the business sphere, it is the drawing together of these ideas which will help you to achieve innovation aptitude.

We'll start with a note of caution. If you are looking here for a 'one-size-fits-all' solution or a list of five values with their associated attitudes and behaviours which will guarantee you a culture of innovation then we are afraid that you are going to be disappointed. As we highlighted early in the book, borrowing or copying another organization's culture is simply not going to work. Neither is following a set pathway, however tempting it looks. Every organization is different and every organization has a different starting place. However, there are a few areas which leaders need to keep at the forefront of their minds if they are to translate the existing culture and behaviours into the desired culture of innovation. These include:

- *Innovation mix* – In Chapter 2 we looked at designing the optimum mix of incremental, differentiated and radical innovation for your organization. Now that we have reached the stage of achieving innovation aptitude followed by (in Chapter 7) embedding a culture of innovation then this mix has to be at the forefront of design and decision making. For example, there is little point in driving employees to create disruptive change if all you have designed is incremental innovation.

- *Operating model* – Have you decided to adopt the dual operating model or perhaps opted initially to introduce change in only one division? Is a culture of innovation to be introduced across the board in one hit or are you initially looking for incremental innovation with a view to moving further towards differentiated or radical innovation over time? Whatever the model, all of your decisions and approaches now will be informed by the pathway which you have chosen.

- *Current behaviours* – Are collaboration, empowerment and ownership already universal behaviours within the organization or is there some way to go before the desired behaviours are evidenced? You know where your start and desired end points are and they are going to influence the way in which you integrate innovation.

- *Management aptitudes* – What needs to happen at the management level to really shift the organizational mindset? What do you need to do to effectively manage your people in line with the new culture? Designing innovation aptitudes is one thing, managing change and instilling the required attributes within the management layer is quite another.

Leadership – its criticality to success

Leaders (and their organizations) get the innovation they deserve.

Above everyone else, leaders must continuously look at their organizations from the point of view of an outsider; seeing the business as a customer or a competitor would in order to spot areas for improvement and opportunity, or to identify weaknesses that would create opportunity for others.

More than that, leaders need to have the ability to look way beyond their immediate market, sector or industry in order to spot potential threats from disruptors. As the cross-fertilization of ideas leads businesses into new fields, the new threat in the world in which we now operate is that in many cases those who will eventually disrupt you probably don't exist yet (PwC, 2015).

Even without cross-sector competition, those who believe they operate in a static marketplace are sadly mistaken. It is a rare sector which doesn't have a continuing feed of new entrants, all arriving without the baggage of past history and all looking to leverage new technologies and new ideas to shoulder aside the more established players. Take the banking and finance sector for example. Challenger banks, payday loan companies, peer-to-peer lending schemes: all are forcing more established organizations to look again at their business models. And these new entrants into the marketplace are being well supported by the regulators. In the UK the Prudential Regulation Authority (PRA) changed its licensing process in 2013 to make it easier for new banks to enter the system, leading to an estimated five to six new licences being granted annually. This has led to PRA comments that new entrants are bringing innovation to banking.

Meanwhile at the same time as tightening up payday lending rules, the FCA's Chief Executive, Martin Wheatley commented that 'There is a lot the payday industry does not do well: but the relative ease of going online, simply choosing the amount you want to borrow on a website refreshingly free of jargon, and to get an immediate decision, for many people, has its merits (Wheatley, 2014).'

Meeting the disruptor challenge requires a multi-layer approach which leverages Next Generation intelligence capabilities. Getting under the skin of the customer base, really understanding what their challenges are will help businesses to create solutions in-house rather than seeing disruptors come in and take the marketplace. But intelligence and insight are only as good as internal capabilities allow; making the ongoing oversight and monitoring of internal innovation adoption levels a continuing priority.

The reality is, if you're not even looking then you'll get the disruption you deserve but if you are looking, thinking about and challenging industry norms and orthodoxies, constantly playing out 'what if?' scenarios, tapping into trend experts and futurologists, you stand a chance of good old-fashioned hard work or even serendipity paying off.

The point about innovation is that if you don't do anything, you'll get nothing but if you do something, even if you don't get what you aim for, you'll get something and, in those lucky serendipitous moments, that might even be a game-changer.

The history of invention is littered with examples of beneficial products being developed by accident. Sadly, one of the best known of these, Teflon, was not, as is commonly believed, developed as a by-product of the space race, having been discovered in 1938. However, even this discovery was an unforeseen consequence of an attempt to create a new type of refrigerant. The discoverer, Roy J Plunkett, credited his success to the way in which 'his mind was prepared by education and training to recognize novelty' (Bowden, 1997).

Those involved in space projects may not have invented Teflon but the space race has been credited with thousands of spin-off developments including:

- Technology developed to take high resolution images on Mars now being used to take in-game shots at baseball stadiums.

- Micro-sensors developed to enable astronauts to measure water content now being used to enable 'thirsty' plants to send messages to farmers.

- Cooling suits used in space walks are now used by those who work in heated environments including racing drivers and shipyard workers.

- Water purification techniques developed to recycle water in space now being applied to simplify kidney dialysis processes.

Even Viagra, one of the most famous and successful drugs of all time, was itself an accidental side effect of drug trials which were aimed at helping to treat abnormal blood pressure and heart disease. Now a related drug is being investigated as a potential aid to reducing the effects of vascular dementia, illustrating how one accidental discovery can have ongoing consequences.

What have these examples got to do with developing the roadmap towards a culture of innovation? Everything! Building a culture of innovation means moving away from a linear development and sales pathway and the limitations of continuous improvement to opening up ideas and mindsets to the potential, which can come from looking at problems anew. The leadership team have to lead the way but they also have to ensure that the infrastructure and environment are changed to enable and encourage others to be open to the possibilities around them. We'll come back to this later in the chapter when we look at building structures to support the innovation ecosystem.

Leaders need to build a compelling vision

Alongside a more open mindset, CEOs and leadership teams need to be clear and aligned on vision. What is the grand vision for the organization, what is its inspiring purpose and what impact does it want to have on the world? Sometimes seen as a bit 'fluffy', creating a vision that sets the course and direction for an organization is absolutely vital yet often approached in a lacklustre way. Creating a compelling vision of the future can become the glue that binds employees to the journey, that moves them to willingly contribute their creativity and ideas because the future destination is something they believe in.

In an earlier chapter we examined the importance of the leadership team assimilating change into their core beliefs and behaviours before they can successfully lead the change. Gaining a deep understanding of the way in which a strong vision can act as a catalyst for change is part of this assimilation. It can be a difficult concept to grasp. As leaders, it can be all too easy to focus first on profit/expansion/market position and so on. So when the idea of vision comes around, the natural consequence is for the vision to be created to support the target areas.

Successfully creating a vision, whether for an innovation-led company or any other reason, which drives the business forward actually requires leaders to turn the pyramid the other way up. Instead of the vision hanging off profitability and other targets, it should be the headline act which, through its success, delivers the end goals. The Prudential case study which we cited in Chapter 1 is a perfect example of the way in which strong leadership and vision combine to create differentiated products and capture the enthusiasm of the marketplace. Without the vision the organization may not have looked to move back into the Polish market and certainly would not have looked to do so in such an innovative way. But without strong leadership the vision would have foundered under the weight of inertia, risk concerns and other barriers to change.

We've looked at the creation of vision and values in earlier chapters but this is where their importance in defining and delivering the innovation agenda truly comes into play. The organizational values that support the vision need to be something that the whole organization believes in and will help define the course of your innovation agenda, the behaviour required and the environment you create and promote inside your organization. Even if the vision is strong, unless the entire organization unites to create systems and processes which align with the vision then the disconnect can ruin any chance of success. So the targets which are set, the metrics which are used, the expectations and bonuses all have to align with the innovation ideal. Balancing the vision with internal processes can be a challenge with the leadership team having to create solutions which best fit key aims.

Example

For an example, let's turn to motor racing and the multi-million dollar business of Formula 1. When a car arrives at a pit stop for a tyre change, the sooner it gets back on the racetrack the better. So do you set expectations and performance bonuses solely in terms of speed? Well no, because although tyre-change times have been slashed in recent years, too much speed could result in an ill-fitting tyre which then needs to be re-sited or comes off at the first corner. Do you prioritize safe tyre replacement? Again no, because that could result in the car staying too long in the pits, thus potentially damaging the chances of a race win.

The challenge to the team therefore has to be to come up with a solution which targets the key aims, namely maximizing the chance of a safe replacement while minimizing time taken. In pursuit of this, those in the pit crew and those in the factory have come up with numerous innovative solutions, from redesign of key equipment to a focus on speed and fitness training and they are rewarded accordingly.

This is a perfect example of knowing what you want to achieve and targeting and rewarding appropriately. Sadly, all too often the opposite is true. We could conversely have used the example of the leadership team which wanted to improve customer relations and yet targeted on number of calls answered; or the organization which wanted to be first to market and therefore skimped on safety testing.

We could even have used the example of the financial services organization which wanted to improve the way they treated their small business customers. The idea which emanated from the leadership team was a desire to train relationship managers to understand customers, their issues, their business and their challenges and in the process learn how to service them better. In other words, a desire to move away from selling products and towards solving issues and building relationships. Unfortunately, by the time the idea had filtered through successive layers of management, none of which had been sufficiently engaged in the original vision, the result was a junior member of the training team being tasked to deliver a half-day behavioural change course while targets for products sold remained unchanged.

The original concept of moving away from selling and towards relationships signalled a move in direction towards a more inclusive and mutually rewarding relationship. Where did it go wrong? Quite simply, in the fact that it was perceived as another *task* rather than a change of approach and culture. The thought that ideas and approaches could be changed by a 'sheep-dip' course completely misunderstood the nature of the challenge and the nature of people. Add in the fact that the metrics still calculated products sold rather than customer satisfaction and the idea was doomed to failure before it even started.

The message to take away from these examples is that the vision is nothing unless everything else falls into line behind it. Here again, it is up to the leadership team to ensure that it happens and that the vision and understanding is not simply retained within the leadership team but is diffused through successive layers of middle management/team leaders and so on. Their support is vital if change is to succeed. We will be examining this area in more depth in Chapter 7 when we look at embedding change.

Moving forward there must also be the recognition that the vision may change and with it the innovation strategy. The world we operate in is in such a state of constant flux, increasing complexity and movement that organizations must be able to 'shift' with the changing times. That means building organizations and most importantly people to be 'dual state', ie solid and impervious to attack but also fluid and dynamic whenever the need arises. Leaders must therefore above all else embrace adaptability and build it into their approach to innovation.

Pursuing the same path and vision long past its sell by date means organizations merely battle to keep or gain market share, desperately trying to compete at the old game while more forward-thinking, horizon-looking competitors have already moved on to win at the new game.

Leading outwards

We couldn't pass onwards without highlighting the importance of not only leading the organization but also looking to draw those outside the organization into the mix. It's a theme that we have touched on earlier in the book but it is one which becomes more important the closer that you get towards achieving your innovation goal. External stakeholders, regulators, governing bodies, suppliers, customers, even organizations with which you have a co-project relationship will all affect and be affected by your change of culture.

For those looking to lead a culture of innovation, leading outwards is as important as leading those within the organization. After all, these are the relationships which may eventually result in the greatest benefit for your customers. Or what about the relationship with regulatory bodies? This is very much more of a two-way street than popular conceptions would have us believe. Although regulators have a duty of care, businesses too have a duty towards their customers and investors. The result is a relationship in which both parties seek to work in tandem for the general benefit of consumers.

And then there is the general relationship which organizations have with suppliers and other third parties. There is no point in being innovative if your suppliers are still treading the same pathway as before. There is little use in looking to go it alone in providing innovative product solutions when there are others within the market who may already have part of the solution; and there is no point in offering to work with another organization to provide a complete solution and then refuse to interact with that body.

When leading outwards the importance of strong leadership which interacts with the different stakeholder groups cannot be underestimated. Even within a large organization, the sponsor of the innovation will probably spend a significant amount of their time doing stakeholder management to align people, rather than working on the actual innovation itself.

Building strong mutual relationships is key to success. It's about influencing people, taking the different groups on their change journey by understanding their situations, constraints, priorities and so on and then creating as much alignment as possible. It also calls for leaders to make it as easy as possible for people to reach agreement. For example, if someone needs to present to a governance board or steering committee, you may need to help them shape a presentation that will have the best chance of a successful outcome. At the end of the day it's the outcome you're interested in, and if that means doing stuff that may not technically be within your remit it may be advantageous to do so.

Understanding the real influencers in terms of decision making is critical for gaining people's emotional buy-in to at least explore the concept; as is having a good stakeholder plan using the principles which we discussed in Chapter 5.

Just as Siemens deployed SpigitEngage to draw ideas from the marketplace, so too can other organizations innovate by collaborating. And for successful collaboration to take place, organizations have to define and share a common goal and that means leading outwards, taking your values into the general business sphere and working together to provide solutions. To illustrate this, the following case study shows how leading outwards turned an idea into a successful business

CASE STUDY Collaborative leadership in action

Introduction

We've just been looking at the importance of leading outwards, collaborating with external bodies to not only develop products but to translate ideas into viable businesses. This is particularly the case when it comes to new enterprises and propositions which are breaking new ground and having to work with external stakeholders and regulators to prove the viability of, and set the parameters for the new product or service. With this in mind we turn to BrightMove Media to see how they successfully launched an innovative product into the advertising marketplace.

Situation

London is a vibrant city for work and leisure, playing host to millions of commuters and visitors every year. It is therefore a prime site for across-the-board advertising and indeed the advertising space in Piccadilly Circus is regarded as one of the most photographed landmarks in the world. Given the size of the potential audience it might therefore be safe to assume that advertisers had fully explored London's advertising potential.

However, the pace of technological change creates fresh opportunities and in 2011 the BrightMove Media founders identified an opportunity to introduce interactive advertising on the roofs of London's iconic fleet of black cabs. The premise behind the idea was that the messages could be changed at will with the added benefit of geo-targeting which enabled differing messages or advertisements to appear depending on the area of London which the cab was passing through at the time.

Approach

With a completely new product there was no benchmark or standard to work from. This created challenges as well as providing an opportunity to not only introduce a new product to the marketplace but also to design the acceptance parameters along the way. Research showed that the product had a place in the media marketplace and could help solve the problem of delivering better and more relevant, targeted advertising as well as being accountable. It also highlighted four key stakeholders, each of which had differing agendas. They were:

- *Transport for London* (TfL) – This body regulates all transport within the confines of London. BrightMove Media not only had to satisfy TfL concerns over safety and risk, they had to work with TfL to define acceptable parameters for the new product. As the displays were mounted on the roofs of taxis, concerns were also raised over the 'changed shape' of a brand which had world-wide recognition.

- *Media planners/buyers and brands* that advertise – UK outdoor advertising is worth £1 billion and advertisers are constantly in search of a new angle. However, although the drive is for new innovative applications, the market is somewhat risk-averse. This brought challenges of its own with an innovative and potentially disruptive idea having the potential to shake up the market.

- *Taxi drivers and the taxi industry* – With a proud 350-plus-year history, black cab drivers tend to be traditionalists. Their way of life is under threat from private hire operators and from other transport sectors and they are therefore naturally wary of change. To gain acceptance and trust took a significant investment in time and money as BrightMove Media worked with drivers to identify the benefits of Taxitop advertising.

- *Investors* – Working with a diverse group of investors brought a wide range of thoughts and input to the project, helping to refine and drive forward the initial idea.

To get its idea to market BrightMove Media had to work closely with all of these key external stakeholders, anticipating and overcoming challenges and proving the safety and viability of the concept. This required strong visible leadership, both within the business and externally, sharing and maintaining the vision and drive which would bring the external stakeholders into being strong collaborators within the project.

This meant that, for example, when working with TfL not only did BrightMove Media have to understand the safety issues and concerns but also in effect had to lead change within the transport body. With no blueprint to work from TfL and BrightMove Media were, in essence, starting from scratch: collaborating to anticipate potential pitfalls such as whether the public would be distracted by the signs and therefore put at risk or whether the change of cab outline would affect tourist perceptions. But while these were prime concerns the BrightMove Media leadership had to balance their work with TfL with the needs of the other stakeholders and the business.

Conclusion

Taking an innovative idea from a piece of paper to successful launch and market is never easy but BrightMove Media has shown how working with and drawing ideas in from others can lead to a successful launch. So much so that in 2014 CEO Piers Mummery was shortlisted for both the Urban Entrepreneur of the Year Award and the Media Disrupter Entrepreneur of the Year Award at the Great British Entrepreneur Awards.

At the time of writing BrightMove Media has successfully installed over 400 Taxitops screens bringing the latest in 'near and now' advertising onto the streets of London, with further expansion planned both domestically and internationally.

Why leaders need to engage HR

We mentioned previously the importance of drawing the HR team into the innovation leadership mix and in a short while we'll move on to examine some of the systems, policies and processes which HR, in tandem with the leadership team, can use to support the innovation framework. But first, we thought it important to take a little time to examine just why the input of the HR team is so vital for innovation to succeed. And we'll start with a reminder that the HR team should be at the table right from the initial discussion and design phase. Bringing them in only when it comes to implementation is asking them to 'catch up' on a project which they should by rights have had a strong hand in developing.

Successful innovation requires collaboration on multiple levels if it is to succeed. This means that in order to build a culture of innovation, innovation needs to be approached as a 'team sport' and when it comes to teamwork and employee engagement, HR are right at the forefront of the knowledge game. This is especially true when it comes to finding those i-agents who can help drive the innovation agenda, inspire people to contribute and support those that do. We've previously highlighted the importance of these champions but when it comes to creating the roadmap which translates vision and ideas into actuality the i-agents role is key. So it is up to the leadership team to find these people, sponsor them, train them and 'unleash' them. In order to do this, leaders must initiate the help and strategic support of their HR director and HR department. Building a culture of innovation requires leaders to utilize every tool they have at their disposal and by the very nature of their roles, HR professionals are front and centre of the people strategy. They are responsible for ensuring that the right people are hired, retained and equipped with the necessary skills to drive the organization forward. This means that HR, often overlooked in the pursuit of innovation, are perfectly placed to start helping build a cultural framework that supports the strategy, vision and drive towards innovation. This in turn helps to ensure that people are at the centre of innovation strategies.

Make no mistake, the HR team are not just there to find and identify those i-agents who will sit at all levels throughout the organization and who will support innovation. We've previously mentioned the importance of including the HR director, at the very least, in the leadership team but when it comes to embedding the culture the HR business partners should be on hand to support the business lines in identifying and nurturing talent, understanding key skill sets and structuring rewards and recognition programmes to support the innovation agenda. Any move towards a change of culture can prove difficult for employees to assimilate. People are by their very nature lovers of stability and whenever we ask people to adopt new values, new beliefs and new attitudes there will always be an element of resistance. Interestingly, even if we are asking employees to change from a toxic bullying culture towards one which is more caring and open there are still barriers to overcome as old habits prove hard to break and the professed new culture is initially viewed with suspicion. So if even small cultural changes can be hard to instil, how much resistance and inertia will leaders have to overcome when they look to adopt an innovation culture? Taken to its full extent, by the time a full culture of innovation has been embedded in the organization, the leadership team may have decided to sweep away job demarcation, silos, fixed processes and strict hierarchy and replace them with flatter structures, open collaboration and a fresh outlook on every process.

The fact is that typically, failure rates in the region of 70 per cent are quoted in relation to culture change programmes. As strategic partners to CEOs and leadership teams we have seen for ourselves the way in which cultural transformations fail because leaders have either tried to impose change by decree or have looked for quick wins, ignoring all of the necessary preparatory work and 'skipping to the good bit'. Well, although you can devise your strategy with some quick wins along the way, the 'good bit' just won't happen and certainly won't be sustainable and repeatable unless the groundwork is in place.

It's probably worth emphasizing here that the nature and extent of the groundwork required will depend on the organization itself and its innovation maturity. So while some organizations may look towards the Holacracy model of distributed authority, others may follow a more conventional route.

That is why it is so important to build the high level innovation team, including i-agents and to ensure that the team is involved in the co-creation and development of an innovation framework and roadmap. And it is why it is so important for HR to be involved at every level – acting as guardians of the plan, sharing learning and feedback, linking goals to innovation and providing ongoing support.

Moreover, one of the first challenges for HR is to act as a voice of reason when the CEO just wants to race off and 'do stuff'. HR professionals understand their people and they can help the CEO and leadership team to understand that people won't be lectured to, won't be dictated to and that the surest way for the culture to change is to take the right pathway.

Identifying and engaging intrapreneurs

In a moment we are going to move on and look at the structure to support innovation ecosystems. Before we do so this is an opportune moment to spend a little more time looking at some of the people who could make or break the change. Those people are the intrapreneurs within the organization.

We took a quick look at the key traits of intrapreneurs in Chapter 6 when we looked at some of the 'influencer' groups but as intrapreneurs play such a strong part in delivering a culture of innovation within an organization it is worth taking time out to really understand these individuals.

You will be familiar with entrepreneurs, those individuals who set out to create something special, generally via a start-up business model. They are the ideas people, the disruptors, the individuals who have seen an opportunity and are out to make a difference. You may not be aware that key individuals within your organization display the same traits. These are the *intrapreneurs*, the individuals who are not content to sit back but who have a burning desire to help their organization to succeed and the imagination and drive to carry change along with them. Intrapreneurs are the organization's natural innovators, comfortable with navigating uncertainty and exploring new terrain. They apply entrepreneurial thinking and actions to the role which they play within the organization and that means that above everything else they embody the fact that innovation is everyone's job.

Organizations that are looking to make innovation a key part of their DNA have to leverage strategy, leadership and culture, and intrapreneurs can add their weight to all three:

- *Strategy* – In previous chapters we've outlined the importance of strategy, and of communicating strategy and this is one area in which intrapreneurs can shine. Assimilating the change, interpreting it for fellow employees and translating it into actions and behaviours are all key intrapreneurial roles. Successful intrapreneurs are likely to have a fairly high level of emotional intelligence and can therefore understand and empathize with people across the organization, helping to share the message. Moreover, as connected thinkers they can add weight to the strategy, helping to take the words and translate them into on the ground actions.

- *Leadership* – Intrapreneurs may not have a title but they are leaders in every other sense of the word. Paving the way, encouraging and enthusing, sharing the vision; these individuals can drive change. With their natural propensity to take ownership and responsibility, they can demonstrate the benefits of empowerment and show how people don't have to wait to be given responsibility, but can take responsibility upon themselves by their actions and attitudes.

- *Culture* – Intrapreneurs are idea-creators, builders and risk-takers; willing to try something new or different yet fully aware of the risks and rewards. Because they generally sit at the heart of the organization they are 'corporately bi-lingual', able to influence both up and down the line, helping to drive the momentum for culture change. Moreover, because they are not content with simply carrying out a task they are more likely to look to co-create with others, in the process helping to break down silos and fostering collaboration.

The structure to support innovation ecosystems

So far in this chapter we have worked on consolidating our understanding of the importance of the leadership team delivering a consistent message when inculcating a culture of innovation. With this firmly in mind, we are now moving on to really delve into the depths of the roadmap, looking first at the systems, policies and processes which will support innovation introduction and then to examine the ways in which innovation success can be measured, before finally looking at one possible method of introducing the innovation process.

We have tried, wherever possible to provide some generic solutions in the hope that they will act as catalysts for your own developmental ideas. Naturally, depending on your sector, there will be some challenges/areas of consideration which are industry-specific. However, these can all be overcome as long as the leadership team concentrate on the key message, which is to create solutions to real problems, wherever they may occur. The ideas which we discuss here will also need to be modified to account for your optimum innovation mix and structure. For example, should you opt for the dual operating system, which we discussed in Chapter 4 then wholesale changes can, and should, only take place if the new systems also support those who are tasked with maintaining the core processes.

With that in mind let's look at some of the systems, policies and processes which will form the basis of the roadmap which will lead towards a new culture of innovation.

- *Performance management* – This is one of the intrinsic elements of employee engagement, particularly if you are moving towards a more self-managed model of engagement. We've already largely covered this aspect earlier in the chapter, so suffice it to say that unless you set and measure performance targets which are in line with the innovation model then you are giving out mixed messages. This is one area in which the HR team can add their considerable expertise to the mix. When you are looking for collaboration, when failure has become a learning point rather than a cause for censure then not only will employees need to be coached in new attitudes, the appraisal/ reward structure may also need to be changed. For example, when intelligence is an intrinsic part of the innovation process, call-centre staff may be at the forefront of gathering customer insights. However, if they are targeted by number of calls handled then they won't have the time to chat to customers and gain an understanding of their wider issues. To overcome this, targets would need to be changed in order to reward innovation-focused behaviours.

- *Pay and reward* – Following on from the above, in a linear structure, pay bands are relatively easy to concoct. When the structure flattens out and when cross-department collaboration becomes the name of the game, then the entire pay and reward structure may require an overhaul. Should bonuses be based on team behaviours rather than individual contributions? Should pay itself be based on rewarding innovation efforts or on other criteria? If one part of the organization has adopted an innovation model while others have yet to jump, how do you structure comparative scales?

- *Internal communications* – Whatever you do, don't just decide that as you now have collaboration you'll simply copy everything to everyone in future. But equally it's a fair bet that your existing communication structures won't support an innovation mindset. So take time to review and overhaul your internal communication system. From bulletin boards to crowdsourcing innovative ideas and solutions and from intranets to instant chat rooms and collaborative idea sharing platforms, there is no shortage of possible systems to choose from when developing innovation capabilities. Even the once ubiquitous 'suggestion box' may have a part to play but you may first have to reinvent it to overcome 'tick-box' perceptions.

- *Systems development* – Much of the work involved in systems development will follow as a consequence of adopting an innovation culture, rather than as a prelude to it. However, the leadership team need to be alive to the possibility of systems development: either to enable employees to collaborate more easily or to provide additional functionality which will enhance the customer experience. In keeping with the innovation model, the way in which systems development is approached may also need to be re-examined. Delivering innovative solutions should not rest on a model which churns through every step at the pace of a snail. Agile is now the name of the game, allied to a 'minimum viable product/solution' which launches to market sooner rather than perfect with iterative development following on.

- *Processes* – Let's be honest, you aren't going to change every process in an instant. Within any organization there is already so much interweaving that unravelling the tangled threads will take some time. But equally there will be some processes of which it could be said that the sooner they are changed the better. Start with the 'Do we really need x?' ones and move on from there. Unravelling and doing away with processes which clog the smooth flow of the system can be seen as useful 'quick wins', especially if they are spread across departments. And when we are talking about process reviews, we should be mindful of the 'start with the customer and work backwards to the technology required' approach. Admittedly this is an approach which is not confined to those seeking to embed an innovation ecosystem but it is an approach which is particularly appropriate as a deliverer of innovation. Remembering back to earlier chapters, innovation looks to solve real problems so if you haven't identified those real problems, your process review is just whistling in the wind.

- *Policies* – HR policies, safety policies, use of personal equipment at work policies – some are necessary to comply with the law but others have grown up over time and quite frankly have no place in a Next Generation Organization. Review them with a critical eye and amend as soon as possible. Here again it is possible to engender some quick wins. And don't forget to be innovative when you are reviewing. For example, why are smartphones banned in work; would 'bring your own device' (BYOD) be a more appropriate response to meet Generation Z expectations; what do we really mean by flexible working?

- *Recruitment* – When the values and competencies of the organization change then inevitably the recruitment processes and policies will also come under scrutiny. Hiring for cultural fit has rapidly gained traction since the end of the recession and hiring those who meet more open, collaborative profiles may be an advantage. However, don't concentrate on these traits to the exclusion of all others. You still want someone who will meet core values such as honesty or accuracy. One point to bear in mind here is the way in which the job market has changed as countries have stepped away from recession. From seeing a number of years in which employers very much had the upper hand, the tide is turning in favour of the employee.

If the falling unemployment rate were not indication enough, the rise in articles on the internet all seeking to show employees how to identify the culture of their prospective employer gives some indication of the way in which the marketplace is moving. This makes hiring for cultural fit a two-way process with both sides looking for meaning from the relationship. But no matter how rigorous the employment process, it is only when new employees experience the organization from the inside that potential matches are confirmed or otherwise. On the employer's side, that is one reason why the probationary period can be invaluable; from the employee side, perhaps the Zappos model is worth investigating with new hires being offered money to leave if they feel unable to embrace the Zappos way.

- *Risk and governance* – Whenever the question of innovation is raised, inevitably the risk matrix comes into question. While innovation requires the acceptance of failure as a learning point, it does not equate to an increase in what we call 'Cavalier Risk'. Rather, it is important that the freedoms inherent in innovation are bound by definitions of acceptable risk or what we call 'Smart Risk'. So while inevitably innovation leads to a reappraisal of the risk/governance matrix it does not lead to them being scrapped. Partly this change is driven by the 4Es engagement process which includes education and empowerment but not only do people have to change, the internal and external approvals process also needs to change to encourage empowerment. For example, taking steps to identify vulnerable customers and taking extra care to ensure that the products/services are aligned to their needs.

- *Training and development* – We've partially covered this area when looking at engagement, above. When behaviours change, so too do the skills which are required to support them. Everyone, from the leadership team downwards, will need training and coaching to develop their personal skills to meet the innovation imperative. This will include the development of a more holistic view of the organization and a broadening of skills and behaviours such as collaboration and customer focus.

- *External relationships* – When the organization changes its focus, so too will the relationship with its partners, suppliers and customers change. Designing an 'open innovation' programme will help to ensure that the innovation ideal is taken up by partners and suppliers while a more open relationship will pave the way for greater interactions and co-creation of aligned, relevant and innovative solutions with customers. In fact, the more you develop the innovation ecosystem, the more you may find opportunities to review contracts and commercials and to change future selection processes. As you then seek to draw suppliers into the innovation mix, there will be a need to explore not only what problems suppliers have that you can solve but also what suppliers can bring to the party.

Before you panic, you don't have to change all of the systems and processes at the same time. The key is to identify what may need to change and then to prioritize to bring the changes in, in a smooth and orderly manner. Only by identifying potential change and then developing a change structure will the leadership team be able to map the pathway from now to the future. To illustrate this, let's have a look at an example of an organization which solved an innovation engagement challenge by leveraging the power of technology.

CASE STUDY   Harnessing people-powered innovation

Introduction

We've just been talking about the importance of placing HR front and centre of the innovation strategy and of the way in which leaders should leverage every tool available to them in order to bring innovation into the day-to-day interactions. As we have moved through our innovation journey we've seen numerous occasions on which technology has been an enabler and when it comes to HR and to engagement this is another time in which technology can help to transform innovation approaches. We turned to Brightidea to see how their crowd-driven software was helping organizations to take advantage of the full creative capacity of their people.

Situation

Brightidea is driven by the concept that organizations not only have to innovate, they have to innovate faster than the market to win. From launching the first online innovation platform in 2005, the company has developed its offering to a point at which it offers a complete suite of capabilities that track the entire idea lifecycle from initial collection through execution. Brightidea is now the partner of choice for leading global companies including Cathay Pacific, BT Group (BT), General Electric (GE), Hewlett-Packard (HP) and Nielsen.

When Nielsen approached Brightidea, as you would expect from a global organization which provides insight into consuming patterns, Nielsen strongly believed in innovation and the ongoing development of customer insight solutions. However, Nielsen lacked a method of tracking and recording ideas in a structured way and this led to:

- Around 65 per cent of employees having no idea where to go to innovate, with those that stated they did know citing over 20 different tools.

- No single innovation portfolio view which caused most employees (80 per cent) to describe Nielsen as 'not innovative'.

- Approximately 72 per cent of employees noted solely using e-mails and conversations to innovate.

- Around 68 per cent of ideas submitted remained open for over six months with no rendered decision, leading to disgruntled employees, hesitant to participate in ideation.

Approach

Powered by Brightidea, Neilson designed an innovation management framework that defined how the company captures, catalogues, decides upon and communicates ideation to both employees and clients globally and consistently, while supporting Nielsen's strategic innovation efforts. This included creating an overall portfolio scorecard that measures the breath, depth and impact of Nielsen's collective innovation efforts.

The result was that Nielsen was able to drive employee engagement, liberate functions to innovate as needed, satisfy corporate oversight and governance *and* increase innovation activity and throughput. With a central innovation programme management team, aided by 'ambassadors' within the functions, the programme not only captures and rewards best practices, it also combines both discipline and freedom in a way that enhances engagement and speeds up engagement. The net result just nine months after implementation includes:

- One hundred per cent of ideas submitted are evaluated and acted upon (previously not measured).

- One hundred per cent of qualified commercially important ideas pass through IP workflow.

- One hundred per cent of employees notified of idea status (previously not measured).

- A 225 per cent increase in ideation challenges offered to employees.

- A 518 per cent increase in ideas submitted.

- A thousand per cent increase in first-time employee engagement of Nielsen Innovation Portal.

Conclusion

Leveraging both the power of technology and people boosts engagement and innovation outcomes. Plus it encourages idea formation and brings those ideas to fruition in a consistent manner. When people are engaged, the results can be game-changing.

How will innovation be measured?

When we get along the path to the future, how will we measure success, or otherwise? The whole concept of measuring innovation is often polarized in that the old guard think it's about measuring everything, after all, you can't manage it if you can't measure it, and the new guard promote the freedom to be creative alongside a looser approach to the creation of innovation. And some argue that innovation is impossible to quantify and that anything that attempts to measure 'creativity' simply stifles it.

But they're wrong. Creativity without measurement is akin to chaos. And while the random patterns which derive from the application of chaos theory may make for pretty patterns on T-shirts, it is of little use in developing innovation-led organizations. True creativity takes hard work and discipline. Aside from that, is disregarding measurement and resting the future of an organization in the hands of creativity a viable business strategy? We don't think even Mark Parker, the CEO of Nike, widely considered the most creative CEO in the world, would follow that mantra.

According to McKinsey (2010), more than 70 per cent of corporate leaders tout innovation as a top three business priority, but only 22 per cent have set innovation metrics.

The problem is, if you don't measure innovation, are you still getting innovation? Well, you probably are but not in a systematic, as-efficient way as it could be. Moreover, if you don't measure innovation then how can you show early wins, which will help build momentum and enable people to feel that the organization is making progress?

The truth, and what this framework is based on, is finding the right balance and getting that balance means finding a happy medium between quantitative and qualitative measurement; so measuring return on investment as well as measuring innovation-focused behaviour for example. Measure too much and you slow down the idea and innovation process, even blocking it if measurement becomes too invasive. Conversely, if you're too slack and 'set creativity free' then how do you know where you are, what's happening and what the ROI is?

Not measuring enough is just as dangerous as measuring too much and you can even end up getting worse results. Information overload is a well known facet of business life and with Big Data rapidly gaining traction, being able to shift through the chaff to get at the wheat is a key skill. In fact the idea of the 'haystack syndrome' was originally proposed as long ago as 1990 by E M Goldratt. Early in his book, he comments: 'We are drowned in oceans of data; nevertheless it seems as if we seldom have sufficient information.' (Goldratt, 1990) Having lots and lots of data can be compelling but when you are moving towards an innovation ecosystem which values intelligence, getting behind the data is a key indicator of success.

Creativity and nurturing differing perspectives, ideas, thinking, approaches etc are all required for innovation and the culture you build will either help promote them or not. But, innovation is actually one of the most process-driven things an organization can do and that means it can and should be measured. With that in mind, how do you figure out what the right balance of measurement is, what to measure, where and how much?

Every organization is unique and will, by the very nature of having an individual culture unlike anyone else's, approach things in a different way. So the best approach is to decide what will help you get better at innovating. Off the back of your innovation strategy, vision, direction etc, what do you need to know about what you're doing and how you're doing it in order to learn and improve, to build an ever-more efficient innovation engine?

Measuring for measuring's sake is wasteful and costly and only serves to appease the bean counters and analysts who thrive on data, numbers and statistics. But, unless that information gives you real, valuable insight into how you can improve your innovation process and move you up the maturity scale it will only serve to strangle it in terms of its cost, the manpower required and its blocking of the core goal of generating useful ideas.

Deciding on relevant metrics

Building the right 'metrics portfolio' of things to measure should focus on the most important innovation drivers that fit your approach. However, there are some typical factors like making sure your metrics portfolio is well rounded and balanced. It must be congruent with what you're trying to achieve and with what you need to know to keep improving in order to get there. It should also include three parts of the innovation process, input, throughput and output, ie: What do we need to put into our innovation process, what does it take to develop viable solutions and then when implemented what are we seeing in terms of a return from the output? However, don't become so tied up with measuring the 'what' that you ignore the importance of measuring *how* people are embracing the new behaviours. This could be a simple addition to performance reviews but unless you track engagement with the culture change then you could find adoption slipping away.

With that in mind it's important to involve key stakeholders and i-agents from across the organization in order to identify an initial set of metrics. These should then be evolved as your understanding of what works and what doesn't increases. Flowing from these learning loops, this then becomes an ongoing process allowing you to continuously innovate your innovation approach.

For example, organizations which traditionally see themselves as innovative, in the invention sense of the word, may decide that the filing of patents is a valuable element of the innovation mix. So, General Electric, whose employees filed some 20,000 patents in one decade, are widely quoted as viewing patents as an essential measurement of innovation. However, to purely concentrate on the filing of patents, and thereby ignore other developmental work which did not reach the patent stage, would give a false picture of the true extent of innovative efforts. Equally, in other sectors, such as finance, where the granting of patents is an unusual occurrence, the patent count would probably be a waste of resources. In those cases measurements may be better focused on areas such as:

- *ROII (Return on Innovation Investment)* – Measuring ROII focuses on measuring the actual cost of the resources required to drive innovation along with the cost of investment into specific potential innovations in the form of prototypes, trials etc and the financial returns gained. It's important to take a venture capital (VC) approach to innovation when measuring ROII, as not everything you do will change the fortunes of the organization. But like any VC the approach needs to take into account the overall portfolio of activity not the returns on individual ideas.

- *Input metrics* – An important factor in measuring the innovation process is the measurement of content into the start of the process. That typical innovation process starts with gathering ideas but our perspective is that 'ideas' are stage two and the first stage is the insight or 'intelligence' gathering process in order to unearth problems that require solutions. Measuring how and where you gather that intelligence from can be specifically aligned to your core purpose and direction and so can be measured to make sure you are gathering the right intelligence and understanding about the world in order to focus your innovation efforts in the right direction. There's no point spending time developing great ideas that aren't actually aligned to your customers or the problems they currently face or that aren't aligned to your core strategy.

Choosing the most appropriate input metrics for your organization will depend on your innovation maturity and expected outcomes, as modified by your business sector. For example, those in highly collaborative environments such as pharmaceuticals or the marketing/advertising sphere may well see external sourcing of ideas and technology as a normal part of their existing methodologies. So, for example, Proctor & Gamble has 'Connect + Develop', an open innovation strategy which seeks to draw in ideas from across the world. Conversely, those who are more used to working in closed systems are more likely to look to internal metrics in the first instance with a gradual widening of the scope as the level of innovation maturity increases.

Once you have an idea of the metrics which are most appropriate for your organization you can then start to look at measuring your ideas and the volume, quality and source of them. They key is focusing on quality of good ideas rather than the usual approach of quantity of ideas; many of which aren't aligned to the problems you've unearthed. However, the obvious goal is quantity *and* quality. Here are a few key ingredients:

- how well you communicate everything about innovation;
- the more 'intelligent' you become about the world in order to inform your innovation process and how well you communicate that;
- how engaged your people are as a result of how great your culture is;
- how easy your innovation process is to work with;
- how inspired everyone is with the future vision of the organization and its purpose;

- the visibility of the senior leadership team's sponsorship of innovation;
- how well you define, frame and communicate the problem or challenge to be solved;
- how much people are allowed (as a by-product of culture) to collaborate.

However, this list focuses on input metrics, the way in which the organization changes in response to culture change. For a balanced viewpoint, you also need to consider output metrics, or IIPP (Implemented Innovations Per Person). This can be measured as a ratio of how many employees you have or how many people actively contribute to the innovation agenda versus how many ideas actually make it to market or get implemented.

Here again, the focus should be appropriate to organizational delivery and sector but output metrics may well include:

- number of new products, services, and businesses launched through innovation and not 'what you would have done anyway' in the past year;
- percentage of top- and bottom-line growth from innovations implemented on an annual basis;
- number of ideas turned into patents by employees;
- royalty and licensing income from patents and IP (intellectual property);
- number of innovations that significantly differentiate the existing business;
- number of innovations that disrupt existing business or create new business;
- percentage of new innovations that come from open-innovation;
- percentage of employees trained in innovation processes, tools and frameworks;
- numbers of customers involved in co-creation through open-innovation.

This list isn't exhaustive so pick a few but create your own in order to create a set of metrics aligned to your organization. The optimal 'metrics portfolio' helps promote the specific actions and behaviours required to increase your innovation capability so make sure you don't focus on general metrics as they won't help you. However, just deciding on the right things to measure is a process in itself but the main thing is to make sure you build a specific 'metrics portfolio' that helps you increase your innovation capability and reinforce the values, vision and ambition that your organization aspires to.

While risk is a fundamental part of innovation, gambling isn't; it's what we call 'cavalier risk' and not measuring innovation is just that. But don't forget that measurements are not set in stone and the areas which are measured will develop over time as the organization becomes more infused with the innovation ideal.

Designing your innovation process

The traditional approach to innovation has historically followed the 'stage-gate' process. For more than 25 years, the Stage-Gate® idea-to-launch process (Stage-Gate, 2015) has helped some of the world's most innovative companies including Du Pont and P&G to develop and launch innovative products.

Our suggestion is to use a simpler model to start with until you find your innovation feet and build your innovation maturity. To start with, try using our *3Is innovation process* which focuses on helping organizations move from inventing to innovating. Unlike most organizations which try and innovate by asking for ideas, the 3Is innovation process builds on the key components of design thinking and the fact that game-changing innovation starts with a question not an idea.

Those three stages are:

1 *Identify* – In Chapter 1 you will recall that what differentiates invention from innovation is that the latter solves a genuine problem and more importantly, makes it to market or gets implemented. To facilitate that we also outlined the first trait of a Next Generation Organization as being 'intelligence', or becoming more intelligent about the world in order to unearth bigger questions and bigger, more relevant problems to solve for their customers. The identification phase is therefore simply the discovery of genuine problems, questions, opportunities etc that require solutions.

Remember, genuine problems may not necessarily be of the 'stand up and hit you in the face' variety. Successful discovery requires those within the organization to keep a broad perspective and an open mind. Identification may come from anywhere so this is where the intelligence element of the Next Generation Organization approach to

FIGURE 6.1 The 3Is innovation process

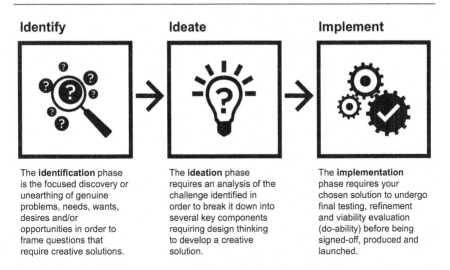

Identify	Ideate	Implement
The **identification** phase is the focused discovery or unearthing of genuine problems, needs, wants, desires and/or opportunities in order to frame questions that require creative solutions.	The **ideation** phase requires an analysis of the challenge identified in order to break it down into several key components requiring design thinking to develop a creative solution.	The **implementation** phase requires your chosen solution to undergo final testing, refinement and viability evaluation (do-ability) before being signed-off, produced and launched.

innovation really comes into its own. Identifying user needs, understanding the customer and scanning the business horizon to pick up potential disruptors will all form part of the identification phase. But although discovery feeds into the second stage, it should be viewed as a continuing activity; so although other innovation activities are in differing stages of progression, 'identification' will be there acting as a continuous and continuing feed into the innovation process.

2 *Ideate* – Now you have identified a problem, what next? Before you can get on and develop a solution that meets the identified need and/ or opportunity there needs to be a deep analysis of the question in order to break it down into several key points or components that need to be solved. In Chapter 1 we outlined the second attribute of a Next Generation Organization as 'collaboration' and that plays a significant part of this phase: working with colleagues, customers, suppliers and others to develop relevant and aligned solutions.

This is where giving employees a more holistic view of the business comes into its own as people who would traditionally be unconnected with a product, problem or department are able to make a valuable contribution to creating solutions. This is also, particularly in the early stages of innovation as an organizational imperative, an ideal opportunity to reinforce the determination of the leadership to work in a new way. Because of the constant questioning nature of design thinking, the solutions you come up with will also create potential alternative routes or even prompt a redefinition of the initial problem you were trying to solve so making sure you're on the right track is crucial. The minimum viable product (MVP) approach is crucial here as it allows you to get something out there and test it in real time on real people in order to evaluate whether your solution meets the invention or innovation definition. Prototyping, testing, evaluating and prototyping again (iterating) cannot be underestimated if you're going to fail fast/learn fast in order to get the right solution to market at the right time.

3 *Implement* – But, once you've got the solution, you need to deliver it. Sounds simple, but don't neglect the importance of user-testing, communication, feedback and evaluation. And here again we are going to highlight the importance of implementation, as from our experience that is one of the weakest parts of the innovation process and as we know, moving from invention to innovation means embracing the third trait of the Next Generation Organization: 'adaptability' and 'getting stuff to market' quicker than the competition. Ultimately, the key to successful implementation is an implementation plan and taking action and executing all the required tasks as outlined in it. Any implementation plan always requires continuous monitoring and review and that's where the process feeds directly back into the 'Intelligence' capability of being a Next Generation Organization and using the deep connection and relationship with customers to help analyse the impact of the solution delivered.

In summary

By its very nature the roadmap has to be specific to each organization. Not only will it depend on innovation maturity levels and expected outcomes, it will also vary according to business sector. In some cases it may even vary across departments within a single organization.

The roadmap draws together all of the background scoping work and looks to put a framework in place which will move the organization forward. Leadership, vision and the early input from the HR team are vital for success but unless systems, policies and structures are put in place with a view to supporting the innovation ecosystem the hard work will be in vain.

The key point to remember is that 'identify, ideate and implement' is an ongoing rolling process and unless there are systems in place to measure success the business will become locked in stasis.

Key insights

- A good idea is a good idea but it is how you link good ideas together, connecting things that on the face of it may not seem to go together to create systems, when innovation changes the game.

- As the cross-fertilization of ideas leads businesses into new fields, your competitors are no longer in the room and in many cases, those who will eventually disrupt you probably don't exist yet.

- Only by identifying potential change and then developing a change structure will the leadership team be able to map the pathway from now to an innovation-led future.

References

Bowden, M (1997) *Chemical Achievers: The human face of the chemical sciences*, Chemical Heritage Foundation, Philadelphia

Goldratt E M (1990) *The Haystack Syndrome: Sifting information out of the data ocean*, North River Press, New York

McKinsey (2010) [accessed 08 April 2015] [online] http://www.mckinsey.com/insights/innovation/innovation_and_commercialization_2010_mckinsey_global_survey_results

PwC, (2015) [accessed 04 March 2015] 18th Annual Global CEO Survey (online) http://www.pwc.com/gx/en/ceo-survey/2015/assets/pwc-18th-annual-global-ceo-survey-jan-2015.pdf

Stage-Gate, (2015) [accessed 04 March 2015] (website) http://www.stage-gate.com/

Wheatley, M (2014) [accessed 08 April 2015] (online) http://www.fca.org.uk/news/competition-in-the-interests-of-consumers

Embedding a culture of innovation

07

The hard work is over and the end of your innovation journey is in sight. You've worked to understand your level of innovation maturity; you've defined vision and values and have arrived at an innovation mix that is aligned to your corporate strategy. The roadmap is in place and the senior leadership team and i-agents have all received the training they need to communicate the new culture.

So what's missing? Why is there a need for Chapter 7 at all? Quite simply, because you are approaching one of the most critical phases of any culture change: making it stick. Now is the time when all of those innovation barriers that you identified at the outset will rise up and consciously or unconsciously work against embedding the new culture. Inertia, fear of change, concerns about loss of status – whatever the reason, if the leadership team take their eye off the ball now, then all the hard work will be wasted.

In this chapter we are going to look at some of the ways in which organizations can embed change so that it becomes a permanent part of the DNA. We'll review how systems and technology can help to boost collaboration and we'll revisit the people dimension, examining how time spent on engagement and alignment can transform resistors into advocates for change and innovation.

Although embedding change is the final phase of the journey towards embracing an innovation culture, it is also the longest phase. If successful, in fact this phase carries on indefinitely as the organization grows in its level of innovation maturity and adapts to embrace the ongoing challenges of changing technologies and expectations. So we are loosely breaking this chapter down into three sections. We start with a general look at embedding change, before moving on to the people dimension. Finally we take a look at the future, enabling your organizational culture to evolve in response to the world around you.

Embedding change

Whether you are looking to change an existing culture to drive innovation or are seeking to create a strong culture following a merger or acquisition or even in a start-up phase or period of rapid growth, the key to success is to get the right vision or mission in place by setting the values which you want your organization and people to hold dear. In essence this means changing or creating the beliefs, attitudes, behaviours and working styles that reinforce the desired culture and putting in place the right structures to make it truly 'stick'.

Regardless of the hours which are spent in drawing up a set of values and behaviours that, it is envisaged, will drive the organization forward, unless you take time, effort and thought to create change then all you have done is indulge in a meaningless exercise. True change touches every structural fibre of an organization, reinforcing and supporting the transformation through the attention paid to the physical work environment; the daily processes; the way in which people are rewarded; the reason people are promoted or leave; customer and supplier interactions; marketing; website design and so on.

It's not necessarily a quick process either, nor should it be. However much you may want them to, epiphanies are not going to happen overnight for every one of your employees, customers and related third parties. Even if they did, it would still take some time for systems and processes to be changed to fit the new model. This begs the question: How do you ensure that as the organization evolves its innovation model, those within the organization are also evolving to meet the new challenge? It's a question that faces all organizations, whether they sit in the more traditional business spheres or in fields such as the arts or sport or even if they are quasi-governmental organizations. Even the military are not exempt and indeed a quick internet search reveals the way in which innovation culture permeates armed forces.

Throughout our journey we have looked at the way in which the leadership team not only has to change but it has to be seen to change; and we have also examined how i-agents, those influencers who sit at all levels within the organization, can make such a difference to embedding innovation change. But for true change, the innovation concept has to permeate the entire organization and that means eventually it has to touch every person and every process.

This brings trust into play, the trust which leaders have in their teams to deliver engaged change. For leaders who have traditionally instructed rather than empowered this can be a difficult transition to make. But trust and empowerment go hand in hand and if you give people the tools to act in an empowered way then they will deliver. To illustrate this idea more fully we turned to someone who has first-hand experience of leading and empowering teams to deliver game-changing results.

Guy Munnoch is now Managing Director of Rupert Morgan, a leadership consultancy, while also holding several non-executive director positions for firms in the UK and South Africa. Prior to this he was CEO of Zurich Insurance Company in the UK and South Africa. The organizations that Guy has been involved with during his 21-year career in Financial Services have benefited from some of the leadership skills developed during his earlier 21-year career in the British Army.

Perspective

The traditional view of military life is that it is rigidly controlled and hierarchical and therefore would not be the best choice to illustrate empowered or innovative behaviour. Guy disagrees and points to three key areas in which the army actually embodies the spirit of an innovation culture:

- Empowerment – The army truly empowers. It pushes decision making down to the most junior soldier. Within certain parameters each individual has total control over their decisions and their actions. Whether on the streets of Basra or the mountains of Afghanistan it is, more often than not, the junior Corporal who is making on-the-spot decisions. Creating a similar environment in business can have massive benefits but it takes strong leadership and a willingness to 'let go' to install.

- Clarity – In the fog of war one needs complete clarity to ensure that the basic mission is accomplished as safely as possible. With the benefit of clear instructions and understanding, soldiers know exactly what is expected of them and are given freedom to innovate within clear boundaries. Clarity of mission provides everyone with the confidence to execute.

- A 'Can Do, Will Do' attitude – The army relies on soldiers thinking 'outside the box', even when the orginal plan starts to unravel. Everyone recognizes that a 'plan' is exactly that – a 'plan'. It is a framework as to what might happen rather than what will happen. But what is critical in the Army is that soldiers are trained to expect the unexpected. It is the 'can do, will do' attitude that secures success through individuals 'digging deep' and using personal guile, cunning and initiative. Essentially, soldiers are trained to innovate even though they might not realize they have this skill.

Drawing further parallels between military and business life Guy says that at heart, innovation is all about how to beat the opposition through creating game-changing solutions. In the army the opposition is the enemy, in business it is the competition – both current and future disruptors. He believes that sometimes we spend too much time looking inwards rather than looking outwards to meet external challenges. His message for success is simple:

- Keep it relevant.

- Keep it simple.

- Encourage 'front line' innovation.

While we were tapping into Guy's knowledge we asked him if there were any 'hidden' themes which CEOs need to be aware of when seeking to link culture and innovation. He pointed to three areas which derive from leadership and which in his opinion, if properly embedded, will drive success:

1 Adrenalin – When life steps outside of the mundane and into an 'act now' phase then most people become more incisive and innovative. Whether reacting to a crisis, responding to an unexpected 'burning platform' or engaged on a pre-designed organizational change programme such as a merger or acquisition, nerve endings sharpen, engagement levels heighten and solutions flow. Similar reactions can be created in an innovation culture where the drive is continually to seek solutions for ongoing problems.

   The challenge for leaders in such a situation is to manage and control the reaction so that the focus remains on creating real solutions rather than leading to 'burn-out'. Managed carefully, this can excite employees and create a very powerful sense of self-drive and self-motivation. Put simply, adrenalin is a natural drug, which in the right dosage can have massive impact on performance and creativity.

2 Execution – Guy believes that success comes from a combination of 'clarity of direction' and 'ruthless execution'. While many leadership teams can create 'clarity of direction', most failures come from an inability to execute. In particular the leadership teams which have not fully assimilated the ideas behind an innovation culture struggle when it comes to putting those ideas into action. As Guy says, most people can understand the difference between ignorance and knowledge but many find it difficult to articulate the move from knowing to doing. This can in some instances lead to corporate inertia, in which talking about change becomes a substitute for action.

3 Empowerment – Drawing on his military background, Guy reiterated the importance of creating an environment of mutual trust to deliver results, to drive change and to stimulate innovation. Trust and leadership are, in his view, one of the same. Furthermore, he believes that you do not need to have rank to lead, emphasizing that leadership is everyone's business. Guy believes that most organizations are 'over-managed and under-led' – the key to success lies in re-ordering the balance between management and leadership. Creating strong leadership at all levels will, in turn, inspire and promote innovative behaviours. As Guy confirms, leadership is simply the 'art of inspiring ordinary people to do extraordinary things' – a theme which lies at the very heart of innovation.

Too short, too sharp, too shallow

For the leadership team, the process of embedding change can be one of the most frustrating of times. It's hard to escape the feeling that all of the hard work, all of the thought and design is leading to the one pivotal moment when the new concept is ready to be launched. In turn this can lead to a hurried and pressured launch that simply does not send the right messages to employees. Then when the quick wins don't follow, the whole concept is dropped, making it harder for any future change to gain a toehold, let alone a foothold in the organization.

In truth, the problem with many culture change programmes today is that they are too short, too sharp and too shallow. In fact they are exactly what one would expect from the 'want-it-now' generation which, in the decade leading up to the recession, ushered in toxic practices such as short-term profits at the expense of long-term profitability. But when we are looking to instil a culture of innovation, particularly when we are looking for an innovation culture to be collaborative and to provide real solutions, then the last thing we should be contemplating is a short, sharp introduction, which skims the surface of the business and everyone in it.

There is another element at work here and that is the way in which culture change is wrongly viewed as a 'programme' with leaders looking to approach change in the same way as they would approach a project plan. This can lead to the view that change programmes are strictly linear. But you can't just tick a box saying, 'Okay, we've completed the launch communications plan, job done, on to the next task.'

This in fact, is one area in which the wider leadership versus management concept comes strongly into play. If those on the leadership team have been drawn from a programme management background then they are more naturally inclined to think and lead in linear project-plan type ways. Their instinct will therefore be to seek a programme-plan style of delivering culture change. But culture change is more about leadership supported by management. It is therefore worth reminding ourselves here of some of the differences between leaders and managers:

- Leaders set direction and inspire others, managers execute and problem-solve.
- Leaders set policy on people issues, managers deal with day-to-day people issues.
- Leaders align and influence, managers control resources.
- Leaders shape culture, managers endorse and reinforce culture.

If they are to avoid a short, sharp and shallow introduction that then fizzles out, leaders have to accept that when building for the long term, it doesn't matter if the entire organization isn't transformed in an instant. Yes, designing some quick wins into the early stages will help to keep enthusiasm levels high. And yes, you can start to see a meaningful shift in culture in a very short space of time but that doesn't mean that everything has to happen all at once. In fact, if significant levels of change happen too quickly then the internal support structure can be destabilized, leading to problems further down the line.

That is one reason why the dual operating model, which we looked at in Chapter 4, can be a useful tool for leaders looking to introduce innovation culture change. Wrapping an innovation layer around core functions enables innovation activities to drive progress without seismically affecting mainstream functions. Continual interactions then gradually move the entire organization towards a fully integrated innovation ecosystem over time.

So when you are trying to convince your employees and others that innovation is not just another passing fad, what key pitfalls should you avoid? Let's look at a few of the most common failure points:

- Too short – In previous chapters we've looked at communicating change and at introducing the roadmap which will drive that change forward. But it can be all too easy to concentrate so much on getting the initial announcement right and on selecting and training i-agents that the longer-term change needs of the organization are ignored.

  Let's be honest: having spent so much time on designing the change and having blocked out time in the diary to accommodate change initiatives, sooner or later the leadership team will start to get twitchy and to look at the other projects that they want to move forward. Mergers and aquistions (M&As), annual returns, commissioning of a new IT system; whatever the reason, there will come a time when the leadership team want to move on and this is when so many initiatives fail. If the behaviours exhibited by the leadership team give the impression that they are no longer focusing on change then the organization will express a collective sigh and mark down innovation culture as yet another passing fad.

  On a positive note, provided the leadership team have assimilated the required change into their every action and decision then they can move on to other projects while still exhibiting innovative behaviours that will encourage ongoing development of the business. But there are also two key ways in which the leadership team can ensure that even after the first flush of change announcements the transformation momentum continues. The first is simply to schedule a series of events and activities that reinforce the innovation ideal. These don't have to be time-consuming or expensive. Even something as simple as a five-minute, fun get-together can do wonders to reinforce the message that the new culture is here to stay.

Secondly, don't underestimate the effect that i-agents can have on change. When the top team sends out a message, people listen and then drift back to the way things were. When leaders throughout the organization reinforce the message, it starts to become real and when i-agents, who may not even be 'official' leaders, start to act as advocates for change then that change has a good chance of becoming embedded into the organization's DNA. In fact this is the very time when mobilizing the management population using the 4Es methodology, which we discussed in Chapter 5, really comes into its own. With the momentum being picked up by management the leadership team only need to maintain a light touch, freeing them up to concentrate on developing future change.

- Too sharp – One of the key barriers to change rises up when people feel threatened. The fight-or-flight response is woven into our being and is as powerful when our day-to-day interactions are threatened as it is when there is a threat to our lives.

   Announcing major change without any thought to softening the blow can throw up so many barriers that they become almost insurmountable. When the announcement concerns something as fundamental as the way in which people follow processes and interact with others at work then the leadership team need to follow change management best practices and phase in the way in which the change is introduced to the workforce.

   Those who have worked sequentially through this book will already be familiar with the idea of following a pathway along which change can be designed and brought to implementation. It is one step further to ensure that the introduction is phased, giving employees time to assimilate the need for change and the way in which that change will affect them.

   That doesn't rule launch announcements out, but it does mean that if you are planning a launch then all of the leadership team, i-agents and other interested parties should be briefed and ready to anticipate and diffuse initial objections. It also means that follow-up actions should be clear and consistent and in place at the outset. This is one reason why we paid so much attention to communications in Chapter 5; it's not just what you say, it's how you say it and how you prepare which makes the difference. It is also worth reiterating here that preparation is everything when looking to share your message. That includes factoring in 'how' to communicate with or engage people and considering what works well for the various populations. It also includes determining and preparing to overcome the kinds of resistance or arguments you may encounter and understanding what communications channels will work best for each segment.

- Too shallow – Earlier in this book we took some time out to look at employee engagement. And the reason we did so is that the level of employee engagement has a profound effect on the way in which employees embrace and align with organizational ideals. In far too many businesses employees still turn up, follow the process and go home again. In these organizations life is lived on the surface, there is little alignment and little depth to the relationship.

  When you are looking for something as profound as a culture of innovation, which requires initiative, creativity, collaboration, understanding and empowerment if it is to have any chance of gaining traction in the organization, then you can't afford to have a surface relationship with employees. Engagement is the name of the game and that means that when you are looking to introduce change, you cannot afford to do so purely on a surface level.

  The introduction of an innovation culture is nothing like the introduction of a change in the payroll system to take account of new legislation. With changes of this nature training may be on the lines of 'make sure that employee details are carefully recorded to avoid errors in tax calculations'. With an innovation culture you can't expect to tell people that in future they will step outside their offices and connect with others and expect them instantly to change their behaviours. They have to be engaged, given the tools, shown the benefits and encouraged to change their behaviours and outlooks and that requires far deeper training and coaching than simple instructions.

  This is one area in which the HR and training teams can make a considerable impact on the acceptance outcomes. It can be all too easy to assume that everyone will react in the same way to change and therefore apply a block approach. Understanding the complexities of human behaviour and the way in which people react to change can make a measurable difference to outcomes. For example, everyone has a different starting point and a varying level of emotional 'buy-in', or reason to change, but needs to get to the same end point. People have to be given time and space to 'practise' and assimilate the new behaviours and this takes careful management.

Moving change forward

Leaders who are aware of the dangers of a short, sharp and shallow introduction and who design the roadmap accordingly have a far greater chance of obtaining employee buy-in at the outset. With energy and vision allied to a strong emphasis on introducing the 4Es (educate, engage, empower, enable) at a deep level the initial impetus is more likely to carry on into lasting change. But that initial effort has then to be sustained, albeit not at the same level of intensity, in order for the momentum to continue.

It is at this point that concerns about change fatigue arise. If you push for change and then take steps to keep innovation culture at the forefront of the business is there not a danger that employees will become weary of the idea? Well no; not if you design and introduce the change appropriately. Change fatigue arises when people are bombarded with a constant stream of changes, all of which make them change their attitude or their behaviour. Changing to a culture of innovation should be a lifelong change. Admittedly it may be a fairly seismic change to introduce, but once innovation ideals have become part of the DNA of the organization then every process, action and interaction will simply be carried out within the innovation umbrella. Here again it is important to remember the difference between 'programmes' and innovation culture change. With a programme you can tick a box and move on, with culture change there is no tick-box and the business moves on with you.

This doesn't mean that in future the business will stand still – far from it. But it does mean that future strategic initiatives will be designed and implemented as a natural part of the innovation ecosystem. In fact, in the early transition stages, organizations that manage systems change with one eye on the innovation model can go a long way towards strengthening innovation adoption.

This is a key message for leaders and HR teams throughout organizations. The more that employees can see innovation culture in action the better able they will be to integrate it into their thoughts and behaviours. There is little point in launching an innovation culture and following shortly after with an imposed change. Demonstrating innovation in action will speak to the heart more deeply than mere words can ever do.

So, with innovation designed to solve real problems, take the chance in the early stages to set the team going on identifying, progressing and creating a solution for long-lasting problems. In a way, it doesn't really matter what these are. The important thing is that employees are encouraged to start to move along the innovation pathway.

In these early stages there is a fair chance the moves towards innovative solutions will bump up against legacy problems. This is where the resolve of the leadership team is really tested. Being realistic, there will be some projects that fail and the way in which the leadership team respond to these failures will send a strong message to the organization about the extent to which the leadership team have truly embraced the innovation model. Censure the project team and innovation is dead in the water. Treat the failure as a learning point and the innovation culture ideal is strengthened. The approach here may include:

- Projects are rarely a complete waste of time. Taking steps to identify elements that have been successful and to see if any of these can be integrated into existing systems and processes either now or in the future will still engender a 'win' scenario.

- Consider how the project has strengthened internal collaboration and enhanced individuals' personal networks.

- Identify how the project has increased shared knowledge and created a platform for the new behaviours to be 'practised'.

- Simply by following the project pathway the team will have strengthened their skill levels. Identify and highlight these as a positive, which can be used to benefit the business in the future.

- Work with the team to identify the reason for failure and look if possible to prevent similar project failures in the future. For example, if the project team felt they lacked the necessary skills or training then help them to acquire the skills required or look to enhance future teams with people from other divisions/departments who can provide the knowledge back-up required. On the other hand if the project couldn't complete due to a lack of technology or infrastructure then this may well need to go on the future development schedule.

- Acknowledge the efforts made by the team. Even a simple 'thank you for exploring this challenge' will start to send out the message that innovation and a new approach is here to stay.

Early stage challenges

Earlier in this book we explored the issue of barriers to change and the importance of planning to overcome them as part of the design and implementation phase. But when innovation culture is in its infancy there are a few challenges which leaders have to successfully overcome if they are to move initial change forward into the long term. These challenges include:

- *Risk* – It's not easy balancing risk within an innovation environment. When you are asking people to experiment, to create solutions, to collaborate both inside and outside the organization and to accept failure then how does risk work within this more open environment? We've touched on this earlier on when we explored how innovation cultures not only require structure, in some instances they may require more detailed structures than before in order to support the innovation ecosystem.

  The same is true of risk monitoring. A change to an innovation culture will require a new risk framework, one which anticipates and manages the challenges which come from both internal and open innovation. This new risk framework will need to be clearly shared with all of those concerned, and their acceptance sought. In essence, people need to understand why things have changed and what the new parameters are. Key here are the risk areas related to compliance, security and confidentiality. For example, it is one thing to collaborate with suppliers on a new solution, quite another to divulge confidential information as a result of that collaboration. In this instance, not only does the risk matrix need to be reviewed, confidentiality agreements may also need to be put in place with third parties.

  Don't forget, risk is only as good as the last person in the chain. If one individual clings to the 'old world' then they will block the innovation flow. Conversely if one individual fails to appreciate the new parameters they could expose the organization to risk.

- *Systems* – The innovation spirit may be willing but the finances may not be there to start again with the systems required to implement all of the innovation initiatives that are proposed. Particularly in larger organizations or those with longevity, replacing legacy systems may have to be done on a more ad hoc basis than the leadership team would ideally like. This may well lead them down the path of End User Computing or of promoting bespoke, discrete developments rather than trying to change the main legacy systems.

  Other options include adopting open-source systems which may go some way towards providing interim solutions or to set new products and services on a new platform with an acceptable and cost-effective interface.

Admittedly, whichever pathway is chosen the organization could be setting itself up for problems further down the road. Within any system there are only a finite number of 'work arounds' which can be accommodated before the system is balanced on a fail point. When continuing operations rely on significant levels of people intervention or on regular refreshes then it may just be time to bite the bullet and make a significant investment in the future.

The other systems challenge that affects larger organizations in particular, is overcoming the test/implementation legacy. Some organizations will release changes whenever they are ready but the larger the organization, the more likely it will be that changes are only implemented on a monthly or quarterly basis. When innovation depends on the iterative approach of rapid deploy, test and learn, then IT will have to face up to the abolition of release 'time boxes'. It is here that the minimum viable product (MVP) approach can come into its own. Leveraging MVP enables organizations to get products and developments out into the market and into user testing as early in the product development cycle as possible. That way organizations can iterate quicker and refine much faster and cheaper until the solution is right.

Originally coined by the CEO of SyncDev Inc, Frank Robinson, the concept of MVP is, at heart, that of finding the optimum balance between launching a product which is so missing in features that it is not viable and one which has so many features that it cuts return and increases risk both for the company and the customer. The SyncDev website (SyncDev, 2015) comments that one of the fundamental principles behind MVP is that it is not just a tool for product introduction but rather is 'a mindset of the management and development-team'. It says, 'think big for the long term but small for the short term'. This is why MVP is such a valuable element of the innovation process.

- *Communications* – We've covered the communication matrix fairly extensively in earlier chapters but it is worth a quick reminder here that the more streamlined and rapid the communication, the better chance collaboration has of taking hold. It's also worth saying that just because you are moving towards innovation, you don't have to only communicate using new and innovative media. Sometimes the tried-and-tested routes are the best. What is important is that there is an open communication stream that enables upward and downward communication throughout the organization.

- *Leadership* – It may seem strange to include leadership team in a list of challenges which the leadership has to overcome, but sometimes leaders can be their own worst enemies. Earlier in the book we discussed the importance of leaders being fully aligned with the change. This is the point at which that alignment is really tested. Clear dangers include leaders who revert to their norms/comfort zone after an initial burst of enthusiasm and leaders who are uncomfortable with the consequences of empowerment, perhaps fearing that they are in danger of losing power. (This can be particularly true if leaders have been promoted based on their technical competence or knowledge rather than their people skills.) There is also a danger that those with lower levels of leadership responsibility are still uncertain about their role within the change process and therefore do not take up the responsibility for change which the higher echelons of leadership may expect.

- *Cost challenges* – When the change programme was devised it will have included certain assumptions concerning costs and funding. But budgets do not equal cash flow and circumstances can change. What happens to the change programme if sales are down or cost/investment challenges are made? These may be due to an external disruptor or to a legal/regulatory/mandatory change which has been imposed on the organization. If the investment spend for change programmes comes under pressure the leadership team have to decide how to manage the change; considering whether to modify, to plough on regardless for the long-term gain or to fold.

The first stage of embedding change therefore is not rocket science but rather comes from a determination to follow the roadmap and to ensure that the initial impetus is not allowed to slide. In fact in the initial stages the main challenge may come from managing the workflow and preventing the organization being overwhelmed with change. Engaged employees will all want to get in on the act and start to find solutions for problems which they have encountered over time; the initial roadmap gap analysis will have thrown up other potential activities; and there is always the outside world, moving the bar forward every day and challenging you to keep up.

Managing these conflicting demands will be a challenge, particularly when you don't want to dampen initial enthusiasms but at the same time can't afford to overwhelm the business. It is here that tools such as the gap analysis and KPIs come into their own. The key is to develop your culture dashboard, using as many of your existing metrics as possible to monitor progress and to ensure that you stay on track. Projects which can't be started now because of potential conflict with others should still be minuted, with interested employees briefed fully on the reasons for shelving their project at the current time. Teams should also be encouraged to retain the concept in the form of a 'virtual project'. This helps to ensure that the idea is not lost with sponsors keeping an eye on market conditions and internal factors, thereby being able to bring the idea back to the table at a future date. Wherever possible, try to find those employees a role on another project to help ensure that enthusiasms stay high.

In essence therefore making an innovation culture stick is simply a matter of:

- design thoughtfully;
- gain momentum;
- sustain effort;
- measure and adapt;
- recognize that it is a journey.

But there is a further element to your journey and that is shaping the business and, in particular, its people around the innovation ideal and it is this stage which we are going to look at next.

Innovation people

Whenever you have change management it is impossible to ignore the people dimension. Adopting an innovation model is no different and as we have moved through this book we have looked at the leadership team and at those further down the organization; we have discussed training needs and we have examined the impact which i-agents can have on creating successful change.

However, so far, all of our reviews have concentrated on the existing team and of their immediate reaction to change. The next logical step is to ask: What of the future? How do we ensure that as the organization evolves its innovation maturity those within the organization are also evolving to meet the new challenge? The optimum answer is three-pronged, namely to lead, to encourage change in the current employee population and then to hire for the future.

We've looked quite extensively at the way in which the leadership team can influence change earlier in the book and we have also talked about identifying and appointing i-agents, those who, through their personality alone, can carry and influence the culture around them. But there is one section of the employee population which will bear the brunt of the ongoing culture change and that is the people who sit at the level of middle and junior management. Call them team leaders, department leaders or group leaders – whatever the title, they are the people who are in close contact on a daily basis with the bulk of your people. It is they who are best placed to judge the mood and it is they who can influence the adoption of the innovation culture on an ongoing basis.

It is possible that these individuals may also be i-agents. It is equally possible that they may be serial resistors, having become used to a level of power and influence, which they fear may slip away under a more collaborative model. Taking the time to ensure that these team leaders are fully engaged with the new innovation culture model is one way of helping to ensure that the culture change will permeate the entire organization. As with so much else this too requires a three-pronged approach: involvement, training and empowerment.

In every change process there comes a time when team leaders have to become involved and for something as fundamental as a culture change, the sooner the better. Admittedly in a large organization it may not be practical to bring all team leaders onto the development panel but the sooner that these individuals are engaged in the process the more ownership they will have of it. With that ownership comes a desire to spread the message and to keep the change on track.

This brings us on to empowerment. With a more empowered way of working forming part of the innovation ecosystem there is no reason why team leaders shouldn't be empowered at an early stage to identify and set in motion the move towards change. However, depending on the innovation model chosen there may be times when some departments are not seen as early adopters and this can cause conflict and distrust. But just because a department is not seen as an early adopter doesn't mean that the team leader shouldn't look to see if there are any small steps that can be taken to prepare their team for future change. By working closely with the leadership team, best practices can be developed which suit the business model and engender faith in the innovation ideal.

Empowered team leaders are not only more likely to promote the innovation culture they are also more likely to influence its adoption and future development. To help team leaders to maximize their influencing abilities, the leadership team, in conjunction with HR, may well need to schedule some extra training in areas such as influencing skills or communication. Closing off lines of training at this stage sends entirely the wrong message so even if the team leader concerned is not in an early adoption team, if it can be arranged it boosts engagement and perception.

If the team leaders have to change, so too do their teams. Even the most enthusiastic adopter may need help to change their working behaviours and attitudes. This is another reason why the HR team have to be involved at an early stage. One method which has been found to work well here is the use of structured support and challenge groups. These groups traditionally tend to be relatively small in size, with colleagues taking it in turns to explain a problem or challenge which they face, while the remainder of the group listens and asks questions to help their colleague to explore the issue more fully and hopefully arrive at a solution. In a change scenario, such support and challenge groups can have a wider remit, enabling leaders to work through challenges/barriers, to share best practices and to celebrate successes.

But with the best will in the world, no matter what change approaches are used there will inevitably be a few individuals for whom the idea of working within an empowered, collaborative agile model is so alien that they are unable to change.

These may be the people who not only don't like change; they find it deeply distressing to contemplate change. They may feel happy working in a structured way or carrying out simple processes and the idea of taking on responsibility or being more empowered triggers such a fear response that they are unable to assimilate change. There may well still be a place for these individuals within the organization, albeit in a different role and the HR team need to be prepared to work closely with these individuals to help them to identify their own challenges and find a way to adjust.

Then there are those whose innate personality and attitude simply rides roughshod over any notion of change. These individuals are so entrenched in their attitudes that they not only find it impossible to change, they don't see why they should. Left unchecked these people can damage the chances of successful innovation integration and therefore eventually there may come a time when they have to be encouraged to move away from the organization.

Aside from these few individuals, with training, with help, with influence, the employee population can be encouraged to move forward and not only adopt the new model but also become enthusiastic supporters of it. That leaves one further challenge: hiring for the future – seeking out and taking on employees who will add to the development of the culture of innovation.

Hiring for cultural fit

Much has been written about this area of recruitment but there is still a basic misunderstanding in many firms. Hiring for cultural fit does not mean hiring a clone, someone with the same personality and qualifications and outlook. Indeed, studies have shown that the richer and more varied the workforce mix, the better the organization can innovate and serve its customers. Hiring for cultural fit simply means choosing people who have the same values and beliefs. People who can embrace the belief and behaviour model of the organization and enrich and enhance it in the process.

This is where the HR team can strongly influence the process. The accounts department may be crying out for a qualified person who can start immediately but it is up to the HR team to moderate their demands and instead work with them to define the type of person who would bring the most to the role. There is absolutely no point in taking on the most-qualified candidate if they are going to upset others in the team or disrupt the carefully nurtured customer care programme.

This brings us on to the next step in the process, the job advert and selecting candidates for interview. Now is the time to be creative if you want someone who will add to the innovation mix. Throw out all of your preconceived processes and ideas and work with the team to really understand what sort of person would best fit; ask the team if they know of anyone suitable and change your selection and interview criteria to meet the new parameters. Most importantly, don't then hand the applications over to someone who will weed out candidates purely on qualification or background or any criteria other than those qualities which you have already identified.

This is your chance to hire individuals who will not only fit into the new culture, but will actively promote the new culture. More than that, this is your chance to employ individuals who will raise the performance bar above that of the existing workforce. It's a concept which is already in evidence at a number of organizations: the deliberate selection of candidates who will play their part in taking a business to the next level. The only caveat here is that if you are in the early stages of your innovation journey and your candidate is already used to a higher level of innovation then there is a danger that they may turn round and say that 'this is not working for me'. Retaining such candidates requires a measure of awareness and leadership to ensure that they not only stay on the journey with you but actively help to promote the journey.

Get the process right and you are well on the way to selecting a candidate who will be a force for good in the organization. Get it wrong and you'll soon be parting company with someone who may be very qualified but is just not right for the culture of the organization. And the failure won't be theirs, it will be yours.

There is one further item to look at when considering hiring for cultural fit and that is the way in which new employees are integrated into a multi-generational, multi-cultural workforce. As the Google diversity report in 2014 said, 'Having a diversity of perspectives leads to better decision-making, more relevant products, and makes work a whole lot more interesting.' (Google, 2014)

Depending on the business the diversity mix may vary across departments or across continents. Integrating new employees into a diverse workforce which also embraces a culture of innovation requires careful planning and may well require organizations to move away from the 'here's your desk' induction and towards a phased blended induction routine. This should encompass far more than simply the immediate task, otherwise the new employee will not be able to participate fully in innovative collaborations.

Evolving innovation

With engaged employees supporting a culture change which is well on its way it is now time to look towards the future. Although the hard graft is over, in a way the journey is only just beginning. Customers and the wider marketplace are starting to wake up to the realization that your business has undergone a transformation. For now they are delighting in your product or service but sooner or later they will start to see this new service level as standard and you'll have to move on again to keep ahead of their expectations.

This though is the beauty of a culture of innovation. It's not like introducing a finite process such as a new health and safety regime. Innovation looks to provide real solutions but it is also a dynamic culture, only satisfied when it continues to grow and evolve. Giving your people time and space to think, to create and to collaborate may take the business into unchartered waters but provided that the innovation hand is on the tiller your employees will be leading the way, mapping out and shaping the future.

It is because of this potential for exponential growth that dual operating systems can work so well in the early stages. Phasing in the introduction of an innovation culture gives the business and its people time to assimilate the change, to reformat their working methodologies and to understand exactly how innovation can be so game-changing. Success breeds success but only if it is introduced in the right way.

Put simply, if you try to go from a standing start straight into a full-blown mature innovation culture the most likely outcome is burnout. It just won't work. As an example, think about one of your departments or teams. It is a fair bet that at present the department is focused on its immediate priorities with targets and achievements being measured accordingly. Whether that department is process driven or sales-oriented, legally minded or technologically focused, the internal culture and perception is likely to be centred around the task in hand.

Now think of the reaction if you asked every person in that department to instantly change focus, change mindset and work in a completely different way! It is unrealistic to ask people to throw out their entire working methodologies and beliefs in an instant. But now consider what would happen if you gradually started to introduce change, if you started to talk about the effects of a more customer oriented or innovative way of working. Perhaps you might challenge and empower them to create a solution or to propose a change which would enhance service. As one success builds on another and as you give people the freedom to think and to explore the ideas become more inventive, more challenging, more constructive; ultimately leading towards being more innovative.

With every failure being a learning opportunity and with every success creating an appetite for further success, once the innovation ball is set in motion it can only accelerate into the future. The leadership role then becomes one of guidance, suggesting and empowering and inspiring in such a way as to encourage innovative actions within given parameters. The roadmap which you created all that time ago is now working every day to create game-changing differentiated experiences. Engaged and aligned employees are now collaborating with each other, with customers, suppliers and strategic partners to create real solutions, which the organization is delivering with speed and flexibility. That is true innovation in action.

In summary

Never forget that culture change is an ongoing journey. It can be tempting to sit back and relax once all of the identification and preparation work has been completed but if you do then all of your hard work will come to nothing as employees yet again receive the message that this change is unimportant. With that in mind, the key elements of successfully moving the culture change forward are:

- Remember, culture change is not the same as project management. With the latter you can tick boxes to measure progress towards a finite end. With the former, the initial preparation is merely the start of an ongoing journey.

- Too short, too sharp, too shallow – Embedding change is not a 'click your fingers and it's done' process. It requires thought, preparation and planning.
- Progressing change – Build success on success, spread the good news until you reach the point at which strategic initiatives start to be designed and implemented as a natural part of the innovation ecosystem.
- Be prepared – Early stage challenges can arise from a number of directions but the more that leaders are prepared and the greater their resolve, the easier it is to meet and overcome ongoing challenges.
- Innovation people – Encourage existing employees to adapt, be prepared to lose those who are unwilling to change and hire intrapreneurs for the future.
- Evolve – Nothing stays the same forever and this is particularly true of a culture of innovation. Each success will lead on to further successes and models which seemed out of reach at the start become eminently doable as people and systems evolve.

Key insights

- The key to embedding change is to get the right vision/mission in place by setting the values which you want your organization and people to hold dear.

- Phasing in the introduction of an innovation culture gives the business and its people time to assimilate the change, to reformat their working methodologies and to understand exactly how innovation can be so game-changing.

- Evolving to an innovation-led culture will require a new approach to risk, one which anticipates and manages the challenges which come from both internal and open innovation.

References

Google (2014) [accessed 27 April 2015] [online] http://www.google.co.uk/diversity/at-google.html

SyncDev (2015) [accessed 26 May 2015] [online] http://www.syncdev.com/index.php/minimum-viable-product/

Conclusion

08

This book has taken you on a journey, following a six-stage process designed to help you build a culture of innovation inside your organization. But this is not the end; in reality, your innovation story is only now beginning. We have given you the tools; we have shown you how you can reframe your world to create a game-changing innovation culture which is agile and inclusive. It is now up to you to shape your future.

Before you started on your journey you may have wondered whether innovation was worth all of the hard work, which inevitably comes with culture change – or you may have been one of the many who knew that their organization was ripe for innovation but didn't know how or where to start.

We hope we have answered your questions and that you are now ready to move forward with innovation. Don't delay; don't make this a *mañana* project that never gets off the starting blocks. If you do then be prepared to watch helplessly as more agile, innovation-leading disruptors take market share or even entire markets away from you.

Innovation is not a 'nice-to-have', it is an imperative for all future-focused organizations. Innovation is not something that you can buy off the shelf unless you want to see the internal capability of your business stagnating. So we are throwing down the gauntlet, challenging you to make a start towards becoming a Next Generation Organization. If it all seems too much then break the task into chunks; start small, grow big; or run a dual operating model that enables the innovation imperative to gradually infuse the organization. Whatever it takes to take the first steps, start your journey now.

Throughout this book we've done most of the talking; sharing our experience and expertise in building high-performing, innovation-led cultures. As we've guided you through the six-stage framework that will lead you towards a fully embedded innovation culture and beyond, we have been ably assisted by both individuals and organizations that have generously agreed to donate case studies and perspectives which clothe our framework in real-world examples.

In this, our conclusion, we are drawing on the world of business again, letting those who have lived innovation and have seen the transformative power of innovation have the final say.

And we'll start with a case study from an organization which is regularly held up as an example of how businesses can flourish when they take care of their employees and their customers. Waitrose is the food retail division of the John Lewis Partnership, Britain's largest employee-owned retail group. It may be well known for its innovative structure but it is also at the forefront of retail innovation. This case study illustrates the way in which baking innovation into the business mould can deliver transformative results.

CASE STUDY   Building a culture of everyday innovation at Waitrose

Introduction

In many organizations innovation sits in the specialist fringes, with a small pool of people responsible for driving growth, cost-savings, operational efficiencies and NPD and developing new services. But for innovation to become a truly successful and sustainable process it needs to be at the centre of everything an organization does, accessible and acceptable for all. It must be baked into the very culture and everyday working practices of the entire business. We look at how Waitrose has successfully done so to make significant productivity and financial savings.

Situation

Waitrose has 338 stores in the UK and is part of the John Lewis Partnership, the largest employee-owned company in the country. It believes that a successful business is powered by its people and ensures that the profits and benefits created by its success are shared with all its Partners (employees), and as such that all co-owners have the responsibility to make the business the best it can be. To better enable this, and ensure the entire organization works towards helping the retailer thrive in one of the most competitive retail markets, Waitrose developed its Partner Ideas programme. The scheme allows all 60,000 Partners, from senior management to those on the shop floor, to submit ideas which can help the business achieve its corporate objectives.

Approach

Waitrose worked in partnership with Wazoku, an organization that specializes in using technology to help enterprises build a culture of everyday innovation to develop the Partner Ideas programme. Behind this was a collaborative idea management platform, Idea Spotlight.

Once the platform was built and proved with a pilot project, Waitrose ensured it developed, and still maintains, a strong culture of innovation and engagement to support it. Those heading the initiative educate store managers about the programme and platform and give them cards to inform and engage in-store staff. Waitrose regularly promotes the scheme and recognizes the best Partner ideas in its internal magazine. People whose ideas are implemented are also awarded bonuses.

In its first 18 months the programme generated:

- over 1,000 ideas from Partners around the business, including supermarket assistants and operation managers;

- an average of 22 innovative new ideas a week since launch, demonstrating just how well sustainable and repeatable innovation has been built into everyday working life in the organization;

- significant company cost-savings achieved with just the initial burst of ideas enabled, with more in the implementation pipeline;

- ideas from a cross-section of the innovation spectrum:

  incremental innovation – an example of which saw the formatting and management of till receipts transformed, allowing the retailer to save over £100,000 annually;

  differentiated innovation – an idea from one supermarket assistant improved the way the audit team deal with temporary pricing tickets, halving the time taken – representing a significant saving of valuable Partner-hours;

  disruptive innovation – a selection of ideas that have a longer lead time to value creation are currently being reviewed by the Partner Idea programme leaders and senior management.

Feedback from Partners is incredibly positive:

The scheme allows Partners to have better input in the business. I have had quite a few go through and it makes you smile on the inside to think you have been heard.
Supermarket assistant

It's great and it makes you feel valued knowing your ideas are listened to.
Supermarket assistant

And it's generated measurable business benefits:

I'm really proud of the success of the scheme. It's fundamental to delivering efficiency.
Alison McGrath, Head of Operational Strategy, Waitrose

Conclusion

Building a sustainable process and culture of everyday innovation that involves people throughout organizations can generate fantastic results across the innovation spectrum which support corporate objectives and measurable ROI, as well as revealing, recognizing and rewarding previously hidden talent and driving employee engagement with a positive purpose.

> *The success of our Partner Ideas scheme goes to show that sometimes the truly great innovations can be as simple as making small changes to the tasks you do every day, rather than the big ideas which transform everything. By engaging our Partners with the right platform and process, we've managed to achieve significant productivity and financial savings.*
> Stuart Eames, Operational Improvement Manager, Waitrose

> *Innovation initiatives work best when they are put at the centre of an organization and everyone across the business is engaged and involved, as Waitrose has shown. With the right platform, process and culture, there's no limit to what can be achieved.*
> Simon Hill, Co-founder and CEO, Wazoku

The above case study highlights the people aspect of innovation, and this is a theme which has been repeated time and time throughout the book. Chapter 2 was enhanced by a case study from QinetiQ, in which they showed how they shifted the organizational culture away from a civil service mentality and towards one which was more commercialized, private-sector- and innovation-focused. Commenting on the transformation Sanjay Razdan, Managing Director New Technologies at QinetiQ said:

> The key to successful innovation is to have a clear understanding of what your start and end point is; what's enabling and what's inhibiting innovation; what are your people's strengths and what's your company's current level of innovation maturity? When you know what your innovation strategy requires, you can work on filling the gaps. As a leader of innovation, I would say that you need to continuously create possibilities that will inspire, touch and move the people around you. Understand the real challenges that exist, be bold and create the environment, inspiration and direction for your people to solve tomorrow's problems today.

In this one short paragraph, Sanjay Razdan highlights the key factor which will make or break innovation: people. Be they employees or customers, suppliers or third parties – regardless of systems and processes, pay or titles, it is the people factor which will turn ideas into reality. It's a lesson that Chris Baréz-Brown, founder of Upping Your Elvis, knows only too well as he illustrates in the following short piece:

Creativity is people

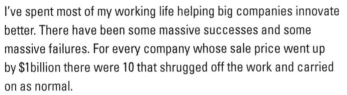

I've spent most of my working life helping big companies innovate better. There have been some massive successes and some massive failures. For every company whose sale price went up by $1billion there were 10 that shrugged off the work and carried on as normal.

To start with it felt like a game of chance with too many moving pieces for me to guarantee success. However, there was a seminal moment. After rolling out an insight process for one of the biggest companies in the world, I was asked if I could run a master class for those who had attended the original programme and needed help moving up to the next level of genius.

I wrote a programme and got them all together in the United States. When I asked how many insight projects they had run since giving them the process, one guy – leaping out of his seat – said, 'Sixteen!'

Impressive, I thought; that's a lot of work. But when he described some of the projects, it became obvious that they were all run identically. They took three days, had three phases and delivered the same average results. I had successfully taught him how to run an insight process but not at all how to be insightful.

Every project is unique. It has different contexts, stakeholders, inputs and outputs, budgets, talent and history. Therefore every project needs a different approach. And that's where people come in. You need creative leaders who know how to inspire innovation and who can create the conditions for others to shine. Laszlo Bock, Head of People Operations at Google, in his new book *Work Rules!* (2015) explains emergent leadership, one of the four traits for him that make a great leader: 'When you see a problem, you step in and try and address it. Then you step out when you are no longer needed. That willingness to give up power is very important.'

It's the *people* that generate the genius, not the tools. That's why culture is so important. We create. We are creation.

From the moment we kicked off our framework by starting to develop an understanding of why change was required, to the final stage in which we made innovation happen, the constant theme throughout the book has been the need to understand the people and organizational culture dimension of innovation. With your people embracing the innovation ideal, change will flow. More than that, you will quickly find that the impetus shifts, from one that is driven by the leadership team to one that is driven by the entire organization and beyond.

It is time – more than time – to commit to making innovation real. So get that i-agent team together, have that conversation and start figuring out how to shape your future by building a game-changing culture of innovation.

Reference

Bock, L (2015) *Work Rules!: Insights from inside Google that will transform how you live and lead*, John Murray, London

INDEX

4×4 innovation maturity model 43–44

Accelerate 108
Accenture report (2013) 82
acceptable risk 47, 56, 74
acceptable value 47
acceptance
  of authority 6, 8, 9
  of failure 46–47
  see also personal acceptance
accidental invention 152
accountability 86–87, 102–103
adaptability 15, 16, 19–20, 73, 75, 79, 103, 176
adrenalin 182–183
advocates 91
affordability 4, 5
agility 7, 37, 104, 109, 165
Alcatel-Lucent 78
alerts 139
alignment 113–115
ambiguity 89
Apple 5–6, 42, 72, 99
appraisal/reward 164
apprentice stage, innovation maturity 43f
assessment
  of employee engagement 36
  of organizational capacity 50
  of readiness for change 50–51
  see also cultural assessment
attitudes
  change in consumer 6
  collaborative 74
  entrenched 195
  innovation as change in 3
  need for change in 59
authority, acceptance of 6, 8, 9
autonomy 105, 111
awareness 90

Baréz-Brown, Chris 205
barriers to innovation 65
  overcoming 24–27
    case study 27–30
behaviour(s)
  and desired innovation culture 150

need for change in 59
reward of innovation-focused 164
translation of strategy into 63, 64f, 128, 129f
translation of values into 14
best guessing the future 72–73
Betamax 6
Bhatia, Abhishek 28, 29, 30
board level, diversity at 85
Bock, Lazlo 205
body language 91, 140
bonuses 164
breakthrough innovation *see* radical innovation
breatheHR 141
brevity, of vision 97
Brightidea (case study) 167–169
BrightMove Media (case study) 157–159
Bristol Brabazon aeroplane 6
broadband 9
business models, need for change in 10
business perspective, Generation Z 10–11

'can do, will do' attitude 116, 182
capability
  as a barrier to change 26–27
  building 87–89
    (case study) 106–108
  buying innovation and danger of disregarding 37
  openness and clarity about 71
capacity-building 26
caring generation 10
Carter, Bob 62
cavalier risk 56, 166, 174
certainty 105
challenges 189–193
change(s)
  benefits of 115–116
  drivers of
    Generation Z 8–11
    regulation 11–12
  embedding 179, 180–183
  innovation as 3, 4

change(s) (*continued*)
    leading through 89–91
    phasing 106
    public appetite for 25
    readiness assessments 50–51
    see also social change
change agents 109
change ambassadors 131
change appetite 51–52
change fatigue 130, 188
'change function' approach 110
'change leadership' style 110
change management 24, 28, 91, 108, 132,
        186, 193
change teams 114
Cisco (case study) 107–108
clarity
    about capability and buy-in 71
    of communication 132–133
    of direction 183
    in highlighting problems 56
    in leading change 91
    of measurement and reward 57
    of mission 181
    of values 100
    of vision 98
co-creation 6, 25, 104, 109, 142, 161,
        163, 167
coaches 88
coaching 76, 136, 141, 147, 164, 187
Coca-Cola 53
collaboration 15, 45–46, 106
    in 3Is process 175
    as an innovation aptitude 103
    cross-departmental 74, 79, 84, 164
    defining strategic mix 73–74
    examples 77, 78
    Generation Z and 10
    global CEOs 16–17
    on innovation *see* open innovation
    leadership team agreement 83–84
    Next Generation Organizations 16, 19
    online (case study) 137–138
    owning the innovation agenda 60–61
    with third parties 62
collaboration tools 136–138
collaborative leadership (case study)
        157–159
collaborative mentality 74
Collar, Ben 137
commitments, exemplary leadership 88
communication(s)
    in 3Is process 176
    challenge 191
    change timeline 144
    cultural due diligence 61

culture change 60, 65
    and engagement 121, 136, 140
    Generation Z 10, 11
    ideals 132–134
    internal 164
    launching innovation (case study)
        146–147
    in leading change 91
    in positioning innovation strategy 81
    successful innovation culture 66
    as a two-way process 135
    of vision 121
    see also body language; social media
communication plan 135
    creating 142–144
    other platforms 138–140
    social media and collaboration tools
        136–138
    verbal communications 135–136
competencies, translating values into
        102–104
competitive advantage 101
concise communication 133
confidentiality 190
congruent communications 134
Connect + Develop 77, 172
consistency, in leading change 91
consistent communication 133
constraints 72
consumer attitudes 6
consumerist order 8
contextual innovation 80
continual feedback 140
continuous communications 134
continuous improvement(s) 39, 55, 80,
        104, 152
control 105
coping mechanism, change fatigue 130
core values 100
cost challenges 192
creativity 10, 72, 169, 170, 205
cross-departmental collaboration 74, 79,
        84, 164
crowdsourcing 37
cultural assessment 38–42
    importance of (case study) 47–49
    innovation maturity 42–47
cultural due diligence 61–62
cultural fit, hiring for 15, 165, 166, 195–197
cultural manifesto 98–99
culture *see* innovation culture; organizational
        culture; sub-cultures
culture change 14, 120
    barriers to 60
    communication and 60, 65
    creating lasting 36

difficulty of instilling 161
failure rates 161
intrapreneurs and 162–163
leadership teams 59, 60, 127
'measure-act-measure' rule 39
perceived as a programme 184
preparedness for 66
successful (case study) 47–49
timelines 144
as too-short, too-sharp, too-shallow
    183–187
culture dashboard 192–193
Culture Hack™ 141
customer empowerment 18
customer expectations, changing 8–11, 16,
    18, 22
customer experience 97, 102, 104, 116, 164
    exceptional 11, 17, 22, 27, 96
    game-changing 15, 91
customer feedback (case study) 146–147
customer loyalty 5, 6, 15, 22, 76, 111
customer relationships 104, 111
Customer Satisfaction Index Report (2015) 16
customer service 15, 20, 27
customer understanding 17–18
customer-centric culture 52

decision-making 80, 150, 157, 197see also
    strategic innovation decision
delegation 41, 60, 61, 116, 122
Department for Business and Innovation
    Skills (BIS) Report (2014) 3
design thinking 26
development see systems development;
    training and development
developmental pathways, measuring 45
dialogue 85, 89
differentiated innovation 50, 51f, 54, 55,
    62, 81, 114
differentiators 8, 11
digital capability 89
digital understanding 9
disruptive innovation see radical innovation
diversity 10, 85, 121, 197
'doable' ideas 4, 5
Drive 37–38
dual operating system 108–110, 114–115,
    163, 185
due diligence (cultural) 61–62

e-mails 139
early challenges 189–193
Economist report (2015) 15
educate (4Es methodology) 122
Egon Zehnder Diversity Analysis report
    (2014) 85

emotional buy-in 157, 187
emotional engagement 129
emotional intelligence 104, 162
emotions 91
empathy 104
employee disengagement 23, 38
employee engagement 79, 111–113, 114
    4Es methodology 122
    assessment 36
    benefits 38, 112, 116
    communication 121, 136, 140
    company vision 98
    cultural assessment 40
    developing 120–123
    embedding change 187
    emotional 129
    employee-led/self-managed programmes
        123–124, 140, 163
    falls in 37, 41
    human resources and 160
    idea/reward mix 58
    in leading change 91
    measuring 123, 140
    performance management 163
    and profitability 23
    responsibility 113
    young people 55–56
    Zappos 14
    see also engagement plan
employees
    Generation Z 10
    importance of knowing 124
    induction 197
    involvement in cultural assessment 42
    knowledge of 124
    resistance see resistance; resistors
    Zappos 15
employers, Generation Z 10
empowered decision-making 80
empowerment 79, 95, 103, 116
    customers 18
    employee-led engagement 122, 124
    and innovation culture 183
    intrapreneurs and 162
    in military life 181
    team leaders 194
enable (4Es methodology) 122
enablers 40
encouragement 59
engagement see employee engagement
engagement plan 124–126
    immersive engagement 141–142
    surveys, feedback and engagement
        platforms 140–141
enthusiasms, developing 55–56, 131
equality 121

espoused values 99
ethical viewpoint 10
European Central Bank 21
European Union 12
evaluating 176
everyday innovation culture, building (case
    study) 202–204
execution 183
experimentation 66
experts, use of 18
external influencers 144
external influences 41, 74
external relationships 156–157, 166–167

facilitated discussion 141
facts, confused with understanding 17
failure 7, 46–47, 57, 71, 189
failure rates, culture change 161
falling sales 23
faltering reputation 24
fast discovery teams 110
fear/risk-averse mentality 7
feedback 176
    continual 140
    gathering and delivering 132
    technology and 141
    see also customer feedback
feedback forms 140
Feefo (case study) 146–147
feeling that something is not right 24
'fight or flight' response 90
Financial Conduct Authority (FCA) 12, 21
Financial Reporting Council (FRC) 12, 85
Financial Services Authority (FSA) 26
financial services sector 20–21, 25–26,
    86, 151
fitness (strategic) 109
Food Standards Agency survey (2014) 18
Ford, Henry 59
4Es methodology 121f, 122, 166, 188
freedom 71–72
future trends 18, 73
the future
    best guessing 72–73
    designing 95–117
    learners as inheritors of 8
Fuzzy Front End 26

G20 12
gambling 174
game theory 141
game-changing customer experience 15, 91
game-changing innovation 3, 15, 44, 49,
    69, 174
gender balance 84–85
General Electric 171

Generation Y 9
Generation Z 6, 8–11, 25, 121, 165
global digital age 7
global financial crisis 11–12
global growth, innovation and 11–12
globalization 37
Goldratt, E.M. 170
good ideas 149, 172
Google 42
Google diversity report (2014) 197
Google Glass 7
governance 166
Grand Tour 8
growth, innovation-led 11–12
Growth and Innovation Fund 12

high influencers 125
hiring *see* recruitment
Hoffer, Eric 8
holacracy 161
holistic approach 19, 26
holistic viewpoint 40, 81, 106, 113, 144,
    166, 175
homogeneity 7, 11, 22
honesty 102
hook, for enthusing i-agents 130, 131
Hsieh, Tony 15
human resource (HR) teams
    hiring for cultural fit 196
    performance management 163–164
    skills needed 132
human resources (HR) 114, 131
    need to engage 159–161
hyperlocalism 11

idea challenges 59
idea creators 124
idea generation 26
idea-to-launch (Stage-Gate®) 174
ideas
    contest (case study) 137–138
    cross-fertilization 151
    dismissal 46
    doable 4, 5
    formation 169
    good 149, 172
    innovation as a search for new 4
    measuring 172–173
    recognition/reward 57
    storytelling and adoption of 129
    valuing 56
ideation, 3Is process 175–176
identification, 3Is process 174–175
IIPP (Implemented Innovations Per
    Person) 173
Immersion Zone 141

immersive engagement 141–142
implementation 128
  3Is process 176
implementation plans 59, 176
implementation teams 86
improvement, innovation as 4
In the Limelight 142
In the Middle 125
inclusion 10
inclusivity 11, 56, 129, 139
incremental innovation 44, 49–50, 51f,
    52, 53, 62, 80
individuality 97–98, 111
induction 197
influencers 124–125, 143–144, 157
influencing skills 132
information
  flow of 89, 109, 110, 115
  gathering 18
  top-down cascade of 124
information overload 170
inhibitors, of current culture 40
initiative 103, 124
'Innovateur' Dramatics 141–142
innovation
  in action, demonstrating 188
  as an imperative 201
  barriers to *see* barriers to innovation
  buying in 37–38
  collaboration on *see* open innovation
  'creative freedom' myth 71–72
  definition of 13
  drivers of 72–75
  evolving 197–198
  intelligent 18
  invention versus 3–6
  leadership *see* leadership; leadership
    teams
  measuring 169–170
  people-powered (case study) 167–169
  purpose 101
  reasons for 6–8
  recognition and visibility of 58
  return 5
  scenarios pointing the way towards
    20–24
  as a strategic priority 15
  sustainable 49, 50, 51f
innovation agenda, owning
  aligning with innovation strategy 63–65
  collaboration 60–61
  cultural due diligence 61–62
  engaging young people 55–56
  positioning ownership 58–60
  risk/reward mix 56–58
  sub-cultures 62–63

innovation agents (i-agents) 114,
    126–134
  appointing at every organizational level
    128–130
  developing 130–132
  intrapreneurs as 125
  involvement in metrics portfolio 171
  middle managers as coalition of 125
  translation of strategy into behaviour 128,
    129f
  translation of vision into reality 160
innovation aptitudes 102–103
  building 149–177
innovation champions 58, 86, 127, 131
innovation culture 1, 12–16
  benefits of a fully developed 38
  building
    human resources 160
    as a long-term initiative 38
    need for careful stewardship 55–56
    need for holistic approach 26
    six-stage framework 2f
    Waitrose (case study) 202–204
  as a business imperative 3, 8–11, 15
  consumer attitudes and collaborative
    aspects of 6
  embedding 179–199
  and growth 12
  key elements for success 66
  leadership and 69–70, 182–183
  military life 181–182
  opening up of new ideas and mindsets
    152–153
  sharing the idea of 131
  see also cultural assessment; culture
    change
innovation directors 86–87
innovation eco-systems, the structure
    to support 163–167
innovation gap 53–54, 114
innovation journey 95
  crunch point 96
  shaping 104–106
  starting 35–36
  see also innovation roadmap
innovation launch event 145
  (case study) 146–147
Innovation Manager: role, competencies
    and skills 87
innovation maturity 42–47, 114
  4x4 model 43–44
  acceptance of failure 46–47
  measuring 44–46
  and successful innovation culture 66
  traps 45–46
innovation mindset 70–71, 112

innovation mix 49–53, 62
  defining for each department/division 63
  as forefront of design and decision-making 150
  intelligence, collaboration and adaptability 72–75
  secret of identifying 55
  sustainable 49, 50, 51f
innovation process
  designing 174–176
  importance of 58
innovation roadmap
  basis of 163–167
  design/make-up 63, 64
  forming of high-level 114
  need for 50
  Ofwat 21
  vision and 98
innovation strategy
  aligning with the appetite for innovation 70–72
  aligning innovation agenda ownership with 63–65
  and culture change 60
  developing 49–55
  examples 77–78
  high-level 128
  intrapreneurs and 162
  level of risk 47
  ownership 78–79
  see also innovation mix
innovation teams
  importance of high-level 161
  shaping 114
innovative solutions 4, 5, 6, 21, 45
input metrics 172–173
insight 97, 172
insight-gathering 18
intelligence 15, 16, 17–19, 72–73, 164, 174
  framework 115
  gathering 172
  leveraging 20, 23, 73, 74
inter-departmental wrangling 23
interaction(s) 106
  customer 17
  digital 89
  Generation Z 9, 10
  'move away' response 90
  and organizational culture 13
  scheduling time for 113
interconnectedness 11, 77, 140
interest 59, 143–144
internal communications 164
internal resource(s), combining external influence 74

internal talent, danger of disregarding 37
international organizations 12
internet 6, 7, 8, 9, 73, 166
intrapreneurs
  encouraging people to be 103
  identifying and engaging 161–163
  as influencers 124–125
  need for harnessing power of 7
  need to find and identify 125
  see also innovation agents
intuition 103
invention 3–6, 7, 152
investors 25
involving 113

Jenkins, Antony 25
job market 165–166
Jostle 141

key performance indicators (KPIs) 45, 65, 66
knowledge 74, 109, 124, 189
Kotter, John 108

larger business, marketplace challenge 7
lead stakeholders 144
leaders
  creating compelling vision 153–158
  differences between managers and 184
  empowered 194
  exceptional 24
  four traits of great 205
  intrapreneurs as 162
  need to engage human resources 159–161
'leaders without a title' 90, 128
leadership
  challenges 192
  change in model of 116
  collaborative (case study) 157–159
  commitments of exemplary 88
  as critical to success 151–153
  external relationships 156–157
  as inspiring, enabling and co-creating 109, 183
  re-ordering balance between management and 183
  restaurant analogy 127
  and successful innovation culture 182–183
Leadership Challenge™ 87–88, 89
Leadership Practices Inventory™ 87, 88
leadership stage, innovation maturity 43f
leadership team agreement
  collaboration and risk 83–84
  ownership 86–87

personal acceptance 84–85
readiness 81–84
leadership teams
building 69–92
collaboration 61, 73–74
creating capability 87–89
cultural assessment 40–41, 42
culture change 59, 60, 127
defining the innovation mix 63, 72–75
employee engagement 124
innovation culture 69–70
innovation strategy 71, 78–79
leading through change 89–91
making the complex simple (case study) 75–77
mission creep 65
positioning innovation for everyone 79–81
status and autonomy 105
supporting middle management 126
translating vision into reality 120
Leading Change 108
learners, as inheritors of the future 8
learning, the basics of innovation 43
learning points, failure as 7, 46–47, 57, 71
legacy problems 189
legacy systems 190
legal profession 21
level playing fields 7
linear project-plan style 184
listening 91, 112–113, 140
listening skills 132
long time horizon 66
longevity 1, 20, 78, 116, 190

McDonalds 11
McKinsey (2010) 169
malpractice 47
management
cultural assessment 41
reordering balance between leadership and 183
management aptitudes 150
managers
differences between leaders and 184
see also middle managers; new managers
marketplace challenge 7
measuring innovation 169–170
mentors/mentoring 88, 125
metrics portfolio 171–174
middle managers 125–126
military life, innovation culture in 181–182
minimum viable product (MVP) approach 30, 165, 176, 191
mis-selling scandals 8, 11–12

mission 100, 181
mission creep 65
mission statements 99
mistakes 47
Mobility Idea Contest (case study) 137–138
mobilization 60, 61
momentum 71, 109
Moore's Law 6
motivation 37–38
multi-communicating generation 10
multi-tasking creativity 10
multi-tasking generation 9
Munnoch, Guy 181, 182, 183
mutual relationships 156–157

Netflix 99
new entrants 21–22, 151
new managers 125
newsletters 139
Next Generation Organizations 9, 16–20, 165
Nielsen 168
non-national board directors 85
novelty 4
novice stage, innovation maturity 43f

Octopus Investments (case study) 75–77
OECD 11, 12
Ofcom Report (2014) 9
Ofwat's roadmap (2015-16) 21
open communication 191
open innovation 38, 77, 166, 172
open-source systems 190
operating model 150
see also dual operating system
organizational capacity, assessment of 50
organizational culture 13–15
as a barrier to change 26
capability for radical innovation 49
consumer-centric 52
definition 13
developing to meet changing dynamics 12
integration of innovation into 35
redesign 42
see also cultural assessment
organizational strategy
aligning innovation to 53–54
as a barrier to change 26
organizations
need to reinvent themselves 7, 22
solutions-based 79–80
see also international organizations; Next Generation Organizations
Oshry, Barry 125
output metrics 173

ownership
    as an aptitude/value 102–103
    Generation Z 9
    innovation agenda 55–65
    innovation programmes 86–87
    of strategy and vision 78–79

parochialism 8
partnerships 89
passivity 9
patents 171
pay and reward 164
peer-to-peer recognition 141
people dimension 41, 193–195, 204, 205, 206
people-powered innovation, (case study)
    167–169
performance management 163–164
personal acceptance 84–85
personal development 88, 89, 130
personality 195
Pink, Dan 37
plans see communication plan; engagement
    plan
Plunkett, Roy J 152
pluralthinking report (2014) 9, 11
policies 165
position of truth 42
Price, Mark 22
PricewaterhouseCoopers' 18th Annual
    Global CEO Survey (2015) 16–17
probationary periods 166
problem-solving 4, 73, 102
    see also innovative solutions
process flows 112
process reviews 165
processes 165
Procter & Gamble (P&G) 77, 172, 174
product homogeneity 22
product similarity 27
professional excellence 102
professional stage, innovation maturity 43f
professionalism 95, 102
profitability 1, 20, 23
programme-plan style 184, 188
project delay 22–23
prototyping 66, 176
Prudential (case study) 27–30, 153
public appetite, for change 25
pulseCHECKER 138
purpose
    of innovation 101
    organizational see mission

QinetiQ (case study) 47–49, 204
questioning techniques 132
quick wins 27, 38, 59, 71, 91, 165

racial diversity 85
radical innovation 49, 50, 51f, 52, 53,
    54–55, 62, 80
Razdan, Sanjay 204
readiness for change 50–51
realistic, being 101
reason, voice of 161
recognition 57–58
recruitment 15, 165–166, 195–197
regulatory bodies
    as barriers to change 24
    dialogue and support 89
    as drivers of change 11–12
    and need for innovation 20–21
relationships 104, 111, 156–157, 166–167
reputation 5, 23, 27, 57, 111–112
resistance 25, 160–161
resistors 90, 125, 194
resources 74, 88–89
respect 102
responsibility
    for engagement 113
    see also social responsibility
restaurant analogy 127
return, innovation 5
review, cultural 61
reward(s) 57–58
    successful innovation culture 66
    see also appraisal/reward; pay and
        reward
risk 166, 190
    acceptable 47, 56, 74
    leadership team agreement 83–84
    and successful innovation culture 66
    third party/supply chain 61
risk appetite 25–26, 41, 55, 56, 83–84, 105
risk averse mentality 7
risk framework 190
risk monitoring 190
risk-takers 124
Robinson, Frank 191
Rock, David 90
ROII (return on innovation investment)
    171–172

sales, falling 23
'sat-nav' analogy 42, 98, 133
saying thank you 58, 113
scandals 8, 11–12
SCARF 90, 105
Securities and Exchange Commission
    (SEC) 21
self-assessment 42
self-managed engagement programmes
    123–124, 140, 163
selling 11

serial resistors 125, 194
services innovation excellence centre (SIEC) 107–108
70/20/10 innovation effort 53
shared knowledge 74, 109, 189
sharing 113
shopping patterns, changing 18, 20, 22
short-term distractions 84
Siemens AG (case study) 137–138, 140
smaller businesses 7
smart risk 56, 82, 166
social change 8, 90
social media 9, 11, 41, 112, 136–138
social order 8
social responsibility 11
Solicitors Regulation Authority 21
solutions, innovative 4, 5, 6, 21, 45
solutions-based organizations 79
space race, spin-off developments 152
sparks & honey report (2014) 10
spatial awareness 10
SpigitEngage 137–138
splinter groups 110
'stage-gate' process 174
stakeholder analysis 144
stakeholder involvement 171
statistics 18
status 105
storytelling 129, 141
strategic creativity 72
strategic fitness 109
strategic innovation decision 49–55
strategic mix *see* innovation mix
strategic priority, innovation as 15
sub-cultures 40, 62–63
sub-values 100
successful discovery 174–175
suggestion box 164
supplier relationships 111
support and challenge groups 195
surveys 140
sustainability 11, 20
sustainable innovation 49, 50, 51f
SyncDev Inc 191
system challenges 190–191
systems development 164–165

taking time 113
team participation 141
'team sport' approach 160
team-bonding 141–142
teamwork 103, 160
technological breakthroughs 7
technological change 6, 8, 15, 37, 73, 101, 158
technological developments 22, 23

technology
    as a barrier to innovation 26
    collaborative 140–141
    as enabler (case study) 167–169
    and engagement 141–142
    spin-off developments 152
    see also digital capability; digital understanding; internet
Teflon 152
terminology 127
testing 176
'thank you', saying 58, 113
third party/supply chain risk 61
threat 143
3Is innovation process 174–176
3M 44
time, for interaction 113
time/cost benefit 5
time/cost measures 61
timelines, culture change 144
TINYpulse 141
Toyota 62
training and development 166, 187
    see also coaching
true change 180
true collaboration 19
true intelligence 115
trust 27, 101, 181, 183

uncertainty 89
understanding 17–18, 27, 104, 131
United Kingdom, innovation imperative 12
United States Securities and Exchange Commission (SEC) 21
updates 144
Upping Your Elvis 205
usefulness 4
user testing 176

values
    aligning employee and company 122
    changes in importance 100
    and culture change 36, 60
    Generation Z 11
    ownership of the innovation agenda 65
    translating into competencies 102–104
    translation into tangible behaviours 14
    underpinning vision 99–101, 154
'venture capital' mindset 70–71
verbal communications 135–136, 140
vision
    communication of 121
    creating compelling 153–156
    and culture change 36, 60
    ownership of the innovation agenda 65
    ownership of 78–79

vision (*continued*)
    regular checks back to 114
    shaping 96–99
    translating into reality 76,
        120, 160
    values underpinning 99–101, 154

Waitrose (case study) 202–204
Water Services Regulation Authority 21
'wear the T-shirt' moment 81, 133
Wellvue 141
Wheatley, Martin 151

Work Rules! 205
workplace, Generation Z 10
workplace diversity 10
world viewpoint 8, 9

Yammer 138
young entrepreneurs 7
young people
    digital understanding 9
    engaging 55–56

Zappos 14, 15, 166

CPSIA information can be obtained at www.ICGtesting.com
Printed in the USA
BVOW06s0837231215

430875BV00024B/187/P